Therapeutic Work with Sexually Abused Children

Randall Easton Wickham, LCSW
and Janet West

SAGE Publications
London • Thousand Oaks • New Delhi

First published 2002

SAGE Publications Ltd
6 Bonhill Street
London EC2A 4PU

SAGE Publications Inc
2455 Teller Road
Thousand Oaks, California 91320

SAGE Publications India Pvt Ltd
32, M-Block Market
Greater Kailash - I
New Delhi 110 048

British Library Cataloguing in Publication data

A catalogue record for this book is available from
the British Library

ISBN 0 7619 6968 3
ISBN 0 7619 6969 1 (pbk)

Library of Congress Control Number: 2001135324

Typeset by SIVA Math Setters, Chennai, India

This book is dedicated to all children who have been sexually abused.

Contents

Acknowledgements

The authors wish to thank Alison Poyner, Senior Commissioning Editor, and Louise Wise, Editorial Assistant at Sage Publications for their contributions and support in writing this book. We are indebted to Pat Walton, University of Leicester, for her assistance in writing Chapter 12.

Randall Easton Wickham would like to thank the following: both her brother, Michael Easton and her sister, Kelly Easton for their intelligence, sensitivity and unfailing senses of humour, and to thank them for always being there when she has truly needed them; her children Celia and Katie, for their affection, spirit and patience with her while she worked on this manuscript; Phyllis Spinal-Robinson, LCSW, for friendship, supervision and co-authorship of the workbooks for sexually abused children and adolescents written in the US; her previous colleagues on the sexual abuse team and staff at Des Plaines Valley Community Centre in Chicago; most notably the following: Phyllis Spinal-Robinson, Avis Shapiro, LCSW, a highly skilled clinician; Beth Forte, LCSW, who supervised her on her first sexual abuse case; the teaching staff at SSA at the University of Chicago where she received her MA in Social Work; her co-author, Janet, for her unfailing sense of humour, dedication, hard work and fortitude; and lastly, and most importantly, all the children and families she has had the opportunity to work with, who have taught her so much. Thank you.

We also wish to acknowledge the following publications:
American Psychiatric Association (2000) *Diagnostic and Statistical Manual of Mental Disorders*. Washington, DC.: American Psychiatric Association for permission to quote from DSM IV and defence mechanisms.

Sharp, S. and Cowie, H. (1998) *Counselling and Supporting Children in Distress*. London: Sage for permission to quote Table 2.1, p. 28.

Spinal-Robinson, P. and Easton Wickham, R. (1992) *Cartwheels. A Workbook for Children Who Have Been Sexually Abused*. Notre Dame, Indiana: Jalice, for permission to quote some of the Worksheets.

Spinal-Robinson, P. and Easton Wickham, R. (1992) *Cartwheels. Therapist's Guide*. Notre Dame, Indiana: Jalice, for permission to quote clinical material regarding feelings of responsibility for the abuse, p. 4.

Please note that the text is based on an integrative approach to treatment including the following orientations: psychodynamic, person-centred, self-psychology and cognitive. We also advocate a psycho-educational approach.

Please also note that the words 'carer' and 'parent' are used interchangeably in our text. We have varied gender pronouns in order to reinforce the reader's awareness that both girls and boys are sexually abused, and that there are male and female therapists. Within England and Wales, the person with overall case-management responsibility for the sexually abused child who is receiving therapy may be a social worker, a child protection officer, or some other designated worker. Only rarely is the therapist also the child's identified worker.

1   The Dimensions of the Issues

An older child:

In
my body
I
never belonged.
Childhood
an empty state,
invalidated and immobilized.

He couldn't help himself
so he helped himself to me.
An item in a menu
to be sullied, dirtied, consumed,
And thrown away.

I sacrificed everything,
but there is no celebration,
And I never had a choice
A body
childhood
A chance.

Child sexual abuse is a wide-ranging problem of long standing that needs to be adequately addressed. Society has to accept responsibility for its causes and contributing factors. While the scale of the problem of sexual abuse is beginning to be recognized and to receive considerable media attention, there are still many individuals and child care professionals who continue to minimize or deny the scope and severity of the problem. Indeed, it is only in the past few decades that the problem has been seriously acknowledged by both professionals and the general public (Sgroi, 1992).

It is essential to learn how to respond effectively to the child victim in a sensitive and timely fashion. This response requires the availability of legal, medical, social work, and therapeutic professionals who are adequately trained and committed to this important task. Although there has been some progress, British society and other western societies have not responded fully enough; the needs of the victim continue to far exceed the available resources.

Sexual abuse of children occurs across a broad range of social, cultural and socio-economic boundaries, is an abuse of power, and attacks those who are vulnerable and at risk. When children are sexually abused, they are treated both as an object and as an adult partner, forced into sexual activities for which mind and body are not ready. When it comes to light, child and family may be subjected to child protection procedures, and the child may undergo a forensic medical examination. In a minority of cases the child may give evidence in court, either through a video link or in the witness box, at the trial of the alleged abuser. The abuse and its aftermath are inevitably deeply traumatic for the abuse victim. Therapeutic help to children suffering from the effects of sexual abuse and their (non-abusive) carers can be an important component of the child's return to a healthy lifestyle and, in due course, to secure adult functioning.

A case example illustrates some of these issues:

Anna was a six-year-old, living at home with her mother and little brother. Her parents had been divorced for many years. Anna used to be a happy child with a zest for life and a love of nature. Then she became increasingly irritable, defiant, had nightmares, and lost her appetite. Her classroom teacher said she had changed and the other children didn't want to play with her. One night Anna's mother heard cries and found Anna fondling her brother's penis. Anna began drawing willies on her bedroom wall, and started wetting her bed. In the bath one evening Anna flinched, complaining that her bottom was sore. Her mother asked her what was wrong, but Anna only cried and shook her head. Mother was aghast at her daughter's distress. She noticed that Anna wouldn't visit her uncle in the next street; she said it was boring. Mother wondered about this. With difficulty Anna blurted out that she didn't like her uncle. She proceeded to draw a picture, which the mother took to the police. Mother hated doing this and was very distressed – to think that her own brother might have abused her lovely Anna. Then there was a medical examination and interviews with the police and child protection officer, who also wanted to talk to the neighbours and to the school. Anna had to go through it all again in front of a video camera. She became increasingly distressed. At home, she withdrew and was tearful. She began having tantrums, and continued to complain of physical symptoms. Her bottom hurt more and more and she had to be treated with tablets and cream. She hated going to the loo.

When the court business was out of the way, Anna had other kids taunting her about her uncle going to prison. Anna and her mother couldn't sort out all their hurt and mixed feelings, so Anna saw a therapist and her mother saw a social worker. Anna played, drew pictures, and talked with her therapist. Mother talked a lot to her social worker, for the first time telling about how her father had abused her when she was little. Slowly Anna and her mother grew and healed and flourished; though the memory of the uncle haunted them.

Defining the problem of child sexual abuse

Sexual abuse covers a range of sexual behaviours towards children, ranging in intrusiveness from exhibitionism to sexual penetration to involvement in pornography. Frequency and duration of the abuse vary, some children being subjected to intense abuse over time. Intrafamilial abuse occurs when someone abuses the child within the family setting, and extrafamilial abuse when the abuser is not related. An early definition of child sexual abuse is as follows:

> Child sexual abuse is a sexual act imposed on a child who lacks emotional, maturational, and cognitive development. The ability to lure a child into a sexual relationship is based upon the all-powerful and dominant position of the adult or older adolescent perpetrator, which is in sharp contrast to the child's age, dependency, and subordinate position. Authority and power enable the perpetrator, implicitly and directly, to coerce the child into sexual compliance. (Sgroi, Blick and Porter, 1982: 9)

We have subsequently become aware of acts of sexual aggression perpetrated by young children.

Workers have identified a cluster of problems exhibited by sexually abused children, varying in intensity, duration and type from child to child (Berliner, 1990; Porter, Blick and Sgroi, 1982). Edgeworth and Carr (2000: 19) cite studies confirming that 'Sexual abuse has profound short- and long-term effects on psychological functioning', two-thirds of sexually abused children developing psychological symptoms, with a quarter developing more severe difficulties (Berliner and Elliott, 1996; Kendall-Tacket et al., 1993; Wolfe and Birt, 1995).

Being the victim of child sexual abuse

How children respond to the abuse depends on:

- the context, frequency, duration, and type of abuse, especially if penetrative;
- whether the abuse is perpetrated by known people or strangers;
- the child's age, stage of development, ego strength and physical and mental health at the time of the abuse;
- the child's coping mechanisms and resilience, including whether the child has a secure background;
- the carers' reactions and coping mechanisms; and
- environmental support and response. (Elliott and Place, 1998: 93; Johns, 1997; Trowell, 1999: 109)

Some children recover satisfactorily. Other, more damaged, children require therapeutic help if they are not to be affected adversely by what has happened. It seems to be agreed that sexually abused children may:

- have distorted views about the purposes of sex;
- not understand the norms for child and adult (sexual) behaviours;

- see adults as abusers and not as protectors and nurturers;
- experience medical problems connected with their mouths or genitals, or as a result of sexually transmitted diseases, AIDS, drugs, or pregnancy;
- have mental health problems caused by fear and coercion;
- exhibit emotional difficulties and problems with trust, boundaries and affect;
- become victims, or abusers; and
- exhibit symptoms of Post Traumatic Stress Disorder (PTSD), chronic stress and traumas. (Wieland, 1998: 24)

Child victims of sexuality, beyond their emotional and physical developmental levels, are violated in every sense of the word: physically, psychologically, emotionally, and spiritually. Browne and Finkelhor (1986) usefully identify problems that may be caused by the *sexual* component of the abuse:

- *Traumatic sexualization*   Conventional sexual behaviour is skewed. The child may develop atypical sexual behaviours as a young person and adult.
- *Stigmatization*   The abused child may feel 'bad', blaming themselves for bringing trouble upon the family and maintaining the secrecy enjoined by the perpetrator. The child's self-esteem may be jeopardized, and some children subsequently turn to self-harm, substance abuse, or even suicide. The child may dissociate from the abusive situation.
- *Betrayal*   The child's trust in adults may have been violated, and suspicion of other people and their intentions may intrude.
- *Powerlessness*   Powerlessness can promote victimization, depression or suicidal behaviour. 'The experience of powerlessness may also lead to the internalization of a victim-persecutor internal working model for relationships, which sows the seeds for the child later becoming a perpetrator when placed in a position where an opportunity to exert power over a vulnerable person arises.' (Edgeworth and Carr, 2000: 19–20)

Survival becomes the key, and the abused child's developing sense of self and self-esteem is severely threatened. It is clear that victims of child sexual abuse may suffer long-term negative consequences as a result of their abuse (Fergusson and Mullen, 1999: 54–7).

The need for more research on the effectiveness of treatment and outcomes

The current trends in the literature suggest that there will be more research available on the outcomes of treatment with children who have been sexually abused. Hodges states that there is not much available research on child psychotherapy. 'Increasingly, child psychotherapists working in some areas of the NHS are under pressure to give evidence of the usefulness and cost-effectiveness of their work.' (1999: 119)

The challenge of providing therapy

Therapy needs to be proven and effective, taking place alongside the important work of carers, educationalists and healthcare workers, and should be separate from child protection procedures (Valios, 2000). Although there is growing awareness of the need for, and value of, therapeutic work with abused children, there is a constant struggle to create, and maintain, resources. The provision of therapeutic services to children in England and Wales is patchy (Audit Commission, 1999; Sharland et al., 1996) and there is a paucity of effective research to help practitioners decide on the most appropriate treatment methods. Only a fraction of abused children and their families are helped (Hunter, 1999: 133), service provision being left to the discretion of the local authority where the child lives (Children Act 1989, schedule 2).

When therapy is available, it is incumbent on all concerned to identify the issues that are to be worked on in the therapeutic setting. Trowell (1999: 114–15) lists the following:

- abuse issues;
- current disruptions, losses, separations;
- earlier childhood issues;
- psychopathology, such as PTSD, depression and suicidal thoughts, anxiety and panic attacks, separation anxiety, attachment disorders, conduct disorders, eating disorders;
- future plans, self confidence, self esteem; and
- family and social relationships.

There is emerging consensus that there are four major areas of therapeutic work (Gallo-Lopez, 2000; Rasmussen and Cunningham, 1995):

1 Treating children as people in their own right, with space to express and explore their own concerns (the child-centred approach) (West, 1996).
2 Treatment of traumatic sexualization, stigmatization, betrayal and powerlessness (Finkelhor and Browne, 1985) with implications for self-image, cognitive work and ventilation of feelings.
3 Helping the child to regain age appropriate functioning, self-confidence and self-respect, aided by therapeutic regression if necessary (based on developmental and child growth theories).
4 Impacting on the child's world by helping the child's (non-abusing) carers and school or daycare staff to respond effectively to the child's needs (systems or ecological theory).

Contextual requirements are that:

- the child is living with appropriate, nurturing carers and is not being abused;
- if old enough, the child has admitted the abuse; and
- the (non-abusive) carers and perhaps the siblings also receive counselling and advice related to the child's abuse.

Therapeutic sessions with the child, within a child-centred framework, call for non-directive as well as focused work either individually or in a group, with another therapist working alongside the child's carers and ecosystem.

Summary

Unfortunately, the sexual violation of children is an inescapable fact. Its effect varies, depending on the nature of the assault(s), the child's developmental stage and level of resilience, and quality of family support. Some children are so badly damaged, psychologically and maybe physically, that remedial help is necessary for child and carers. Therapeutic paradigms are emerging for individual and group therapy with children, plus help for carers and siblings. The professionalism of the therapist is vital and integral to the whole book, and we pay particular attention to it in the next chapter.

2   The Therapist's Clinical Skills

The nature and quality of the therapeutic relationship with the child has a profound influence on how successful the therapeutic work will be. The relationship with the therapist needs to be one in which the child feels safe, supported, respected, valued, and empowered, a relationship within which healing can begin.

This chapter describes the clinical skills and functions of the therapist, and many important elements of the process are examined including the following:

- the acceptance and integration of the sexual abuse into the child's psyche;
- boundaries and feelings of powerlessness;
- empathy;
- trust;
- the holding environment;
- education about abuse and normalization of symptoms;
- the self-observing ego;
- enjoyment of the child and engagement in play; and
- sensitivity to danger of replicating the abusive relationship.

You never laugh at me
when I tell you that all men with beards
frighten me,
that I can't stand the smell of men's cologne,

that I get scared every night
at sunset,
and need to hold
someone's hand.

You only listen and smile at me,
and in that smile,
I know that I am important,
and worthwhile.
And that it is OK to be scared.

And in your eyes
I see understanding
and caring.
In your face

I see hope
that I will feel better.

You never laugh at me,
you only smile.
And I know that you
believe in me.
It makes me wonder
if maybe, I am worth that belief
after all.

Thank you

The central task of the therapeutic process: acceptance and integration of the sexual abuse experience

In order for the child to begin the process of healing from the experience of the abuse, the child has to acknowledge the painful experience and accept it as something traumatic that has really happened. If the abuse is not acknowledged and accepted, the child will invest tremendous energy in minimizing, suppressing, repressing, and dissociating the experience, in order to cope with and defend against the trauma. 'The trauma can be re-experienced and reworked – either directly or indirectly through the verbalization of details, emotions, and memories surrounding the abuse, or indirectly, symbolically through play therapy.' (Strand 1999: 105)

Although the child's defences (Chapter 10) provide a means to survive and cope with the trauma, they gradually need to be replaced by more adaptive ways of coping and functioning. Many defences, when left in place, are maladaptive and result in dysfunctional behaviour as the child matures. They also interfere with the child's processing and resolution of developmental tasks, which is a necessary part of the child's psychological and emotional evolution.

The exploration and processing of the trauma is necessary for several reasons:

1   Becoming aware of and experiencing the affective and cognitive aspects of the trauma helps to lessen dissociative tendencies.
2   Uncovering and exploring misconceptions about the trauma prevents false beliefs from being repressed. These often include negative beliefs about the self and feelings of inherent badness and responsibility for the abuse.
3   Returning to the trauma and/or processing feelings, cognitions, and beliefs related to the experience help to make the trauma less powerful and overwhelming. The therapist can help to contain and soothe the child, and can strengthen the child's capacity to provide these functions for herself.
4   Therapy helps to strengthen the child's self-observing ego. Gaining some understanding and insight about the abuse helps the child to feel less overwhelmed and powerless, thus providing a modicum of relief and sense of control to the child.

5 The child is helped to tolerate painful affect. Children are afraid of emotional pain, and much dysfunction and symptomology are caused by the avoidance of natural or necessary pain. With the therapist's assistance, the child learns that feeling badly is a natural response to being traumatized.

Over time, the child learns that talking about the effects of the trauma, in the context of being listened to, supported, and understood, will be helpful. Children have a remarkable ability to adapt to positive and negative circumstances, and some can resist or recover even from the negative effects of maltreatment, once they are given proper opportunities and protection (Cicchetti and Rogosch, 1997).

Over time, and with the help of the therapist, the child will also experience a lessening of painful feelings and begin to feel better. The therapist can place the child's healing process in a context in which the child gains emotional strength and courage for having confronted the pain.

The therapeutic relationship

One of the most important functions of the therapist is to provide containment, support, and what Winnicott refers to as a safe holding environment. The term 'the holding environment' denotes not just the physical holding of the baby by the carer, but the provision of or functions of protection, support, caring and containing that envelops the child. According to Winnicott:

> The important thing ... is that the mother through identification of herself with her infant knows what the infant feels like and so is able to provide almost exactly what the infant needs in the way of holding and in the provision of an environment generally. Without such an identification ... she is not able to provide what the infant needs at the beginning, which is a *live adaptation to the infant's needs.* (1990: 54)

Functions such as soothing, security, tension regulation, and self-esteem regulation are initially provided by the 'good enough or adequate mother', or other external sources. The child is gradually able to internalize and take on these functions which become part of the child's own mental structure.

According to Kohut, the therapist becomes a 'self-object' (Kohut, 1971). The self-object is similar to a 'transitional object' in Winnicott's words. The therapist provides these functions for the child in order to help the child experience and process the trauma experience, while at the same time being soothed and contained. These functions are provided until the child is able to internalize them. 'The self of the child expands and achieves cohesion through innumerable transmuting internalizations of self object functions into self functions' (Elson, 1986: 11). The ability to do this is dependent somewhat on the child's age and developmental level. The therapist helps to re-stimulate psychological growth, development, and healing.

This holding environment needs to be established in order that the child may feel safe, as well as engage and progress in the therapeutic process. 'Consistency, regularity, and reliability, the combination of warmth with firm boundaries, are basic requirements in any psychotherapy and are clearly related to the ingredients of effective parenthood' (Margison, 1991).

Consistency in the behaviour of the therapist, an essential element, is equivalent to safety and a prerequisite to successful treatment. Consistency is established by elements such as always being on time, being reliable, being unconditionally accepting and responsive to the child, remembering what the child says, doing what you say you will do, achieving continuity from one session to the next, being calm, and acting in the child's best interest.

The therapist needs to be patient and able to tolerate silence. It is important that the silence is not of an uncomfortable length or it may be experienced as punitive by the child. A child's tolerance of silence is highly variable. Often, a therapist will be surprised by the insightful comments that come from a child as a result of waiting that extra moment or two.

Boundaries and feelings of powerlessness

Establishing boundaries and letting the child know what to expect during the therapeutic process is empowering to the child. The child abuse victim has frequently been robbed of having a choice and of being in control. 'Many children hold on to the powerlessness they experienced when traumatized, and that feeling expands to become their self-image. The clinician needs to help them recognize that they have power and choices, and that their powerlessness as victims does not extend to other areas of their lives' (James, 1989: 22). The child needs to become aware that the traumatic experience does not define either who they are or who they will become.

It is an essential part of the therapeutic process to empower the child whenever possible. One way of accomplishing this is by letting them know that you, as a therapist, have respect for their right and ability to choose. This needs to be reiterated many times during the process, both covertly and overtly.

Boundaries have been blurred and violated as a consequence of the sexual abuse, which is an extreme violation of the boundaries of the self on every level (physically, emotionally, psychologically and spiritually). The differentiation between self and other has often been blotted out, leaving the child feeling powerless, vulnerable and confused. Furthermore, the normal boundaries between adult and child have become distorted or non-existent.

The child is certain to develop some degree of boundary confusion:

> Typically this is manifested as an over-intrusiveness on their part with little or no understanding regarding privacy or personal space. For children who are sexually abused after establishing personal boundaries, the feelings of violation and intrusion are often much greater. They often feel as if they are 'damaged goods'. Indeed Sgroi (1982) goes so far as to label it the 'damaged goods syndrome'. (Smith, 1992: 140)

Subsequently, the child may now feel that he has no control over his own body or life. Re-establishing ownership and appropriate boundaries is an ongoing focus of the treatment process, with the therapist facilitating the re-definition and strengthening of boundaries. The process of maintaining safety and therapeutic boundaries for the child provides a new and healthy role model of boundaries. This is a process which occurs through the child being safe, being educated about the abuse, and being respected and valued in the therapeutic realm.

Identification with the victim or abuser

Many children who have been sexually abused view the world in a polarized way. As a result of the abuse, they may now believe the world is made up of two types of people: abusers and victims. This belief places the child in the difficult position of identifying with either group. A child may wonder whether he will remain a victim or become an abuser. Some children decide, consciously or unconsciously, to be in the more powerful role and become aggressive, controlling or begin victimizing others. Other children become self-punishing and/or identify with the victim role, becoming submissive, or place themselves in positions (unconsciously) in which they are likely to be victimized.

The experience of sexual abuse is best placed within the context of an abuse of power and authority, largely dependent on the age of the child and his developmental capacity to understand this concept. This issue also has strong implications for the treatment process, in which there is an imbalance of power and authority. The therapist needs to be aware of the abuse of power dynamic, which can also be a factor in unintentionally replicating the abusive experience. The therapist has to be vigilant and work hard to establish a partnership with the child, one in which the child feels empowered, respected, and valued at all times.

Empathy

Carl Rogers was one of the first theorists to include both understanding and feeling in his definition of empathy. Rogers wrote of *accurate empathy* as one of the central conditions that is necessary to bring about change in clients:

> The fifth condition is that the therapist is experiencing an accurate, empathic understanding of the client's awareness of his own experience. To sense the client's private world as if it were your own, but without ever losing the 'as if' quality – that is empathy, and this seems essential to therapy. To sense the client's anger, fear, or confusion as if it were your own, yet without your own anger, fear, or confusion getting bound up in it, is the condition we are endeavouring to describe. (1957: 99)

Empathy thus includes understanding and feeling with the child. The therapist who communicates with the child comforts the child, and increases the child's own understanding and awareness. Introspection can be used to facilitate the child's awareness of what he is feeling, and why he is feeling a certain way. In order for positive change and growth to occur, empathy needs to be a central component in the therapeutic relationship.

Therapists do their best to understand how the child has felt or is feeling at the moment. If the child is quite young and does not have a suitably developed 'feeling' vocabulary, the therapist needs to help the child to develop words that identify the feelings. In order to accomplish this, feelings may first need to be described and named. Often, the therapist initially has to provide the emotion for the child. This may be accomplished verbally or through play, using puppets, toys, art work, and so on. Note the example below:

> The therapist is using a finger puppet in her session with Poppy, age 6.
>
> 'Joey, the bear is feeling sad and cross today. He misses John. He is not sure why he went away. Joey feels sad. He also feels cross because John didn't say goodbye. One minute he feels like crying, but a few minutes later, he feels cross, and feels like punching the pillow. It is confusing to him. He wonders why John went away. He wishes John would ring him or send him a letter, or better yet come back home.'
>
> The therapist looks at Poppy, who nods and gives a small smile. The therapist's puppet addresses Poppy's puppet. 'Do you ever feel that way … sad and cross at the same time?' Poppy bends her finger to make her puppet nod. 'My daddy left home too,' she says. 'It makes me cross sometimes, and I don't think he will come home.'

The therapist facilitates the child's understanding and awareness of her feelings, in a non-judgemental fashion, through the process of mirroring and reflecting emotions back to the child. Allowing the child adequate time to experience and reflect upon her feelings and experience is an integral piece of the process. Next, the therapist may choose to validate with the child, either staying in the play metaphor or speaking with the child directly, about whether the child's experience or feelings are similar to what the therapist has described.

The therapist offers compassion and empathy to the child, who often feels ashamed, isolated, and negative about herself. During sessions, the child experiences empathy, understanding, and compassion, and gradually, bit by bit, internalizes the therapist's functions and makes them her own in her own way.

Trust

Trust is inevitably a central treatment issue with a child who has been sexually abused. A child's capacity to trust has been shattered by another person. This is particularly so if the perpetrator was a 'trusted' or 'intimate' other or family member. In these cases, the abuse is more devastating.

> Betrayal and the child's subsequent loss of trust disturbs the very foundation of her development. Betrayal by a loved carer is translated into 'I am no good. I don't deserve better treatment. The world is threatening.' If a child cannot trust her primary carer, she cannot help feeling that literally no one in the world can be trusted. (James, 1989: 25)

A child who has been sexually abused is frequently overwhelmed and confused; the child may no longer trust her own feelings, instincts, perceptions or emotions. The child may doubt herself because she had trusted the individual who then went on to abuse her. As a result, the child may either consciously or unconsciously believe that *it is not safe to trust anyone*. The child may become increasingly isolated and alienated from others as a result of this belief.

In addition, the child may now display impaired judgement and an inability to differentiate between safe and non-safe situations, and healthy versus exploitative relationships. The child may be at an increased risk of being traumatized or abused again because of this dynamic.

In therapeutic work with adult survivors of sexual abuse, we have heard of many situations in people's lives when they lacked good judgement skills, and made negative, risky or even dangerous choices. Many survivors have chosen and remained in unhealthy, even destructive, relationships. Part of this can be attributed to feelings of low self-esteem and self-worth. They did not feel that they deserved to be treated differently or in a nurturing fashion. It can also partly be attributed to Freudian repetition compulsion (an unconscious process to resolve the past trauma through repeating it, and attempting resolution).

In addition, many adult survivors show severely impaired judgement in being able to differentiate between healthy or destructive relationships. There is a lack of awareness and dissociative nature in their choice of relationships, and many such people appear unaware of their responsibility and power to end these relationships. In some cases such as a woman finishing a domestically violent relationship, ending the association could and does have serious and dangerous, even life-threatening, repercussions.

Childhood sexual abuse frequently leaves adult survivors vulnerable to future maltreatment. Many survivors have not had previous therapy, or have not addressed the sexual abuse trauma. Many have never considered the link between their sexual abuse victimization and the unhealthy or destructive relationships they may be involved in, or other symptoms they may be experiencing. Some of them may have been sexually assaulted on one or more occasions, or may describe a dissociative response being triggered when in danger. In situations resembling aspects of their abuse trauma, they may become incapacitated or dissociative, and be unable to pick up on 'danger' signals or clues, leaving them increasingly vulnerable and at risk.

However, this does not mean that all survivors of sexual abuse are prone or likely to be re-victimized. Many survivors do not place themselves in risky situations or become involved in unhealthy or abusive relationships. However, there can be a correlation between the two that should be explored and addressed in therapy.

Therefore, helping the child victim to develop self-preservation skills, and to develop good judgement, is important. The child needs to be able to trust her own feelings, instincts and perceptions. Over time, the child needs to be able to trust other people again, whilst being aware that not all people are trustworthy. This can be complicated for children to understand and needs to be done in a manner that is appropriate for the age of the child.

The therapist needs to be worthy of the child's trust and slowly to help her gradually to rebuild trust and faith in herself and the outside world.

Functions of the therapist

Being the victim of sexual abuse will significantly impair any capacity the child might otherwise have developed to regulate emotions, or to soothe or nurture herself. The child tends to regress due to the trauma. The therapist needs to be able to contain the child, and to nurture the child in the therapeutic setting, until the child is able to provide them for herself. Extensive work with the carers may be needed. The partnership between therapists and carers is addressed in Chapter 6.

Starting where the child is

As with adult therapy, it is essential to accept and respect the child for who she is. The child needs to experience the therapist as non-judgemental and someone who accepts the child's feelings whatever they may be. A child needs to be able to express feelings and thoughts that were previously repressed, suppressed, denied, or considered unacceptable in other settings.

Since much of the child's intra-psychic energy is spent defending against, or coping with, the trauma and its after effects, it is essential that a child is able to express and act out aspects of the trauma, and parts of the self, that have been buried or deliberately hidden as a result of the shame she has experienced. This process can only occur in a setting that the child experiences as safe, with the therapist establishing boundaries in a reassuring and consistent fashion.

Furthermore, the therapist needs to respect the child's pace, and let the child control how fast or slow the process will be. Respecting the child's pace requires having faith in the therapy process, based on the belief that the child will gradually bring in the necessary material to work on, due to the child's innate capacity for self-healing. The therapist enables, facilitates, and strengthens this capacity throughout.

There is often a tendency for a therapist to want to rush the process, due to the vulnerability of the child or the therapist's protectiveness. Such feelings are often evoked naturally as a result of working with traumatized children. There may be a tendency for the less experienced therapist to want to protect the child, which may run counter to reawakening memories of the abuse. Therapists need to be aware of such feelings on their part, since they may interfere with the treatment process. More is said about countertransference issues in Chapter 4.

The following case example illustrates some of these dynamics:

Sophie, aged four, had been brought to treatment following sexual abuse by her grandmother, to whom she had been close. The sexual abuse had been ongoing over a two year period while Sophie's mother, a single parent, had been at work. The grandmother provided child care at this time. The abuse consisted of the grandmother fondling the girl's genitals. The mother did not report the abuse at the time it occurred, as she believed it would distress Sophie, and she could not tolerate action being taken against her mother. She and all other family members had no further contact with her mother following the abuse.

Sophie was depressed, sad, and tearful. She was also reluctant to talk about the abuse. The therapist, who was a counselling student on placement, was concerned about Sophie's reaction whenever she mentioned the abuse. It was difficult for her to tolerate Sophie's tears, and she felt guilty and responsible for upsetting her. The therapist found herself avoiding talking about Sophie's feelings towards her grandmother, or the sexual abuse she had suffered. Fortunately, the student realized her countertransference feelings were interfering with her provision of treatment, and she subsequently approached her supervisor for help.

Her supervisor agreed that she needed to be sensitive to the child's feelings, but that it would be beneficial to approach issues slowly at the child's pace. However, avoiding talking about the abuse was counterproductive, and was probably confusing to the child, who might wonder why she was in treatment. Furthermore, the child might perceive the therapist's avoidance of the subject as proof of her inherent badness. She might also feel that the therapist could not tolerate hearing about the abuse.

The supervisor felt that Sophie needed to be gently encouraged to speak about the abuse. The supervisor tried to help the therapist normalize and support Sophie's despair, and to talk about her ambivalent feelings towards her grandmother, particularly her feelings of sadness and loss. The therapist was unable to work through her own feelings, and unable to tolerate and empathize with Sophie's sadness, and limited in her ability to contain and comfort Sophie. She still felt she either had to take away, or avoid talking about, the issues that caused Sophie so much pain.

The student began using puppets, toys, and pictures to help Sophie express her feelings in ways that were less painful than direct communication about the abuse. Sophie especially enjoyed doing puppet shows and would act out different scenarios with her 'grandmother' and the puppet. The therapist felt safer using this medium. Over a treatment period of seven months, Sophie reached a point when she no longer needed to use the puppets, as she was able to verbalize and process her feelings directly with the therapist. This, again, evoked strong countertransference issues in the therapist.

The outcome of treatment was very impaired largely due to the unresolved issues on the therapist's part.

The approach to the abuse

Previous disclosure of the abuse may have evoked disbelief or other strong and negative responses from people in the child's life, or precipitated negative repercussions for the child who may now understandably feel reluctant to talk about the abuse. A direct approach by the therapist is strongly recommended. Speaking about the abuse encourages the child to talk more openly about her experience. Being direct strengthens the child's awareness that the therapist can tolerate hearing about the abuse, and reinforces the child's belief that the therapist is there to help with issues or symptoms that have been caused by the abuse. If the therapist does not talk about the abuse directly, the child may perceive this as dishonest, and this may intensify any shame the child may feel. It may also interfere with the child's development of trust in the therapist and the therapeutic process.

Letting the child know that you, the therapist, have helped other children who have also been abused, and will do your best to help her, decreases the possibility of any need for secrecy. In addition, the child may be less prone to harbour fears that she is being seen by the therapist because she is bad, or is being punished because of what has happened. If the abuser is not receiving treatment, it is more likely that the child will feel she is in treatment because she is inherently bad or responsible for the abuse.

The child will probably need time to feel safe and to have control over the process. She will generally disclose the least shameful material first, and the worst material later. This is natural and the therapist should anticipate that this may occur. The child will often *test* the therapist, being highly perceptive about the therapist's reactions to the material presented. It is important for the therapist not to appear shocked otherwise the child may hold back on further disclosure.

The therapist may experience strong emotional reactions to some of the child's disclosures. This is particularly true if the material is sadistic or involves ritualistic abuse. The therapist should try not to respond in too strong a fashion. It is most beneficial if the therapist is able to stay calm while the child is discussing the abuse. If the therapist appears upset or alarmed, the child may feel guilty and blame herself for upsetting the therapist. Shame, shock, or anger expressed by the therapist may be interpreted by the child as revulsion or anger directed at herself. Almost all child victims feel some level of responsibility for the abuse. The child may assume that the feelings should be directed at herself if the therapist 'only knew or realized' that the child was really to blame. As a result, the child may withhold important information.

A child may be eager to please or protect the therapist, and may not present information that she imagines will upset or be in disagreement with the therapist. This may be exacerbated if the child is in role-reversal with carers in the family, in the role of a parentified child, which will be acted out in the therapeutic transference. The parentified child typically is hyper-aware of and concerned with other people's feelings and needs, rather than with her own.

If the therapist is experiencing strong feelings of distress due to a child's disclosure or the nature of the abuse, the therapist must seek supervision. Some therapists have experienced a form of secondary post-traumatic stress disorder resulting from providing therapy to severely abused children. Supervision can be important for preventing 'burn out' and providing support for the therapist. It is also extremely helpful to have support from, and to network with, other professionals doing the same sort of work (Hawkins and Shohet, 2000; Knapman and Morrison, 1998; Pritchard, 1995).

Education about abuse and normalization of symptoms

This aspect of treatment is important and beneficial to the child. Normalizing the child's symptoms and issues provides relief to the child victim of sexual abuse and to the carer. From their reactions, children often fear that they are going mad or that something is truly damaged or permanently wrong with them. Letting children know that what they are going through is a normal reaction to abuse can be tremendously reassuring. Repetition is often very necessary to accomplish this task.

A therapist can anticipate some of the child's current feelings and symptoms, helping the child to identify when they started and how they may have changed or become more severe. Frequently, the child has no clue that any of the symptoms are linked to the sexual abuse. It is important to help the child to see the correlation, if at all possible. The therapist often needs to let the child know that the painful feelings and symptoms will take some time to go away, but that they will lessen and get better eventually.

It is useful to explore children's concerns, fears, and fantasies regarding their symptoms. Being open, encouraging questions, and offering information throughout the therapy is empowering, as well as letting them know that you will help them recover from the experience of abuse.

It is therapeutic for the child to be aware that other children have been sexually abused and that the child is not alone in this respect. Telling stories of other children's experiences (while always respecting confidentiality) can provide tremendous relief. Hearing other children's stories reinforces the fact that other children have been abused, and that other children may share similar feelings and experiences. This helps to decrease the child's feelings of being different, damaged, and alone.

A child victim, especially young children, may believe that other people can tell that they have been abused simply by looking at them. This belief increases the child's self-perception of being damaged goods and increases self-consciousness. Group therapy sessions are an excellent adjunct to individual treatment in this respect (Chapter 11). Stigma and shame can be more effectively alleviated in such a modality.

The following example illustrates many of these aspects:

Jean, aged six, was engaged in treatment following abuse by her mother's boyfriend, Richard, aged 27. Richard had abused her over a five-month period after moving into the household. The abuse had begun with Richard showing Jean pornographic videos. The abuse progressed as Richard fondled Jean, forcing her to perform oral sex on him.

Jean began manifesting many symptoms including tearfulness, depression, somatic complaints, nightmares, and her schoolwork deteriorated. She felt increased confusion and shame, believing that other people could tell that she had been abused by looking at her. Her self-esteem lowered and she began avoiding her peers due to her increased self-consciousness. She wondered why her mother didn't respond to her and protect her from Richard. Jean had stomach pains and believed that she was probably pregnant even though no intercourse had taken place.

Jean told her biological father about the abuse. He informed the mother who contacted the police. Richard was arrested. Jean's mother supported her and immediately put her into treatment.

During therapy, Jean's beliefs and misconceptions about the abuse and her body were gently challenged and gradually replaced with accurate information. If the misconceptions had been left in place, and most likely repressed, they would have been detrimental to Jean. The therapist normalized her symptoms in the context of the abuse and supported and contained her.

After three months of individual treatment, in which she made good progress, Jean joined a group for sexually abused children. The group successfully helped Jean to process her shame, self-consciousness, isolation, and feelings of responsibility. She was a member of the group for the next six months at which time she felt much better about herself and treatment was terminated at her and her mother's request. The therapist encouraged Jean to come back in the future if she needed help with unresolved issues, or during her progression through a later developmental stage.

Facilitating a self-observing ego in the child

Children are naturally very perceptive and show uncanny understanding of complicated situations. Clinically our experience validates our inherent belief that children are capable of understanding a great deal more than many adults credit them with. Children often see things clearly, and speak truthfully, because they are still innocent, and have not yet been socialized to dissemble or dilute what they experience.

It is essential to help the child to understand her experience in a physical, psychological, emotional, and cognitive context. 'Through telling her story, the child has the opportunity to clarify and gain a cognitive understanding of events and issues. Additionally, she can ventilate painful feelings and gain mastery over anxieties and other emotional disturbances by active rather than passive means' (Geldard and Geldard, 1997: 41).

When therapists make an interpretation, they should speak directly using simple language, confirming with the child how she has interpreted what the therapist has said. It is helpful to encourage the child to ask questions. It is often surprising how much a child understands. If the child does not initially appear to comprehend the therapist's interpretation, she can simply let it go. The therapist may repeat it at a different point, and it may be more salient and understandable at a later stage when the child may be better able to process and take in the information. Let children know that it is fine if they do not agree or do not want to answer questions, or if they simply do not feel ready to respond.

As with an adult client, timing is important. A child will hear and internalize an interpretation or insight only when ready. There is some debate about how much interpretation is therapeutic for children, but our experience suggests that an interpretation given in a sensitive fashion can increase and facilitate the development of a child's self-observing ego and promote healing and recovery.

At the same time, it is necessary to let children know that you respect their own insights and beliefs. A child who is engaged in the therapeutic process may be hyper-aware of and eager to please the therapist. Getting it across to the child that you are separate individuals, perhaps with different feelings and beliefs, is an important lesson in healthy separation and individuality.

Enjoyment of the child and engagement in play

A child's ability to engage in and enjoy playing can be impaired. Often children feel withdrawn and depressed following abuse, which can interfere with their ability to engage with other children or to enjoy playing. Many carers express concern when a child's behaviour changes dramatically following abuse. For example, a child who was previously outgoing can become a loner and spend a lot of time in the bedroom. The child no longer wants to partake in usual activities that were previously enjoyed. It is helpful to let the parents know that a child's withdrawal can be a normal response to being abused, and that this can be alleviated and change over time.

Another dynamic sometimes present is the child's increased anxiety regarding play. The child may be afraid of suppressed or repressed feelings that come forth when they are playing. Issues regarding the abuse often surface during play, which is normally a child's natural medium of communication and facilitates the resolution of intra-psychic issues and conflicts. The child may restrict play in order to avoid painful emotions or thoughts.

The child may also experience memories or flashbacks of the trauma while playing. Therapists present at these times can contain and soothe the child, and facilitate the child's psychological return to the present. However, due to the reasons already given, it may take some time for the child to be able to play in a spontaneous and enjoyable fashion again.

The therapist's engagement in and enjoyment of playing with the child is important. Sincere and genuine pleasure of being with the child enhances the child's self-esteem. Once engaged in the therapy process, the child is usually responsive to having the complete attention of the therapist, and will frequently enjoy playing.

Trying to see and experience the world from the child's point of view is crucial.

The adult world is very different from a child's world. However, as adults we have not lost our child: it is still a part of our personality. This inner child is available to us if we learn how to access it. Accessing our inner child doesn't mean being childish, or regressing to childhood. It means getting in touch with that part of ourselves which fits comfortably with a child's world. (Geldard and Geldard, 1997: 15)

Play therapy can provide a cathartic experience for the child. Emotions can be experienced, acted out, and released to someone else in the person of the therapist who helps and contains the child. Play therapy can be fun, creative, interesting, stimulating, and is an excellent tool for providing insight and healing.

Sensitivity to danger of replicating the child's relationship with the abuser

There is a slight possibility that the therapeutic relationship may trigger feelings, or in some cases even flashbacks, of the abuse situation. This can be attributed to the fact that some aspects of the therapeutic relationship may resemble the abusive one, ranging from the power imbalance (mentioned earlier), to talking about private matters, or to promises of keeping matters secret due to confidentiality. Engaging in a relationship that is based on trust and intimacy may also contribute to possible flashbacks; the child may have been abused by a trusted person with whom the child was close. The therapist needs to be aware of this potential danger. These issues should be addressed immediately to the best of the therapist's capacity.

Summary

In this chapter we have discussed the primary task of the therapeutic process: the acceptance and integration of the sexual abuse trauma into the child's psyche. This process is best facilitated by the development of a safe, supportive, and empathic relationship with the therapist, a relationship in which the child's healing process can begin.

Conversely, if the trauma is not addressed, the child will spend tremendous energy in minimizing, suppressing, repressing, and dissociating the experience, to cope with and defend against the trauma and its aftermath. This will ultimately interfere with the child's development, and may result in low self-esteem, depression, dysfunctional and/or self-punishing behaviour, and potentially psychiatric disorders.

The skills the therapist needs to possess, and important elements and tasks of the therapeutic milieu, have also been defined. Ultimately, the nature and quality of the relationship between the child and the therapist is of great significance in determining how successful the outcome of treatment will be.

Exercise

Think back on your relationships when you were a small child.

Which adults in your life were meaningful? Think particularly of adults you trusted, who comforted you and helped you to feel safe and secure.

Who gave you attention and validated you?

Who made you feel proud and good about yourself? What were the qualities in these people that you especially appreciated?

If you were a small and vulnerable child going to see a therapist, what would be important to you?

---

3   Beginning Phases of Treatment

A poem written by a male survivor:

Speak to me
And I will speak with you.
I need to reclaim my body
                    my spirit
                            my peace of mind.
I want you to hear me
to understand
how I was forced
not to be a child.
A childhood taken away
destroyed
never to be reclaimed.

I need you to listen
not to speak, but to listen
Will you help me?
Can I be reclaimed?

I am asking you to believe me.
And more importantly
to believe in me.
It makes all the difference.

Listen carefully
For my voice is soft
like that of a child.
And if you speak
I will listen.
I am waiting.

There are many important issues that need to be considered at the beginning of
the treatment phase. These include:

- the referral source and available information;
- the safety and protection of the child;
- confidentiality issues;
- the assessment process;
- obtaining a history of the abuse;
- the child's relationship with the abuser and the nature of the disclosure; and
- the child's feelings of responsibility for the abuse, and how these may be best addressed.

The therapist can best anticipate and prepare for the start of the therapy process by considering these issues, as discussed in this chapter.

Referral source and information

Contact with the referral source, together with gathering and reviewing documentation and information, are important aspects of the initial phase of treatment. Important questions to be addressed include:

- Who is the primary referral source?
- Why is the child being referred at this time?
- Is the child involved in court procedures or on a court order?
- Are other legal proceedings taking place?
- Is the child known to social services or on a child protection register?
- Are the carers participating in the decision about bringing the child to treatment?
- Has the child been involved in the decision to come for therapy?
- Has the child or its family engaged in therapy before, and if so, was the experience positive or negative?
- What information is available about problems, issues or symptoms?
- What is the history and background of the abuse?

It is essential to gain parental consent before obtaining information and records from hospital, medical services, social services, legal records, school, and other pertinent sources.

Safety and protection of the child

The ongoing priority in treatment is maintaining the child's safety. The therapist needs to be in contact with social services or the appropriate legal organization to ensure that the child is continuously protected. Not only is the cessation of abuse essential for wellbeing and healing but, if not protected from re-victimization, the trusting relationship between therapist and child can be damaged. If abuse continues, the child may lose hope, faith, and trust in the ability of therapist, family, and social services to provide protection. The child may also inadvertently encourage further traumatization, as noted by Furniss:

> Sexually abused children can induce secondary traumatization through their own behaviour. They often provoke rejection, punishment, or re-abuse through sexualized behaviour or victim behaviour, which makes them more vulnerable and unable to protect themselves from the consequences of their own sexualized communication and victim messages. This process can easily lead to the induction of entirely new cycles of secondary victimization and abuse. (1991: 17)

The therapist should assess this risk as well.

Assessment of the family's level of functioning is integral to the safety process. In some cases, the family may be dysfunctional or temporarily fragmented due to the additional stress of having an abused child. In addition, the family may have shown, and continue to show, poor judgement in exposing the child to unnecessary risk. Carers who are themselves survivors of sexual abuse may have impaired ability to protect. Assessment of the family's capacity to keep the child free from abuse is necessary and needs to be ongoing.

In some cases, family members blaming the child for the repercussions of the abuse may make the child into a scapegoat. The child may not be believed, or held responsible, being accused of being seductive or initiating the sexual experience. Excuses such as drunkenness or being under stress may sometimes be made for the abuser. According to Furniss:

> The abuse might be denied by the abuser, by the mother, by the child, and by other family members. Each party might deny different aspects of the abuse. It might be total denial that any abuse has taken place at all or it can be partly denial:
>
> 1 of the abusive circumstances;
> 2 of the damaging effects;
> 3 of the addictive and repetitive nature of sexual abuse; and
> 4 of the abuser's responsibility. (1991: 244)

If there is extrafamilial abuse, the child can often be allowed to remain at home. The family may need assistance to learn how to take care of and protect the child from further victimization. Sometimes the family is unable to do this and it will be necessary to remove the child to a safe place. The child may perhaps be put into a temporary foster home or placed for adoption if the family is unable to prevent further exposure to victimization.

In cases of intrafamilial abuse (incest), various solutions are possible:

- the child may be removed from the home;
- the perpetrator may leave the home voluntarily or on a court order; or
- the family may be kept together and supervised.

Removal of the child from the incestuous home provides the greatest protection for the child. However, it can be traumatic for the child, who may view the removal as punishment, and proof both of inherent 'badness' and responsibility for the abuse. If siblings and family members are angry and hold the child to blame, this exacerbates the child's feelings of guilt and shame. The child feels isolated and rejected, often resulting in increasingly low self-esteem and depression. The child may be further traumatized by the losses that occur by removal from friends, relatives, family members, and familiar environment.

Whenever considered feasible by child protection personnel, the abusive carer will be removed from the home as this is considered less traumatic for the child. Family members may sometimes respond to the aftermath of this situation with anger and hostility towards the child. Furthermore, the remaining carer may experience conflicts over loyalty to the child versus loyalty to the alleged abuser. The carer may initially support the child and take legal action, but may later not believe the child and withdraw emotional support. The function of denial can relate to anxiety about:

1　the legal consequences;
2　consequences for the family and relatives;
3　psychological consequences;
4　social consequences; and
5　financial consequences and consequences on work and professional career. (Furniss, 1991: 244)

When the remaining carer experiences emotional and financial difficulties due to the removal or incarceration of the partner, the carer may be unresponsive to the child, and may be resentful, angry, and punitive. The child then inevitably feels like, or is pressured into, retracting the disclosure about the abuse in order to protect or take care of the carer's needs. This can be distressing for the therapist and other professionals involved in the case. If the repercussions of the disclosure are very negative, the therapist should anticipate that this might occur. It can be beneficial in these cases to offer support and advocacy, and to recommend counselling for the carer (if appropriate).

Confidentiality

Because a therapist often acts as a 'safe container' for dangerous feelings shared by a client, confidentiality about these feelings is essential in the therapeutic relationship (Bannister, 1992: 11). In the early stages of the therapeutic relationship, the child needs to be involved in discussions about confidentiality, the limits of confidentiality, and the expected level of parental involvement. It may be advisable to share some of the information about the content of the sessions with carers and/or relevant professionals. If this is necessary, the child should first be asked if it is all right to share information with the carer, and/or be encouraged to share information himself. The child may or may not be present during this period.

Children may also be told that if they would like the therapist to share some information with carers, they can ask the therapist to do so. There may be occasions when other levels of confidentiality are negotiated.

It is essential to establish clear understanding of the requirement for the therapist to report further abuse if it comes to light. This is best presented in the context of the therapist's ongoing need to protect the child from harm. During the course of treatment, the child may present additional information which will need to be reported to the authorities.

If the child reveals further abuse, or more severe abuse than was initially disclosed, the therapist needs to let the child know that a report will be made to the proper authorities, and that the therapist will help the child with this process. Many children exhibit feelings of anxiety or express concerns about what may happen as a result of the therapist's report. The therapist needs to be able to support and reassure the child, but at the same time to help the child tolerate uncertainty. It may be tempting to offer the child reassurances and false promises or platitudes, such as 'everything will be all right' or 'it will all work out for the best', when this may not be so. Therapists have to be honest and let the child know that they will do their best to support and help the child to deal with whatever happens next.

In addition, the child will inevitably have feelings about their confidentiality being broken. The child may experience the filing of a report by the therapist as a *betrayal*, and trust may to some degree be temporarily severed. The issue needs to be acknowledged and addressed sensitively by the therapist. The safety of the child is foremost, and the child may need to be helped to understand the therapist's role and responsibility regarding this process as essentially being about the welfare of the child.

The assessment process

The assessment process is an ongoing and central task. In the beginning phase of treatment, it is necessary to identify and normalize the child's symptoms, and to assess the child's current level of functioning. Contrasting this with the level of functioning prior to the abuse can give the therapist strong diagnostic information. Part of this process involves the child's role and functioning within the family.

The following questions provide some guidelines for the assessment process:

1 What are the child's current symptoms?
2 What is the child's ego strength?
3 What are the child's internal strengths and resources?
4 What is the child's temperament?
5 Is the child generally able to seek out or elicit positive responses from others?
6 Is the child able to accept and internalize positive feedback and sustenance from others?
7 What is the child's sense of self-esteem?

8 What was it like prior to the abuse?
9 What is the quality of the child's relationships with peers, teachers, and significant others outside the home?

In the assessment of the child's family, the following questions need to be considered:

1 What is the child's experience in their family or with other central carers?
2 Who is responsive and nurturing to the child?
3 Who is antagonistic or hostile to the child?
4 Is the family generally functional or dysfunctional?
5 What is the child's family role and relationship with siblings like?
6 What are the spoken and unspoken rules, and communication processes in the family? Are issues and concerns openly addressed and talked about? If so, is the child appropriately involved?
7 How are feelings perceived and expressed? Is the family able to tolerate or encourage the child's expression of emotion?
8 Are there family secrets, loyalties, and alliances? Is there a family scapegoat or a person who is labelled as the 'bad one' in the family?
9 Are there problems in the family that have diminished the child's self-esteem and ability to function?
10 Are there hidden or denied dysfunctions such as alcohol or substance abuse?
11 Is there conflict? If so, is the conflict resolved?
12 How are children punished when they have done something wrong?
13 What is the extent of physical or emotional neglect or abuse?
14 What is the marital/carer dyad like? Do carers operate well together?
15 What is the child's relationship to extended family members and how significant a role do they play in the child's life?

Answers to these questions help the therapist to understand and assess the child's ego strength, symptoms, and functioning. If the family is dysfunctional, the child is likely to have various unresolved issues from the family of origin as well as from the sexual victimization. Many of these issues will likely need to be addressed during therapy.

The following example illustrates how unresolved issues and problems in the family can negatively affect a child and his capacity to recover from the abuse. The majority of the therapeutic work was not directly related to the child's victimization. Tony was seen over 18 months for weekly individual sessions:

Tony, aged four, was brought into treatment following several incidents where a neighbour's boy (aged eight) had fondled him and made him perform oral sex. The older boy, John, threatened to hurt Tony and his father if Tony disclosed the abuse. Following the abuse, Tony had become more aggressive at home and at playgroup. His father, Peter, eventually found out about the abuse from Tony and sought treatment for him.

Tony was an unhappy and angry boy. His mother, Rita, was a drug addict, who had abandoned him on several occasions beginning when he was six months old. Peter, a recovering alcoholic, had poor parenting skills. Rita had recently abandoned Tony at precisely the time the sexual abuse began. Tony believed that the two incidents were linked somehow and that his mother had left him because she 'knew' about the abuse and thought he was bad or disgusting.

Tony felt frightened and powerless due to the sexual abuse. He frequently engaged in aggressive tantrums at home. He was also traumatized by his mother's sporadic abandonment of him. Tony was troubled by his father's alcoholism, manifesting in the father's emotional unavailability and depression. Peter had been unable to soothe or nurture Tony, nor to set appropriate boundaries for him, particularly in relation to his aggressive tantrums. Furthermore, Rita had been allowed to enter and exit Tony's life with no consequences for her irresponsible behaviour. This was in large part due to Peter's collusion in the denial of Rita's addictive behaviour. It was due in part to her constant promise that she was trying to get better.

At the start of each session, the therapist entered the waiting room and invited Tony to join her in the therapy room, but he refused. Next the therapist would tell him to come when he felt ready, and then go into the room and begin to set up toys and play. Within a few minutes, Tony shyly peered round the door and reluctantly entered. He then stood and watched for a short time before joining in. This ritual went on for the first two months of therapy. Understandably, people coming and leaving were emotionally laden issues for him and had to be handled sensitively. In addition, it was his way of being in control and rejecting the therapist before she had the opportunity to reject him.

Tony suffered from physical symptoms such as stomach pains and headaches, which were alleviated in the first few months of treatment. He also suffered nightmares, which he processed utilizing drawing and colouring. He changed these nightmares into stories in which he eventually became the heroic figure who annihilated the various monsters. In these pictures he became very large and the 'bad' figures diminished in size. His nightmares began to cease at that time.

During the first five months of therapy, Tony had tantrums. His play contained angry and aggressive themes often revolving around him being violent and seriously injuring others, the violence being directed at his abuser. The therapist set limits and boundaries around his behaviour, letting him know that it was safe to express his anger, but that he could not destroy objects, hurt himself, or the therapist in any way. After a few months of therapy, there was reparation after his violent play themes. This play paralleled a decrease in aggressive tendencies at home.

By this point, the father had become better at setting boundaries and containing his son. Tony was bright for his age, and was able to understand, in a limited capacity, that his 'acting out' was related to feelings of hurt, sadness, and powerlessness. He became aware of previously repressed affect and began portraying some of these feelings during the therapeutic work. As a result, his feelings of loss and powerlessness, relating largely to abandonment by his mother, were the central issues next manifested in the play therapy sessions. Tony wanted to play a game he entitled 'animals'. This game was repeated over and over during a six-month period. The therapist would be an animal of his choosing, trapped in a cage. He pretended to be asleep (defenceless), but he woke and captured the therapist-animal whenever she tried to escape. He pretended to cry if it took him a while to catch her, but inevitably was able to capture her every time.

Tony was determined to play hide and seek with objects at every session. He became frustrated and angry if he could not find the object immediately. His level of frustration tolerance increased over time, and he was gradually able to trust that the object was present even though it was not within his eye's view (object constancy).

Peter was also actively involved in Tony's treatment. Much of the adjunctive therapy focused on assisting him to develop healthy parenting skills. This work helped him to become more confident so that his self-esteem improved. Peter engaged in Alcoholics Anonymous, and was able to remain abstinent from alcohol and deal with many of his own unresolved childhood issues.

Peter was finally able to set boundaries and limits for Rita as well. She was given an ultimatum that she needed to seek professional treatment and get better, or she could not be involved in Tony's life. Peter maintained full custodial rights. Rita was unable to follow through with any treatment, and was therefore unable to see Tony any more.

An important piece of the subsequent therapeutic work with Tony was grief work involving the loss of his mother, helping him to realize that his mother had a problem, and that 'he' was not the problem. Tony had been continuously re-traumatized by his mother's appearances and disappearances. He had felt rejected, hurt, and powerless which manifested in his aggressive behaviour. Tony had previously been unable to rely on his father for appropriate parenting. Tony's self-esteem had been very poor before the victimization, and it had plummeted following his abuse.

After a year, Tony's favourite game became 'baby' in which he was the baby, and the therapist the mother. He sucked on the baby bottle and lay under the table. His therapist sang or spoke to him in comforting tones. Tony expressed feelings of loss related to his mother and sadness about what she had been unable to give him, particularly consistent affection.

Tony made use of the play telephone to communicate his feelings to his absent mother, feelings that he had been unable or afraid to express because of his fear of her leaving him if he displeased her. Towards the end of therapy, Tony sometimes played the mother figure, and the therapist was directed to be the baby. He sang and spoke in a soothing, caring voice, which indicated that he had internalized the experience of being nurtured, and could be nurturing as well. His father validated this hypothesis by saying that at home Tony was able to stay at one activity for longer, and was playing in a gentler, calmer fashion.

Tony utilized therapy successfully. A bright and sensitive child, he worked hard in the therapy process. His self-esteem improved considerably and his range of affect broadened. The aggressiveness and fear that he felt upon his arrival in therapy was strongly alleviated. Much of this can be attributed to the work done with his father, both in the adjunctive therapy and in his own process. Over the period of Tony's treatment, the father became a much more competent parent on whom Tony could now rely and depend for nurturing and support.

Establishing the therapeutic relationship

The initial contacts and sessions should be used, amongst other things, to establish rapport, safety, and trust, and to explore the child's subjective experience of the abuse. What are the meanings and interpretations the child places on the experience? What are the child's thoughts and feelings about being with the therapist, and about being in therapy?

Letting the child know what to expect from individual and group therapy is empowering and helpful in establishing the relationship. The first few sessions give the atmosphere of the therapeutic experience. Empathy, acceptance, positive regard, compassion, and understanding within safe boundaries, demonstrated by the therapist, can facilitate the start of a strong therapeutic alliance, and the beginning of the child victim's healing process.

Obtaining a history of the abuse

The initial sessions are used to gather information about the abuse and the child's perception and understanding of what has occurred. It is helpful to find out as much as possible from the referral source and the carers in advance. The following are important questions to ask:

1 When did the abuse begin and how long did it last?
2 What is alleged to have happened?
3 Was the abuse ongoing?

4 What is the child's perception of the abuse?
5 How was the abuse uncovered and what happened then, particularly as far as the child was concerned?

Is the child willing to talk about the abuse right away? If so, can the child tell you about what happened and how the abuse was experienced? (Depending on the child's age and developmental capacity, the child may or may not be able to give you this information.) Remember that children may have been given the message, explicitly or implicitly, that it is best not to talk about the abuse, because it will upset them, or it may upset adults to hear about it.

It may be difficult for professionals to hear if the child experienced physiological arousal and pleasure. Children will feel confused and guilty about their physiological response. The child has been sexualized prematurely and the sexualized experience cannot be undone. As a result, children may engage in compulsive or sexualized behaviour as a means of tension relief or gratification. The child may feel ashamed and feel 'bad' because of driven sexual behaviour. Most children will not admit to or disclose details about this behaviour until feeling safe with the therapist, and unless they are asked. Their behaviour needs to be normalized in the context of the abuse. This will probably need to be discussed more than once.

The child may also make a connection between a completely unrelated incident and the start of the abuse. If so, what is the incident that occurred at the same time? If the connection is not explored and processed, the child may engage in avoidance behaviour or phobias may develop.

The child's relationship with the abuser and disclosure

The following are pertinent questions:

1 What was the child's relationship with the abuser? The child may have ambivalent feelings about the abuser, especially if he had a close and intimate relationship with them, or if the abuser is a family member. The child may still have strong positive feelings. Accept and normalize these feelings, and let the child know that it is normal to have ambivalent and/or conflicting emotions. The child may feel guilty about experiencing negative feelings.
2 How long did the child hold the secret?
3 What did the child believe would happen if the abuse was discovered or disclosed?
4 What was the child told, if anything, by the perpetrator about what would happen if the child disclosed the abuse? Were implicit or explicit threats made?
5 When and how did the disclosure come about?
6 If the abuse was discovered, and the child had wished it to remain secret, the child may feel an increased sense of powerlessness and shame.
7 If the child disclosed the abuse, whom did the child tell?

8   Was the child initially believed, or did the child have to tell the same person more than once?

9   Did the child have to tell more than one person before being responded to or believed?

10   What were the repercussions of the disclosure? Was the child dealt with in a positive or punitive fashion?

11   What has taken place since the disclosure?

If the child has undergone abuse for several years and is now old enough either to talk about it or to attempt physical resistance, the child may be angry with himself for having allowed the situation to persist for so long. This dynamic is particularly true with male victims. The therapist may need to help the child see that he was more vulnerable in the past, and unable to respond or seek protection at that time.

Some young children believe that other people can tell what has happened by looking at them. They may think that others have ignored the situation and wonder why they have done so.

Sometimes a child will have been told by the abuser that sexual abuse is a normal part of their sexual education or that it is a normal way of expressing affection. The child may then feel that he is stupid and should have known differently. These erroneous beliefs often intensify a child's self-contempt and decreased self-esteem.

Treatment implications

All these dynamics have implications for treatment of the child victim. Helping the child to talk about, and develop, a more realistic and self-compassionate understanding of what has happened is essential. At the same time, it is important to acknowledge and accept the child's current beliefs and misconceptions about the victimization.

It is important to explore fully the child's feelings and beliefs, informing the child that their reactions are normal, similar to how other children feel about an abusive experience. During treatment, misconceptions need to be gently challenged, and gradually replaced with more accurate and realistic appraisals of the abuser and abuse situation. At the same time, intervening too quickly is often perceived as negating the child's feelings, and may cause the child to censor or withhold important information. Interventions must be handled delicately and only when the child is ready.

Sexual abuse should be placed in a context of power and violence by letting the child know that children should never be touched in a sexual way by older people. Sexual abuse is a degrading violation of the self, and is experienced as such by victims whose negative feelings may be quite strong and projected on to others as well. It may take time for the feelings to diminish. Normalizing and placing feelings into perspective can be enormously comforting for the child.

Addressing the child's feelings of guilt and responsibility for the abuse

The child victim carries the burden of guilt and shame for the abuse. Lamb states that guilt will eventually become an issue for all sexually abused children and will be accompanied by anxiety, anger, or depression. Often the parents' response, their own guilt or their tendency to blame the victim, will foster or increase feelings of guilt in the child. Children may blame themselves for the physical contact, for any sexual pleasure experienced, or for not having prevented the abuse. They may also feel guilty about causing a family crisis through revelation of the abuse. (1986: 304)

Children inevitably feel some degree of guilt and responsibility for the abuse that they have suffered (Spinal-Robinson and Easton Wickham, 1992b). This can be partially attributed to their developmental level; children are egocentric and view the world as revolving around them to a significant extent. Children are largely dependent on their carers and other significant adults in their environment. They tend to idealize and view such adults as caring and all-powerful. Children would rather blame themselves than jeopardize their idealization of their carers. In addition, children are usually very loyal to parents and other significant adults in their environment, finding it difficult to attribute blame to them.

When children are abused by a significant other, they usually believe that somehow they must have done something wrong, or something about them caused the abuse. Ironically, this erroneous belief seems to the child to place the abuser in a more powerful role. Children then believe that they have some control over the situation, and that if they change or do something different, the abuse will stop.

This belief system provides a survival strategy. The child feeling responsible for the abuse is a more powerful and less anxiety producing position to adopt. To acknowledge vulnerability and dependence on the abuser would be even more devastating. Lessening or eliminating the child's feelings of responsibility for the abuse is frequently a central goal of treatment. This process occurs gradually, and needs to be addressed many times throughout the treatment process.

Note the following:

Lisa, aged ten, had been sexually abused by her father since the age of six. Lisa was a child in a parentified role. Her mother suffered from depression and chronic illness and was often bedridden as a result. Lisa believed that if she took on more household responsibilities, took better care of her sister, and improved her grades at school, her mother would recover (and be emotionally available), and the abuse would stop.

Lisa believed that she had failed somehow and the abuse was her punishment for being a 'bad' girl. She felt guilty because she had previously resented taking on so much responsibility in the house. The abuse had begun about the same time as her mother's illness. Her father told Lisa that she had been seductive, and she believed that perhaps she had wanted to replace her mother, and that she had caused her mother's illness. Lisa felt that she was 'being good' protecting her mother's marital happiness and her sister's innocence by not telling about the abuse. Issues related to responsibility and guilt were a strong focus of treatment over a two-year period.

The following issues often increase children's feelings of responsibility:

- Children may feel that they contributed or willingly participated in the abuse because they continued spending time with the abuser after the abuse began. The child may feel responsible even if implicit or explicit threats were made by the abuser.
- The child may have enjoyed certain aspects of the relationship, such as being given special attention, presents, money, or being taken on outings. The child feels that if he accepted and enjoyed these secondary gains, he must have condoned or even encouraged the abuse.
- The child may believe that he encouraged the abuse through seduction. Sometimes children are told this by the abuser, subsequently believing that the abuse was a result of their own behaviour.
- The child may believe that he should have been able to stop the abuse, that he should have said no, protested, or physically prevented the abuse.
- The child may feel that it must be something about him that caused the abuse, because he is the only one in the family to be abused. On the other hand, if another sibling has been abused, the child may blame himself for not stopping that abuse as well. In some cases, the child sacrifices himself in the hope that siblings will be left alone. When the child discovers a sibling has also been abused, he may experience a sense of failure. Indeed, the child's discovery that a sibling is being abused may also be the precipitating factor in disclosure of the abuse.
- The child may have attempted to disclose the abuse and it was not recognized, or the child was not believed. If there was no response, children may then assume that the matter is their own responsibility. In addition, if the reaction to the disclosure is punitive, or has strong negative repercussions for the family, the child may feel responsible for this as well.

If beliefs such as the ones listed above are not uncovered, and replaced with more accurate appraisals of the situation, the child may continue to experience feelings of shame, guilt, and self-hatred.

Child victims who carry the burden of guilt and responsibility also commonly engage in self-punishing feelings, thoughts, and behaviours. They view themselves as responsible for any and all misfortunes that befall them. They feel ashamed, guilty, and inherently bad, deserving the abuse they have suffered. They do not seek out or feel worthy of positive experiences or relationships. In addition, as children or later in life, they may seek out or tolerate relationships in which they are maltreated. The underlying belief of the survivor may be 'this is what I deserve anyway'. Some survivors experience relief, and find that their self-punishing thoughts and tendencies lessen when in a dysfunctional relationship in which someone else is doing the punishing. They may alternate between being in unhealthy and destructive relationships, and engaging in self-punishing behaviour. These negative feelings and self-beliefs, when left in place, can be powerful and damaging, especially when they become an intrinsic part of the child's developing psyche, identity, and self-esteem.

Treatment implications

Helping the child process feelings of guilt and responsibility is an important and central task of the treatment process. Working through this with the child must be addressed sensitively. In the first place, it may be difficult for children to understand or verbalize the ways in which they feel responsible for the abuse. The therapist may have to help by elaborating on other child victims' experiences regarding feelings of guilt and responsibility.

The child may also be afraid that the therapist will judge, no longer be as sympathetic, or experience disgust towards him or her (projection). The therapist should anticipate that the child may have feelings of apprehension regarding this possibility. Children often need reassurance that the therapist will be accepting and non-judgemental, and not think badly of them following their disclosure of feelings of responsibility. The therapist can also anticipate what some of the child's feelings might be, based on the child's previous relationship with the abuser, and the abuse situation. The therapist can then normalize the child's feelings regarding their perceptions.

At this time, countertransference feelings may easily be evoked. It may be painful to listen to the child berate or blame himself for a situation that was so obviously out of his control. If the therapist prematurely tries to reassure the child that he is not responsible for the abuse, he may feel that the therapist cannot tolerate his feelings, or that the therapist views his perceptions as wrong or incorrect. As a result, the child may feel misunderstood, or may not want to disagree with or displease the therapist. The child may then decide not to discuss his feelings of responsibility in future sessions.

The most helpful strategy is simply for the therapist to listen, and then to help the child explore his perceptions and feelings. The therapist can then empathize with how the child feels. The therapist can let the child know that all children who have been abused to some extent feel this way. The therapist validates, but does not necessarily agree with, or strengthen, the child's feelings and perceptions.

The therapist can take this opportunity to reiterate that *the adult is responsible for the abuse*, and that older people should *never* do sexual things with a child. In this way, the therapist places the responsibility on the abuser, but does not devalue or dismiss how the child feels. It is helpful to tell the child that any feelings of responsibility will take some time to go away, that the therapist respects the child's feelings, and appreciates that the child is confiding in the therapist. The child should be encouraged to talk about such feelings or thoughts whenever they surface in the treatment process.

Ideally, over time, the child should gradually be able to relinquish feelings of responsibility for the abuse, and completely attribute the blame to the perpetrator. However, in some cases, the child continues to feel some level of responsibility. If so, it is beneficial if the child can forgive himself for some individual aspects of how he feels he might have contributed to the situation.

The following examples illustrate issues related to secondary gains and feelings of responsibility for the abuse.

Case 1:

Joel, aged ten, was brought into treatment after having been sexually abused by his stepmother, Margaret, aged 29. Joel's father and stepmother were now divorcing, and the case was being investigated. Joel had also been sexually abused by a male friend of his stepmother, Jack, aged 22. Joel had discovered that Margaret and Jack had been engaging in sexual intercourse. This discovery was the precipitating factor for Joel's disclosure to his father.

The sexual abuse began when Joel was eight years old, under the guise of caregiving. Margaret often bathed Joel twice a day, frequently fondling his penis. When Joel was nine, his father was often away on business trips. At these times, Margaret insisted that Joel sleep with her, and masturbated him. She referred to him as 'my little man' and treated him as a replacement for his absent father. She told Joel that he was lucky that she was helping him to become a man. She bribed him with money and special outings, and told him not to tell anyone or she would get into trouble because other people would be jealous. As soon as his father returned, Joel would be ignored.

Joel was confused. He felt hurt, angry, and displaced upon his father's return. He felt ashamed and guilty about the physiological pleasure he experienced during the abuse. He finally realized that Margaret had lied to him and that the situation was not normal, as he had previously been told. Joel felt that he was betraying his father by having a sexual relationship with Margaret, and that the abuse was his fault, because he had encouraged Margaret by agreeing to come into her bed. She had told him that nothing would happen if he didn't want it to, but each time 'something' had happened, which was very confusing. Did he always want something to happen and not realize it? He felt that he was inherently bad and a 'pervert'.

Margaret was nice to him, and gave him money. This made it difficult for Joel to be angry with her. He spent all of the money and knew that he could not return it. He became depressed and began acting out at school. The abuse continued and one day Margaret brought over her male friend, who came in while Margaret was bathing him, and the male friend began fondling

Joel as well. The friend also made comments about sexual acts that made Joel realize that this friend was having a sexual relationship with Margaret. That night Joel disclosed the abuse to his father.

Joel was seen in individual treatment over a period of eight months and was subsequently in a 12-week treatment group for boys who had been sexually abused. During the first four months of individual treatment, Joel had a difficult time working through his feelings of responsibility. He continued to believe that the abuse was his fault, and he suffered extreme shame and guilt. He felt guilty about the betrayal of his father, manifested in Joel's sexual relationship with Margaret. It took him a while to engage in therapy as he believed he deserved punishment instead of help. The therapist encouraged Joel to discuss his feelings, and empathized with how his appraisal of the situation made him feel. Over time, she gently challenged his beliefs and attempted to help Joel replace them with more accurate appraisals of the situation.

At the end of the eight-month period, Joel had attributed much of the responsibility for the abuse to Margaret. He was able to understand how she had manipulated and exploited him. However, he still felt ashamed of his acceptance of money and the special attention he had received from her. It was only during the group process that he was gradually able to forgive himself for what he termed 'taking advantage' of the situation. His acceptance of himself was facilitated by his experience of hearing other children in the group describe how they had gained or benefited from the abuse in some way.

Joel was eventually able to stop punishing himself and instead to experience self-compassion and self-acceptance. He made strong progress towards his recovery.

Case 2:

Drew, aged eight, an only child, was molested over a period of ten months by a neighbour, Philip, a close friend of his father. Drew's parents were recently divorced, Drew residing with his mother, Elaine. His father maintained joint custody, but rarely spent time with his son. Elaine had ended the marriage and the father felt very bitter. Drew felt isolated and lonely.

Philip, aged 42, began taking an interest in Drew who was grateful for the attention of an older male. During weekends, Philip offered to take Drew on outings, which gave Elaine time to catch up on household tasks. She also felt grateful because Drew appeared to be less angry now that Philip had befriended him. She viewed Philip as a 'surrogate father' figure, and became friends with him as well.

Philip courted Drew. He gave him special attention, took him to child oriented places, spent money freely on him, praised him, offered him presents, and eventually began giving him money. These 'special gifts' were to remain their secret, in case Drew's mother did not approve. A few weeks later, Philip began placing Drew upon his lap and rubbing against him until he ejaculated. Next, he began insisting that they engage in mutual masturbation. Drew refused, but Philip insisted. The sexual abuse eventually increased until Drew was anally penetrated by Philip, even though Drew refused. Philip was physically forceful on these occasions.

Drew was frightened and confused. He felt responsible for the abuse, believing that he had asked for and consented to the abuse because he had accepted Philip's gifts. He worried that he was homosexual, and that was why the abuse had occurred. Drew believed that he should have been able to resist Philip's advances and that, because he had not, people would believe that he had wanted the sexual contact.

Drew cared about Philip and believed that he should not betray him by disclosing the abuse. Furthermore, he was fearful of what Philip would do if he told anyone, even though no explicit threats had been made. His central fear was that Philip would hurt his mother or his dog. Philip had been very forceful with Drew during some of the sexual molestation.

Drew began engaging in fantasies of revenge against Philip. At the same time, he began acting out in school and being aggressive towards other males. During break times, he often pushed and hit younger children, and began calling them names. His behavioural problems were immediately noticed by his teacher, who attempted to find out what was wrong.

At home, Drew became withdrawn and depressed. He began suffering from stomach pains and headaches. His mother took him to the GP who could find nothing wrong physiologically. His mother believed that his symptoms were linked to his feelings about his absent father's continued unavailability.

Drew eventually confided in his teacher, who was supportive and responsive to him over the remaining six months of the school year. Philip was subsequently arrested, Drew's mother engaging Drew in treatment at the time of the arrest. Drew was seen over a 12-month period, both individually and later in group treatment. The treatment was successful and Drew was able to understand how the secondary gains he had received had been part of Philip's 'courting' process. Drew was gradually able to relinquish feelings of responsibility for the abuse.

Summary

In this chapter we have examined the beginning phases of treatment. There are several important aspects and tasks facing the therapist. An awareness of these issues can help the therapist anticipate and prepare for the beginning of treatment. Gathering the necessary information and documentation, finding out who is involved or potentially will be involved in the case, and speaking to the referral source, may be first steps in this process.

The safety and protection of the child is foremost. Some guidelines and possible social services procedures to ensure the child's safety are briefly discussed. We address the importance of confidentiality, and stress that confidentiality and its limits need to be made clear to the child at the very start of the initial therapy session.

The assessment process is an important and ongoing process. In this chapter, we provide guidelines or questions for the therapist to consider and/or ask of the child and family. Part of this involves assessing the child's symptoms and functioning (past and present), as well as the child's role and functioning within the family, and an assessment of the family's functioning as a whole. If the family is dysfunctional, there may be many additional issues that will need to be addressed during the treatment process. A case example was given which illustrated this process.

Obtaining a history of the abuse, and exploring the child's perceptions and feelings about the abuse and the relationship with the abuser can begin during the initial phase of treatment. Addressing the child's feelings of guilt and responsibility is inevitably a central treatment issue, and one that may need to be re-addressed many times. Once again guidelines and a case example were given.

Overall, the beginning of treatment is an opportunity to develop the atmosphere and tone of the therapeutic relationship, by letting the child and carer know what to expect from therapy. This can be empowering for the child. Exploring the child's subjective experience of being with the therapist, and about being in treatment, should also be explored. The therapist can demonstrate acceptance, empathy, positive regard, compassion, and understanding to the child. This can set the stage for a good therapeutic alliance.

4   The Therapist's Experience of Working with Abused Children

Cameos from new and experienced therapists:

Susan speaks: 'I hadn't anticipated how working with a sexually abused child would affect me. Initially it was such an incredibly painful experience. I found myself feeling as Rose did – vulnerable, sad, powerless, and hopeless. She was such a small child who had been traumatized so greatly. I found it more and more difficult to leave therapy sessions behind me. I felt protective and I cared so much. Gradually, I came to realize that treating Rose brought back memories of my own childhood. I, too, had been unloved and ill-treated. Part of the pain, for me, was that I saw so much of myself in Rose. It was as if by saving Rose, I could save myself. This was something I really had to work at in my own therapy. My supervisor helped me to separate myself and my own issues from Rose's. It took some time, but it really helped.'

Jane speaks: 'The work was so richly rewarding and challenging. It was difficult and emotionally draining, but completely absorbing. I knew that I needed to take very good care of myself if I wanted to continue treating sexually abused children. I needed to replenish and reward myself, so that I could be more available for the children. I felt that I had discovered an area of work where I could use my full potential, and I learned so much from the children I worked with. I remember being very enthusiastic, and five years on, I continue to be the same.'

Richard speaks: 'I felt that I began to lose my faith in humanity. I became bitter and enraged during the first few months. I couldn't comprehend how anyone could be so cruel to the child. She was so degraded and betrayed. It was painful at times to be with and stay with her, and I had to work hard not to let this experience affect my personal life and my relationship with my two young daughters. You see, I was so aware of the limitations of the work. I caught myself fantasizing that my wife, children, and I could make a home for her. It was so unfair. I felt so angry at the family who had been unable to respond to her, and to protect her adequately from harm.'

Tina speaks: 'I found it stressful and painful doing this work. I hadn't quite realized the damage and severity of symptoms I would encounter. I found it disturbing. I must admit I found the work to be both challenging and very rewarding at the same time. In retrospect, I wish I had been more aware in the beginning of what I was letting myself in for. I'm not sure, but I think it would have made a difference. On the other hand, maybe I wouldn't have taken on this work. I do know that I have made a difference in many children's lives, and I have been there to help them to pick up the pieces, and to make a new picture, one that they can be proud of and live with. I have felt privileged to be part of this process.'

The following material is discussed in order to help therapists anticipate and deal with some potential problems and issues that may arise when they begin to work with sexually abused children. It offers suggestions for therapists in taking care of themselves, both personally and professionally. The issues considered include:

- taking care of yourself;
- emotional demands;
- countertransference issues;
- countertransference issues for the survivor therapist;
- hypersensitivity to child sexual abuse;
- possible effects on the therapist; and
- support for the therapist.

Taking care of yourself (the therapist)

Therapists who possess good mental health are more likely to be free and emotionally available for their clients. Therapists deserve to have their mental health needs met and should take good care of themselves. According to West (1996: 151) 'Therapeutic effectiveness is often proportional to the therapist's personal "togetherness", and to the success with which rejected or discarded parts of the being have been welcomed back into the adult's personality with love, tolerance and understanding'. In other words, the more comfortable and accepting therapists are of themselves, the more accepting they can be of the child.

Therapists engaging in this demanding work should ensure that they are replenished, with adequate time for relaxation and leisure and strong enough boundaries between work and recreational time. Having time for themselves and emotional support in their own lives, as well as having their own needs met, are vital parts of the process (Figley, 1995; Pearlman and Saakvitne, 1995). Workloads should be adequately balanced, without too many severe clients or too many sexually abused children at any one time. This is a judgement call for each individual, and will vary from therapist to therapist.

Therapists choosing this work should have undergone personal psychotherapy, which provides an opportunity to explore and deal with unresolved issues from one's family of origin, as well as current concerns or difficulties. Getting in touch with the therapist's own childhood experience facilitates a deeper understanding of the child being worked with. Personal therapy also serves to strengthen one's understanding of, and faith in, the therapeutic process, and reinforces for the therapist how vulnerable, as well as understood and supported, a child may feel in therapy.

Emotional demands and countertransference

Emotional demands on therapists working with child victims of sexual abuse can be great (Kirk, 1998). The work is often lengthy and emotionally draining. Furthermore progress can seem slow, especially if there has been severe and ongoing abuse.

There are many potential countertransference issues facing the therapist. Countertransference reactions are caused by the interaction of the child's issues and behaviours with the therapist's beliefs, emotions, and experiences. Often the process is unconscious on the part of the therapist and may result in responses to the child that are non-productive and anti-therapeutic. For these reasons therapists should be vigilant about assessing their own emotional reactions and beliefs.

> Throughout the treatment, a traumatized client will evoke a number of countertransference roles in the therapist, including those of perpetrator, helpless bystander, collusive parent, nurturing figures, and even voyeur. These feelings can be extremely disruptive to the therapist's sense of his or her professional identity as compassionate, understanding, interested, and helpful. The therapist may begin feeling guilty and frightened about these feelings and about assuming these roles, particularly in play therapy. (Ryan, 1999: 475)

Therapists need to accept these feelings as normal responses to the work, otherwise they may feel ashamed and their self-esteem and effectiveness will be diminished.

Therapists may also find themselves feelings frustrated, angry, ineffectual or powerless due to the potential involvement of so many other professionals and agencies (medical, social services, legal, and so on) in the case. Many of these professionals will have authority, and be in the position to make important decisions about the child's future. The therapist may or may not be considered a vital part of this decision-making. It can be frustrating and discouraging if the therapist feels that the process is not in the best interest of the child's welfare and well-being. It is enormously helpful if the therapist can provide advocacy for child and family, when necessary.

In order to be most effective, it is important to establish good working alliances with the individuals and professionals involved (Chapters 5 and 6). Unfortunately, it can be disheartening when the therapist is not listened to or valued, which is sometimes the case. It is important not to let these feelings interfere with or contaminate the therapy process.

In some cases, therapists may have unresolved issues that seriously interfere with or impede the therapeutic process. If so, it is essential that therapists engage in their own therapy. Utilizing supervision (Lawton and Feltham, 2000) is also important if therapists are experiencing difficulties due to strong anti-therapeutic countertransference.

Therapists may find some traumatized children difficult to work with because of their acting out or aggressive behaviour. Anger, aggression, tantrums, and other destructive behaviours may be difficult to contain. The therapist needs to establish firm and consistent boundaries and limits regarding the child's behaviour, so that the child is aware of what is and is not permitted during sessions. Let children know that they are allowed to experience and express anger, but are not to hurt themselves or the therapist, or to damage toys or furniture in the therapy room.

It is essential to examine countertransference reactions to difficult or acting out behaviour. The therapist often works hard to understand the child's symptoms and behaviour in the context of the child's unproductive attempt to cope with trauma, and to have needs met. Acting out behaviour masks other underlying emotions as well. Establishing firm and consistent boundaries regarding the child's behaviour will help to contain the child. It can take a good deal of time for the behaviour and symptoms to lessen or go away altogether. The therapist needs to be patient with the child in the meantime.

If the therapist feels powerless, overwhelmed, or even angry as a result of the child's difficult behaviour, it is clearly non-therapeutic. The therapist should never react punitively to the child. Therapists may need to work through their own feelings and issues which may possibly be correlated to negative experiences in their own childhood, particularly with regards to punitive or abusive carers.

The child's aggression may be directed towards the therapist in a more subtle form such as when the child devalues the work done in the therapy process or makes negative comments about the therapist. The child may speak of feeling angry at 'someone else' which may be a metaphor for the therapist. This possibility should be explored with the child. The child may be afraid to speak directly about angry feelings directed towards the therapist for fear of reprisal, or of displeasing the therapist.

Alternatively, the child may engage in *testing out behaviour* or try refusing to co-operate in the therapy and appear disinterested. The therapist needs to be patient, giving the child the opportunity to explore the relationship and situation. Time is often needed before the child is willing to engage in the therapeutic process. As stated in Chapter 7, the child's attachment difficulties will be manifested in the therapy room. The child may reject the therapist outright. This is usually a defence mechanism (Chapter 10). The child unconsciously rejects others because it is less painful than potentially being the object of rejection. Trust and engaging with others is almost always problematic for abused children. Therapists need to be aware of feelings of hurt, anger, or rejection, and not to respond in a punitive fashion to the child. The child's defences and style of attachment should always be respected.

The therapist may be confused if the child behaves inconsistently, for example by being clingy one session and difficult to engage the next. Once again, the child's ambivalent feelings about trust and bonding are being manifested in the therapy process. Children may fear the intensity of their needy feelings evoked as a result of the therapist's responsiveness, and may desire to distance themselves from the therapist. A gentle interpretation can be made about the child's ambivalence and feelings, accepting and respecting that this is what the child needs to do at that time.

As stated earlier, a child may appear to be needy and clingy, demonstrating a desire to merge with the therapist. The child's intense neediness may be experienced as emotionally demanding and depleting. In addition, the child may be depressed, sad, or withdrawn and therapists may find themselves feeling intense pain simply by being with the child, due to the child's vulnerability and experience of trauma. In this scenario, therapists may find themselves emotionally distancing from the child as a way of emotional protection. This can be damaging, as the child will experience this as rejection and further proof of inherent badness. It is important that the therapist be aware of this possibility, seeking supervision when necessary.

Another countertransference response might be that therapists find themselves becoming overprotective of the child, even experiencing fantasies of rescuing or accepting complete responsibility for the child. These countertransference feelings can intensify the child's feelings of powerlessness or being *damaged goods*, because the therapist is unintentionally conveying the message and reinforcing the child's belief that she is unable to make choices and take care of herself. This can be exacerbated if the child's family is dysfunctional or unable to nurture the child. The therapist may feel powerless or angry towards the carer, and this dynamic may interfere with the therapist/carer alliance that is so important when working with young children.

A case example illustrates some of these issues:

John, aged nine, was brought into treatment following his abuse by a friend's teenage brother, Stuart, aged 14. John's mother complained of his angry and aggressive behaviour. She had difficulty knowing how to set appropriate limits or boundaries and felt overwhelmed in her parenting role.

John was clearly unhappy during the first few sessions. He appeared sulky, uncooperative, and said very little. He sat stiffly in a chair, with his hands folded protectively across his body. He challenged the therapist by saying it was stupid to be there and that he knew that it was a waste of his time. The therapist acknowledged his feelings and sympathized with his situation. He asked John if there was anything he felt he would like help with, because John felt that the underlying agenda was to fix his difficult and aggressive behaviour, viewing therapy as a form of punishment.

John became talkative when he described his angry feelings towards Stuart. John described violent acts he could have performed to punish Stuart. However, when the therapist reflected back his feelings, John began saying that the therapist didn't understand and that it was really no big deal.

John was trying to push the therapist away, and to test out the therapist's response. John was clearly surprised when the therapist did not react punitively. The therapist resonated with John's feelings of not being understood. He realized that John was defensive in a self-protective fashion, being in denial about the abuse and the effects it was having on him.

During supervision the therapist discussed his experience with the child. He sensed that John's reaction made him feel insecure about his clinical performance. He was relatively new to the work and felt hurt by his perception of John's rejection. He discussed these feelings with his supervisor and subsequently felt that his own feelings would not interfere with the treatment process.

During subsequent sessions, John continued to be sulky, irritable and difficult to engage. Even on those occasions when the therapist engaged John momentarily, John would catch himself and recant what he had been saying. He continued to devalue the therapist and the therapy process for the next six sessions. The situation was exacerbated by the fact that the therapist was male and John, aged six, had been abandoned by and had no further contact with his biological father.

John also tested the boundaries of the relationship and process by telling the therapist how destructive he could be to the room and the items therein. The therapist let him know that John was perfectly justified in his anger, but could not act on these impulses. He asked John if he was afraid of how powerful his anger might be if he let it out. John was able grudgingly to acknowledge this as true. Interestingly, during these earlier sessions, John's aggressive behaviour at home lessened, appearing to be vented verbally during therapy.

Over a period of seven month, John began engaging more in the treatment process, although his ambivalence and distrust were still evident as he vacillated between being open and friendly with the therapist, and quiet or challenging. The therapist continued to comment on this behaviour, accepting John's ambivalence as necessary for him at this time. Sometimes John smiled and warmed to the therapist after such an interpretation. John and the therapist were able to share humourous anecdotes, and John created several cartoon characters to express different aspects of himself.

John gradually acknowledged and accepted the abuse experience. His anger lessened, and previously unacceptable feelings of fear, sadness, and powerlessness surfaced. John's range of felt and expressed emotions broadened, and he gradually found healthier and more acceptable ways to be assertive and express his anger.

The termination process of therapy was lengthy and difficult for John. A strong positive transference had developed, and John's longings and desire for a male authority figure had finally materialized in the relationship with his therapist. John had even fantasized briefly that his mother and the therapist would become romantically involved and engaged to one another as a result of their mutual concern for John's wellbeing. Gradually, John was able to accept the limitations and inevitability of the relationship ending with his therapist. At this time, the treatment focus shifted to helping John to grieve over the loss of his father as well as the loss of the therapist.

John suffered some regression during the termination phase of treatment which the therapist acknowledged and normalized. Gradually John realized that he could function well enough on his own, and began to relinquish his desire to have the therapist involved in his life forever. The functions of compassion, understanding, containment, and acceptance the therapist had provided for John had become functions he could provide for himself.

Hypersensitivity to child sexual abuse

It is important for therapists to realize that many professionals working in this specialized area experience a heightened sensitivity to noticing or suspecting sexual abuse, even when it is non-existent. Therapists beginning to work with sexually abused children may suddenly perceive the world as a dangerous place for children. The therapist's world view may be challenged, and the potential for child sexual abuse may seem to be everywhere.

If the therapist has young children, this feeling can be intensified and the sense of protectiveness may be increased. The knowledge that child sexual abuse occurs frequently, and in any setting, is disconcerting. Mental health professionals may need to examine and process their own thoughts and feelings about this sensitive issue. Many therapists working in this area initially experience such *hypersensitivity*, but the tendency lessens over time and with experience. It is natural and fairly common for this dynamic to occur. Conversely, the heightened sensitivity the therapist may possess can also facilitate the identification of sexual abuse as a central treatment issue, even when it has not necessarily been identified as a concern.

Countertransference issues for the therapist who is a survivor of sexual abuse

Many mental health professionals choosing to work with child victims of sexual abuse are survivors themselves. Some feel they have special expertise to offer, or are committed to helping others to recover from a painful experience. The therapist who is a survivor may have increased sensitivity and understanding to offer the child victim. In addition, many people want to assist others as they themselves would have liked to have been helped. There is no doubt that the therapist who is a survivor and who has come to terms with the abuse can contribute an enormous amount to this work.

At the same time, it is important to be conscious of potential countertransference issues. The most likely could be the survivor/therapist's over-identification with the child, or projection of unresolved issues on to the child. In over-identification due to their own experience of trauma, therapists may lose objectivity and confuse their own experience with that of the child. As a result, assumptions about the child's feelings, issues, and experience may be incorrectly based on the therapist's own abuse experience.

Briere discusses this dynamic:

> Over-identification occurs when the therapist's empathic response to a client is unconsciously intensified by his or her own abuse-related affect and cognitions. For example, the therapist with untreated sexual abuse trauma might feel unusually intense anxiety, sadness, or anger when hearing the sexual abuse experiences of a client with a similar childhood. The critical issue here is not the appropriate empathy and compassion for the client, but rather the point at which the therapist's own abuse-related responses significantly add to the process. As a result of these unresolved issues, the therapist 'overreacts' to those aspects of the client's experience most reminiscent of his or her own experience. (1992: 159)

In projection, the therapist to some extent uses the child in order to resolve his or her own issues. The therapist is unconscious of this dynamic and, as in over-identification, the survivor/therapists confuse their own issues with those of the child.

The following case example illustrates these potential difficulties:

> A student therapist was working with Jade, aged seven, who had been sexually abused by an uncle. The therapist had developed a good alliance with the girl and felt treatment was progressing relatively well. She felt that she empathized with the girl's experience because she had also been sexually abused, at about the same age, by a relative whom she had trusted.

> At this point in the treatment, Jade started to talk more about the sexual abuse, beginning to discuss some of the positive aspects of the sexual relationship, and her positive feelings towards her uncle. She described her feelings of loss because she no longer was able to see her uncle. The therapist found it difficult to hear about positive aspects of the experience or relationship. She felt disgusted or angry, and shifted the conversation to focus on the negative aspects of the girl's experience. The student therapist was not conscious that she was influencing the focus of the session, but was aware that her strong negative reactions might be related to her own abuse experience.

Over several supervision sessions, the student therapist was able to realize that her strong reactions to the material presented by Jade were related to unresolved issues about her own abuse. She had over-identified with the client and assumed that the child's experience and feelings were similar to her own. She was projecting her negative and unresolved feelings onto the child. After this realization, and by processing her own feelings during the supervision period, she was able to tolerate and even encourage Jade to express all her feelings.

The survivor therapist may also experience additional difficulty when attempting to maintain appropriate boundaries between the child and herself. There may be an increased tendency to become overly protective of the child in a way that is not therapeutic. This over-protective or over-nurturing stance can prevent the child from exploring all the feelings about the abuse, particularly those that are most emotionally painful.

This tendency may also be manifested in the therapist becoming too involved or overly invested in the child's daily life. In some cases, the therapist may feel competitive with the carer and assume that the therapist is the only one capable of looking after the child. Resentment and anger towards the family and/or perpetrator may intensify. Such feelings may seriously limit the effectiveness of the treatment.

If therapists remain unaware of why they are feeling or responding so strongly, they may continue to over-identify and try to deal with their own unresolved issues by projection, inadvertently using the child as the vehicle. All these potential countertransference issues could be detrimental to the child, and may reduce the likelihood of a successful treatment outcome.

It is useful for therapists to work through abuse-related phenomena in their own therapy. Supervision can also be instrumental in helping therapists determine, and process, countertransference issues that may impede the treatment process. If there are remaining difficulties, the supervisor can help the therapist decide the most appropriate intervention.

Support for the therapist

Working with sexually abused children is stressful and demanding. Some therapists emerge unscathed, but for others it is a different story. Figley identifies compassion fatigue as a possible secondary traumatic stress disorder: 'Professionals who listen to children's stories of fear, pain, and suffering may feel similar fear, pain, and suffering because they care. ... the most effective therapists are most vulnerable to this mirroring or contagion effect' (1995: 1). Therapists may also experience 'significant disruptions in one's sense of meaning, connection, identity, and world view, as well as in one's affect tolerance, psychological needs, beliefs about self and others, interpersonal relationships, and sensory memory, including imagery' (Pearlman and Saakvitne, 1995: 151). These authors point to the importance of personal, professional, and organizational strategies to avoid the risk of harm, and Yassen (1995) discusses the merits of physical, psychological, interpersonal, and professional intervention.

Supervision is essential in helping to support the therapist and preventing 'burn out' (Kirk, 1998). It is particularly helpful if the supervisor has worked in this area as well. It may be beneficial to form a support group with other professionals doing similar work. Since sexual abuse therapeutic work requires special skills and knowledge, it is important for the therapist to engage in ongoing training and education, as well as continuing to read the current research literature. The therapist should be accredited to a professional association and continue to search out new sources to inform practice methods.

Summary

This chapter has focused on the experience of the therapist in working with sexually abused children. The first part of the chapter discussed the importance of the therapist taking good care of himself/herself on a professional and personal level. The central premise is that by taking care of themselves, and having their own mental health needs met, the therapist will be in a much stronger and healthier position to nurture and meet the needs of his/her child clients.

The emotional demands and possible countertransference issues were then briefly discussed. A case example was given. The therapist needs to examine and be aware of any issues that may interfere with the treatment process. Seeking supervision, or engaging in one's own therapy, may be necessary. Some additional countertransference issues were discussed, which are particularly relevant for the therapist who is a survivor of sexual abuse himself/herself. Once again, a case example was given.

Lastly, support and supervision for the therapist were discussed as being essential components in preventing the therapist from becoming 'burned out'. Working with trauma survivors, and particularly children who have been traumatized, can be incredibly demanding and stressful. During this process, it is also important for the therapist to engage in continued reading and professional development, and to seek professional support as needed.

Exercise

---

1 As a therapist, how do you feel about your work with children?
2 What are your countertransference feelings? Are there certain emotions, behaviours, or issues that you find difficult to contain or address in sessions?
3 If the answer is yes, is this in any way related to your own experience in childhood?
4 What level of support do you need to do this work effectively, and to prevent yourself from becoming discouraged or burned out?
5 Is there a healthy balance between your work and leisure time? How do you replenish and reward yourself?

---

5 Children in Society, Cultural Considerations, and Alternative Care Provision

A poem written by an adolescent survivor:

There is a hole that remains inside me.

If you fall in ... breath and thoughts evacuate. Hopes are imprisoned, dreams extinguished.
And you are all alone. The hole began when I was six. It got larger and stronger, more sinister with every passing year. I kept people away. Don't you see it wasn't safe? I often wondered if other children had a deep dark place inside. Did they collect darkness the way other children collect stuffed animals? Did they too dream of sunlight?

My dark hole has a name. It is called daddy.

What about you?

To form a therapeutic alliance, it is important that therapists have a working knowledge of, and respect for, cultural differences between peoples (Keats, 1997) and can relate to the child and carers in a range of family situations. Children are an integral part of all societies, but ideas on childhood and child-rearing practices differ between and within cultures. The structure of families varies, in some cases being complex. The child's intimate carer(s) may change, siblings may live apart and 'new' children may become part of the household. Some children do not grow up with natural parents and have several carers during their childhood. Therefore there are added dimensions to be taken into account when working with children living with foster or adoptive parents, or in a residential unit.

Children in society

Childhood is not always idyllic. Over the centuries children have been viewed variously as goods and chattels, of little importance and sometimes a nuisance, or perhaps as mini-adults capable of fending for themselves and making their own way in the world (Ariès, 1973; Cunningham, 1995; de Mause, 1974; Hoyles, 1989; Humphries et al., 1988; James and Prout, 1990; Jenks, 1996; Stainton Rogers and Stainton Rogers, 1992). Nowadays in the western world it is generally agreed that children should be safe, valued and encouraged to grow and develop. Physical health, warmth and nurture, free emotional expression and opportunities to learn about, and explore, the world, plus encouragement to feel roots and trace a spiritual identity should be available (Maslow, 1954; Pringle, 1980; Winnicott, 1986). However, the adult world usually predominates, and when things go wrong unfortunate children may be shuffled between carers, or locked away and neglected, or may themselves take on a caring, parenting role.

Children who have been sexually abused are caught between two worlds. They are there for the abuser's use, pleasure, or money-making, but are expected to remain quiet and to get on with their growth and lives as though nothing painful or worrying is happening. Present-day society has a curiously ambivalent attitude towards child sexual abuse, turning a blind eye and pretending it hardly exists, or exploiting it in the sex trade, child pornography on the internet or otherwise, and in extrafamilial, interfamilial, intrafamilial, and institutional abuse.

Sexual abuse usually also includes physical, emotional, cognitive, spiritual abuse, and neglect. Many sexually abused children suffer a great deal, some exhibiting medical and psychiatric problems (Merry and Andrews, 1994), with difficulties in school, family and daily life.

Relevant professionals strive to develop and commit specialized resources to helping abused youngsters and their families (Crowe and Kettle, 1992; Wieland, 1998). Children thus assisted may be less prone as adults to psychiatric, sexual, parenting, and social problems that beset some adult survivors of childhood sexual abuse (Bass and Davis, 1990). Bifulco and Moran highlight the intergenerational cycle of abusive behaviour that is apparent in some families, and the problems to adults caused by damaged self-image and distorted views on human relationships. Poor parenting may be perpetuated, and some people abused as children tend to be attracted towards abusive relationships and situations (1998: 95, 138).

Daniels and Jenkins (2000: 53–69) point to society's dilemma: are children the 'belongings' of their parents, or are they people (albeit young) in their own right? Society mostly operates the 'welfare' model whereby adults make policies and decisions about the child's life and future. The Children Act 1989 moves towards the participatory model where children have a say but adults make the final decision. The independence, or child-centred, model, where young people make up their own minds, is rare though there is provision in Scottish law for young people aged 12 and over, with mature minds, to make decisions affecting their own lives (Age of Legal Capacity (Scotland) Act 1991; Children (Scotland) Act 1995, s.6 quoted in Daniels and Jenkins, 2000: 18). Giving young people more responsibility for decision-making is supported by the United Nations Convention on the Rights of the Child (1989).

On the whole, British and other western societies have not responded adequately to sexually abused children and their carers (Kennedy, 1997), the needs of the victims far outweighing the available resources (Colclough et al., 1999: 175–7).

In view of the findings that 'women who experienced the combination of neglect, physical *and* sexual abuse had the worse outcomes in adulthood' (Bifulco and Moran, 1998: 183), it seems that resources put into remedial work with children could have a cost-effective outcome.

Professionals are doing their best to break down barriers of silence about child sexual abuse. Progress is being made in seeking the best ways to facilitate children to make the initial disclosure and to attend court as witnesses (though there is room for improvement). It is hard enough for able-bodied children to reveal that they have been sexually abused. Children with special needs offer ongoing challenges as professionals seek to unravel the complexities of sexual abuse perpetrated against youngsters with impaired sight, hearing and speech, learning disabilities or physical problems, and who may be ill (Aldridge and Wood, 1998: 188–217; Westcott, 1993; Westcott and Cross, 1996). Sexually abused children with disabilities may have their own special requirements, including a suitable venue and materials (Lear, 1996). Informed, empathic and flexible therapists should be able to provide for children with a range of problems and family backgrounds.

Sensitivity to cultural issues

The Children Act 1989 (s.22 (c)) stresses the need to take into consideration the child's racial, cultural, religious, and linguistic background. It is tricky enough trying to engage with children and their families when therapist and family share the same racial background. Professionals need to be aware of and sensitive to the family's cultural heritage, and to respect a diversity of family lifestyles.

In maintaining an appreciation and understanding of cultural diversity, therapists have a commitment to understand the various ways in which history, politics, and economic considerations influence cultural expressions of affect and behaviour (Barn, 1999; Thomas, 1999: 65–78). This includes developing an appreciation of how the family's cultural heritage influences the development of symptoms, coping skills, and response to external resources such as therapy. Allowing for cultural diversity, the therapist recognizes that certain so-called adaptive or maladaptive behaviours may be appropriate within the culture of origin. If the therapist does not understand the values, beliefs, and behaviours of the relevant culture, there may be a tendency to pathologize the child and/or family in terms of symptoms or functioning. There are variations in cultural beliefs and values, traditions and religious practices. Diet, family structure, language, childrearing customs, and the baseline of what constitutes child abuse may differ, as may attitudes towards women, the sick, the infirm, and the elderly. What are the family's perceptions of the host culture and do they share its values about success and status (Palmer and Laungani, 1999: 2)? What is the role of children? Are there different expectations between boys and girls? Are there rites of passage, or standards of expectable behaviour, at certain ages? Does the child's position within the family (for example first born or youngest) influence how the child is perceived?

It behoves therapists to check whether values inherent in western psychotherapy are appropriate for children and families from other traditions. The child-centred approach, working non-directively without a specific agenda or undertaking free-flowing work rather than an educational stance, and approaches that appear to ignore the role of the head of the household, may not be appreciated (Laungani, 1999; Palmer, 1999: 153–73). Some cultures find it inappropriate for the child to participate in unstructured sessions, to work with a therapist of a specific gender, or to initiate communication with adults (O'Connor, 1991: 53–5). Play is an alien notion to some peoples (Roopnarine et al., 1994). In cultures that place value on the family or extended family, working with the child and carer or other family members may be more effective than working with the child alone (Eleftheriadou, 1997: 72). Is it possible to get a linguistic match between therapist, child and carers?

Being an effective helper requires a commitment to be watchful for ways in which minority families may be vulnerable to additional stresses as a result of having to function in an alien culture. Potential problems experienced by minority communities include poverty, prejudice, isolation, and racism. Discussing abuse, especially sexual abuse, may be taboo, and the family can feel particularly shamed to have a sexually abused girl. Naomi illustrates some of the issues, in a United States context.

Referred for therapy by the child protection team, Naomi, aged four, was brought in by her mother and grandmother following sexual abuse by her mother's boyfriend. Naomi's mother, Chelsea, had ended the relationship with the perpetrator following Naomi's disclosure of the abuse. Naomi's grandmother, Henrietta, provided full-time day care for Naomi while Chelsea, a single parent, worked full-time.

Naomi, a black child, was born in the United States where her mother had also been born. Henrietta, widowed three years ago, had been an indentured slave in the South, and had brought up Chelsea. Chelsea became pregnant as an adolescent. She had a strong extended family network that helped her throughout her pregnancy and parenting. She had begun dating the perpetrator of the abuse six months before seeking therapy.

When the therapist met Chelsea and Henrietta for the first time, it was clear that both women were reluctant and even defensive. Henrietta did most of the talking. They were unsure about bringing Naomi to therapy. Henrietta elaborated on her belief that therapy was designed for 'white' people, or people who were mentally deficient. The therapist acknowledged her view and gently challenged it, addressing the dynamic that 'a part of her' might feel differently or believe that the therapist might be able to help Naomi, since Henrietta had followed through with the referral. Henrietta acknowledged her ambivalent feelings.

Chelsea raised concerns about therapy being 'non spiritual'. This was discussed in some depth, the therapist seeking to reassure them that, as a therapist, she was not a 'replacement for spirituality' but more of an additional resource. She let them know that she considered people's spirituality to be important and valuable in the healing process. Both women appeared satisfied with her response.

The women addressed their preference for a black therapist. Unfortunately, a black therapist was not available at that time. Cultural issues and differences were discussed, the women sharing the reluctance they felt about Naomi working with a white therapist. They were afraid of the potential values and beliefs that might be imposed on her, and on the family. The therapist tried to reassure them that she would not do this, and would do her best to be aware, and respectful, of cultural differences.

Resources and support within the extended family and the outside community were discussed, the family having a strong support network. The therapist did her best to be non-threatening to their perception that their existing network was adequate, presenting herself as another link in the system, and not as a replacement for what was already there. She explained that both women would be included in the therapy process, as it was clear to her that the grandmother was threatened by the therapist's potential role in her granddaughter's life. And, more importantly, the grandmother provided most of the child's daily care.

Naomi was suffering from strong negative symptoms, which the therapist felt were the deciding factor in their decision to engage in therapy on a 'trial basis'. The therapist believed that her openness and encouragement in discussing cultural issues at the start of treatment facilitated a good working alliance. The cultural considerations were subsequently discussed many times. Each time, the therapist felt that they were adequately addressed to the extent that child and family felt safe and comfortable with her as their therapist.

Naomi was motivated and engaged easily in therapy, which lasted for eight months with a successful outcome. The therapist had developed a strong working relationship with the mother and grandmother based on mutual respect and understanding, and learned much about their culture and heritage.

In the consultation period prior to starting therapy, the therapist should acknowledge cultural issues and differences that may exist between therapist, child and carers by asking the child and family about race and ethnicity, and whether they are willing to work with a therapist from a different ethnic group. The therapist should gain consent to ask questions about the child's culture and experience. Expressing an openness and willingness to learn should help bridge cultural barriers. The focus should be on making ethnic, cultural, racial, and gender issues and differences safe for child and therapist to discuss. 'True cultural competence requires that the therapist has good understanding of her complete ecosystem and her place within it as well as the ability and desire to become fully aware of her child client's ecosystem and the child's place within it' (O'Connor, 1991: 56).

Acculturation

It is important to be aware of how well an immigrant child and family have settled into a new 'host' culture yet also retained their own cultural heritage (Coward and Dattani, 1993: 248). This varies from family to family. Assessing acculturation within the family may take some time, and will most likely happen by degrees as the child becomes more comfortable.

Typical information therapists might seek include the following:

- When did carers and child immigrate to the country?
- What is their immigration status?
- Where is their family of origin?
- Are they first or second generation citizens?
- Where are their relatives?
- How often do they see their extended family or return to their place of birth?
- What is the child's and family's level of acculturation?
- How much have they integrated into mainstream society?
- Do they accept the values, norms and behaviours of the majority population?
- What are normative practices within the culture that they accept or reject?
- How open are they in discussing these issues with the therapist?

Family dynamics

Children and adolescents tend to acculturate faster than adults, and this may pose a problem within the family. Children frequently learn the new language quicker than adults. The child may subsequently be in an abnormally powerful position in the role of interpreter. This situation can create tensions within the family. The child may develop a social network more quickly through school. As a result, the child may begin to question or reject family norms and cultural heritage. The therapist should seek to know how these issues are addressed within the family.

Is the child's more rapid acculturation viewed as a betrayal, and does the child feel confused and conflicted about having a role in two cultures? Are siblings' experiences and roles similar? Acculturation is bound to be an issue in ethnic minority families, and it may be helpful if the therapist can determine whether these issues are being resolved in a psychologically healthy fashion or if there is conflict and/or dysfunction. Furthermore, individuals from ethnic minorities have a mixed acculturation level; acculturation is frequently less developed in areas related to child rearing practices, psycho-sexual development, coping patterns and outside support and family relationships. This is a normal dynamic.

Many cultural issues and beliefs are normative, adaptive, deeply embedded, and do not necessarily occur on a conscious level. These accepted ways of functioning might be in opposition to those of the majority culture in which the family now lives. This can increase stress levels and cause depression and anger in family members. Having to function in two cultures can cause guilt, conflict, confusion, and a decrease in self-esteem or ethnic pride.

Engagement in therapy

Cultural beliefs, perceptions and values may influence the family's willingness or reluctance to engage and remain in the treatment process. The following key questions should be discussed when establishing whether therapy is appropriate:

- How is therapy viewed within the family's culture? Are carers and child able to discuss their views with the therapist?
- What are the carer and child's preconceived notions about engaging in therapy? (The biggest task facing the therapist may often be engaging child and family in the therapeutic process.)
- What are the family's feelings about being in a relationship with a therapist from a different culture, religion, or gender?
- What are the expectations of therapy and hoped for outcome?
- What meaning do family members attribute to therapy sessions?

It is helpful to gain the family's view regarding the child's abuse and aetiology. How is sexual abuse seen within the relevant culture? The family may experience additional stigma, shame, and less support from their community as a result which can increase the family members' sense of isolation, and sometimes result in depression. If the problem is denied, child and family may experience more stress.

External resources

External support systems and the use of extrafamilial resources vary within different cultures. The therapist and key worker need to be aware of the role and importance such support systems may offer child and family. What is the family's existing support system?

If the family indicates this might be helpful, therapist or key worker may encourage family members to link with existing support, such as family, friends, relatives, clergy, teachers, or alternative healers. Many minority cultures rely heavily on extended family members or have a more elaborate support system than the majority culture. The family may need encouragement from the therapist to utilize their support systems, particularly if there is a sense of guilt, shame, or feelings of responsibility for the abuse.

How does the child and the family's religion affect symptomology and available resources? Is spirituality a source of consolation and comfort? How do religious beliefs affect their view of the child's victimization, symptoms, and the recovery process?

Another significant factor leading to possible reluctance to engage or stay in therapy is the socio-economic status of the family. There may be certain value attitudes deriving from the family's socio-economic status about whether treatment is worthwhile. For example, therapy tends to be viewed as more acceptable within middle or upper socio-economic classes. Generally, individuals from lower socio-economic classes feel more reluctant, embarrassed, or ashamed about seeking counselling services. Their view of therapy tends to be less positive, and therapists often have to work harder to engage them in the treatment process.

In addition, economic deprivation will increase the family's stress level and most likely decrease available resources. In some cases, it may be advantageous for the key worker (or family's designated worker) to recommend that the family supplement or strengthen social resources, and to suggest additional contacts or services for them. This should be sensitively assessed and handled as it may invoke strong emotional reactions from the family. Many clients experience shame and stigma related to economic difficulties. Furthermore it may be necessary to explore with child and family feelings about utilizing information or resources. If they are unable to accept help, the key worker can assist by exploring and processing with them the meaning the family attributes to seeking aid. It is generally more empowering to encourage the family to do things for themselves before offering to intervene.

Special considerations when working with children placed in substitute care

Children from any culture who remain in an unsafe, stunting environment, or who are not wanted, may have to be re-homed, ideally within the extended family but otherwise with foster carers or in small residential units. Therapists working with children in many types of setting, including schools, hospital units, or secure accommodation, need to be aware of the opportunities and constraints in these environments.

Research findings have shown that sexually abused children in substitute care are likely to spend longer in care than non-abused children. Educational problems plus rejection, disrupted parenting, and emotional and behavioural difficulties, are recognized to be significant. Children suffering faulty parenting, and/or changes of carer have inevitably undergone significant loss, and may have poor attachment skills and maladaptive behaviour patterns. The therapeutic task is often multi-faceted (Farmer and Pollock, 1998: 229–30; Fitzgerald, 1991; Livingstone Smith and Howard, 1994).

When the child is placed outside the home, the context of therapy broadens (Cipolla et al., 1992; Doyle, 1997: 97–113). The therapist may be involved with social workers, foster or adoptive parents, natural parents and, in some cases, institutional settings. It is advisable to explore and define the roles of carers and professionals to avoid misunderstandings and crossed boundaries. Collaboration and co-ordination of services becomes part of the therapeutic process. The natural family should be included in the child's treatment process, unless, for example, the family supports the abuser and not the child, or denies that the child was abused. Will the family of origin have contact with the child and to what extent? How long is the child expected to be in placement? Is it the intention of the various agencies to reunite the family at some point? These considerations impact on how the family of origin is involved and how the treatment process is organized. It is important to determine the substitute carers' view of the child's family of origin and their potential role in treatment. The therapist should also ascertain the implications of pending court proceedings.

If the therapist was working with the child's family of origin prior to the child's placement, the therapist will usually have been able to develop a therapeutic alliance with child and carers. Carers may feel intimidated and powerless when dealing with the various individuals and agencies involved, and may blame the therapist for the child's removal. Professionals should not underestimate the importance of the child–parent–sibling bond, and the subjective meaning that the family may attribute to the child being placed away from home. Taking the child into care, or placing the child with another family, often represents a crisis and a deep sense of failure and grief to the family members.

When placed in substitute care the child too often feels a sense of loss, anger, confusion, shame, anxiety, and sadness. Conversely, the child may be relieved, which may intensify feelings of guilt, particularly if a sibling remains in danger. Children bring with them unresolved issues pertaining to sexual victimization and other problems. The child often feels rejected, but may displace these feelings on to the professionals, blaming them for the rejection. This may be more tolerable than blaming the family. Allegiance and loyalty issues may come into play. The child may long for its family of origin, idealizing them even if a member of the family carried out the abuse. Children may believe that the abuse is their fault and that they have been removed from home as punishment.

The substitute family may find it strange that the child can be upset about leaving an abusive or neglectful family, and may need help in the conflict between acknowledging the child's grief and their own repellence at what has happened to the child. Children placed with families from another culture, or even within the same culture, may have problems relating to identity confusion; cultural, religious, and social skills; racism, prejudice, and disadvantage (Mehra, 1996).

Engagement of the child with foster/adoptive parents often takes time, and may be difficult. From the child's viewpoint, intimacy with others may now be perceived as dangerous and to be avoided, or the child may want an 'instant relationship' with the new carer and family. The child will most likely initially feel insecure and powerless. It may be less painful to remain emotionally distant and unattached from the new family, particularly if in a short-term placement.

Living with, and caring for, sexually abused children is a demanding process. Children in substitute care are often more troubled than children who remain with a parent. Abused children may abuse other children, perhaps fail to attend school or have been excluded therefrom. They may be involved in sexual behaviour outside the home, introducing other children to prostitution, pornography, and drugs. Substitute carers are often lacking information about the child's history. Carers may feel vulnerable to (false) allegations about abusing the child, and complaints from the child. Keeping confidentiality to relatives, neighbours, and friends about the child's personal affairs can tax the adult who also feels responsible for ensuring the safety of other children. Court appearances and problems over seeing parents and/or siblings can be stressful.

Many foster/adoptive parents are overwhelmed if the child acts out or exhibits challenging symptomology, and may find it difficult to respond to a child who is sexually precocious (Davis et al., 1991). Transition of a child from one family to another is stressful enough without the added dimension of the child's victimization, betrayal, stigmatization, and powerlessness. The therapist can anticipate some of the central issues and help to normalize them for the substitute family.

In a survey conducted in 1989 of 60 families adopting or fostering a sexually abused child, Macaskill (1991) found a mixed view of therapy and therapists. Out of 80 children, 25 (31 per cent) received individual therapy after placement. Little explanation of therapy was given to the family, and rarely was the family asked about the impact of therapy. Some families felt that the child could not get necessary therapy, whereas other families thought that the work the family undertook was equivalent and that therapy was unnecessary. Some families disliked the 'aura of mystery' emanating from some therapists; others valued open sharing of information. It was often appreciated when the therapist continued as a consultant to the family after therapy ended. Key issues arising from the research were:

- Is an exclusive relationship between child and therapist appropriate?
- Carers may feel they should care for the whole child.
- Communication between therapist and carers is vital.
- Joint training between professional carers and therapists would help.

Have things changed since that research was reported in 1989?

The following example illustrates some of the potential issues and complications that can arise when a child is in foster care:

Tara, aged 11 who had been sexually abused by her stepfather Rod, was brought into treatment by her foster parents. Upon disclosure, her mother, Eileen, initially supported Tara and reported Rod to the police. However, after a few weeks her mother recanted, accusing Tara of lying and attempting to seduce Rod.

Tara was articulate and bright; she told the social worker about the sexual abuse and was subsequently removed from the home. She was placed with a supportive foster family who engaged her in therapy at the recommendation of the social worker. In the meantime, Rod left the mother's household due to allegations he insisted were false.

Tara's biological father, Steve, who was still involved in her life, participated in the treatment process to help support her, and to strengthen the father–daughter relationship. Steve was currently considering remarriage, and he and his prospective wife, Ella, wished to gain full custody of Tara. Tara had ambivalent feelings about this arrangement as her parents had divorced when she was six years old, and she felt she did not know her father very well.

Eileen decided she wanted Tara back. She engaged in her own treatment at another agency and requested that she be included in the treatment process with her daughter. Tara felt betrayed, did not trust her mother, and did not want her included in her therapy, so Eileen's request was turned down.

The foster parents were also involved in treatment as they were experiencing difficulties with Tara who was angry and acting out, flouting rules and limits her foster parents tried to place on her. Tara felt confused and powerless about the custody situation, her feelings towards family members and the foster family changing drastically from session to session.

Tara continued in therapy for a year, remaining with the foster family. At the end of treatment, it appeared that she would be placed with her father who had established good parenting skills and a healthy relationship with her. Tara saw her mother regularly whom she felt was doing much better, but Tara had no desire to live with her mother again.

Tara's treatment was time consuming and complicated, by having so many different individuals potentially involved. Considerable liaison was required with the various parties' social workers. The therapist had to make several decisions about whom to work with and to what extent, while at the same time respecting Tara's desires. She also needed to clarify what her role and responsibilities were regarding the legal aspects of the case. Much of the work involved establishing appropriate boundaries and limits around what could have been a chaotic system.

Residential considerations

Another level of complexity is added when a team of residential staff cares for the child. Most residential homes operate the keyworker principle with at least one (sometimes two) staff members nominated to be the child's main care worker(s). Inevitably other staff are involved, and on top of that there will be a management structure. Therapy will be part of an overall child care plan:

Staff need to know what is happening in individual therapy particularly when children become upset as a result of feelings aroused in sessions, leading possibly to agitated or disruptive behaviour or sometimes self-destructive activity (e.g. suicide attempts, self-harming, absconding). Progress, too, in individual psychotherapy can often be improved if the child psychotherapist is informed of significant events and experiences in the community. (Wilson, 1999: 161)

When undertaking therapy with a child in a residential setting, it may prove helpful to check out the following:

1 The unit's commitment to therapeutic work. Does the unit subscribe to a therapeutic ethos? Will staff support therapy? What happens if some approve of therapy, and other members of the team rubbish it? What effect will this have on the child?
2 Can staff of the residential establishment adopt a uniform, therapeutic approach to the child?
3 Is the child attached to someone who could regularly, reliably and consistently escort the child to and from therapy sessions, and be available to the child between sessions?
4 Does management recognize the need for children to have therapy? How will management support the keyworker and team members to care for a child receiving therapy?
5 With whom will the therapist liaise? Will it be someone from management (who perhaps does not have much direct experience of the child in a daily context)? Could it be the keyworker who might have problems implementing a team approach to dealing with the child? What is the role of the keyworker's supervisor?
6 How will information be shared between therapist and key personnel? What sort of information systems are available?
7 How can the therapist share information with residential staff about meeting the child's needs?
8 Does the therapist have a role in the unit's team meetings and training sessions? Many residential staff, as with some carers, may not have much understanding about therapy, or about children's normal and abnormal responses to abuse.
9 Who holds the power, and how will decisions be made? How effective is the child's social worker in the residential setting?

Therapists working with children in residential units

Unit therapists may undertake individual, group, or sibling therapy with children, and/or may provide consultation to the staff group and to individual staff (Wilson, 1999: 160). Partnership becomes more complicated. The child's residential key worker, or named member of staff, are important people who have taken on, albeit temporarily, some of the parenting tasks. Other staff are influential, and can have a disproportionate impact on the child and child's therapy. Therefore, the therapist has to adopt something of a team approach when liaising with institutions, and to take the time and trouble to seek out influential personnel. Feedback the therapist gives should be carefully handled so that the messages get to the right place (or people) at the right time, and are not distorted, so that children are not made to feel that they are being picked on or penalized in any way. Staff need to understand that sometimes children choose not to attend therapy sessions, and should not exploit this to undermine the therapeutic process. As well as all this, it may be appropriate for the therapist to liaise with the child's parents (or carers) in the home setting, as well as with the usual range of professionals.

Liaison with other professionals, child and family or residential setting

The social worker (or key worker) usually undertakes planned work with the carers to help them to cope with the child's removal from the family and the effects of the abuse, including pointing out community resources that might be helpful. Additionally the social worker might undertake specific tasks with the child such as life story work, preparing for court, making arrangements for the child's future, getting medical treatment, and often acts as a link between therapist and family.

The therapist gathers and studies the initial referral information, meeting with the referrer and/or key worker to discuss the best way forward. The therapist meets the keyworker(s) and, if appropriate, the child's previous carers, to get their perceptions of what has happened to the child, and the child's reactions to the abuse and life experiences. The therapist will also elicit the current carers' perceptions and concerns. Together they explore the appropriateness and feasibility of therapeutic work. If all this is in order, the therapist should then be able to offer a tentative treatment plan to the child, carers, and relevant professionals, including:

- aims of the therapy sessions;
- number of sessions, time and place;.and
- arrangements about how the child will be taken to therapy sessions, and the availability of a positive attachment figure near the therapy room if this seems important.

Remember that carers and children have their own agendas, and are assessing the therapist. Part of the negotiations includes working out the most appropriate way for the therapist to liaise with the carers. It is helpful if the therapist is informed about changes in the child's life and behaviour, and carers often want feedback about major areas of therapy, plus suggestions about how the child can best be helped at home and school. Issues such as confidentiality, and liaison with the courts (if appropriate), will also be discussed.

Contact with school or nursery personnel is usually helpful. Key staff will have useful information about the child, can offer support during the child's therapy and can facilitate the child's attendance at therapy sessions (if these are to be in school or nursery time).

When all this has been accomplished, child and therapist are probably ready to meet to discuss the child's understanding of what has happened and why a referral for therapy has been made. The child will also want to suss out the therapist, and the two of them will start to build the therapeutic relationship.

Summary

In this chapter we have highlighted the confusion in western society about the roles of children. Are they the belongings of their parents? When do they become people in their own right? In real terms children have little autonomy, yet can be treated as mini-adults. Bullying and abuse by older children, adolescents, and adults is not uncommon.

In the interests of the therapeutic alliance, it is important that therapists are aware that norms and expectations can vary both inter-culturally and cross-culturally. Patterns of child-rearing and expectations about the child vary, and carers' views on child care and what is, or is not, suitable for their child need to be understood. The therapist working with a child and family from a different culture needs particular sensitivity to ensure that inappropriate stereotypes and expectations are not imposed.

If suffering from a breakdown in family life, the child may live with foster or adoptive parents, or in a residential unit. The therapist may therefore have to respond to the additional dimensions of the 'new' carers and their approach to the child, plus the child's relationship to former carers and/or natural parents and siblings.

If the child is in residential care, it will help the therapist to understand the ethos of the establishment and to form creative lines of communication with the child's designated careworker(s) plus significant people within the unit, such as manager, team leader and other professionals working with the child. Additional factors of group living and peer pressures also need to be taken into account. The child may also be the subject of a court order.

In many cases the child's natural parents have rights about the child's treatment and well-being, and the child may still be seeing the natural parents, sometimes with supervised contact.

The therapist's sensitive and informed approach to these dimensions is crucial in creating a therapeutic alliance with child and carers, be they substitute or natural parents.

6 Carer Involvement

In this chapter the task of relating to, and involving, child and carers with the therapeutic process will be discussed. We will be thinking specifically about:

- the importance of the relationship between carer and therapist, including the formation of the therapeutic alliance;
- the child's perspective;
- information the therapist will seek from the carer about the child's history, present circumstances, response to the sexual abuse, and symptoms since the abuse;
- the relevance of assessing the carers' parenting skills and their ability to participate in the therapeutic process;
- typical reactions from carers;
- the carer's ongoing relationship with the therapist; and
- the social worker's role.

Initial goals of partnership and liaison work

A good liaison between the social worker, therapist and other professionals is highly desirable, with agreement at the outset about their respective roles. It is highly beneficial to develop a positive working relationship with carers, whenever possible. Occasionally a carer might directly approach a therapist. More often the child's carer is invited to consent to an intermediate person, such as a social worker or police officer referring to the therapist details about the child, the presenting problems, and circumstances of the abuse. If carer and child seem happy at this stage, a preliminary meeting between the therapist and carer (sometimes with referrer and child) will be arranged. The therapist will gather more details about the child's background and present situation, about the sexual abuse, and about the family. The therapist will want to talk about what is involved in therapy sessions. Things to be discussed include:

- the purpose and type of therapy;
- the time and dates of sessions;
- place for the therapy;
- who will accompany the child (it is important that the child be escorted to sessions by a known and trusted person);
- the number of sessions to be undertaken;

- who will be told about what happens in sessions and what the level of confidentiality will be; and
- reports the therapist might have to give, such as to the court or the referring intermediary.

Children are free to tell carers whatever they like about their sessions, but there is a measure of confidentiality as far as the therapist is concerned. One option is for the therapist to meet the carer, on a monthly basis, to hear the carer's concerns and to learn about the child's progress, to pass on the main therapeutic issues in sessions, and to offer messages about how the carer can best meet the child's needs. Alternatively, the therapist may discuss these issues with the child's main worker, who in turn meets with the carer. An important point to establish is that there should be a reliable method for the therapist to receive information about changes in the child's life. Changes may include additions or departures within the family, changes of house or school, significant illnesses of family members, and the present circumstances of the child's abuser. Such knowledge may help the therapist fully understand what the child is presenting in sessions.

The therapist normally asks the carer, or sometimes the referrer, to talk to the child about the possibility of therapy. The therapist also arranges to have a brief introductory meeting with the child. This may take place in a setting familiar to the child, or more commonly in the therapy room. Carers will be reminded whether the social worker or some other person will be helping them with their issues, and of the level of liaison anticipated between the therapist and other involved professionals. This starts the therapeutic relationship with the carer, who is consulted about a number of things and in turn can discuss queries and doubts. Preliminary work also goes on between the therapist and others in the child's environment.

The child's age and level of understanding are taken into account when engaging the child. It is helpful for children to participate in the planning stage and to tell the therapist what is worrying or concerning them, describing the sorts of things they like doing, and to have a say in the scheduling of appointments. Some therapists like to put down on paper what has been decided, and issue a 'contract' or 'agreement' for the child to sign and/or retain.

There are occasions with older children when therapist and referrer consider that the child has a right to confidentiality within the therapeutic relationship (Daniels and Jenkins, 2000: 75, 80). It is in any event instructive to ask:

- Will the parents' permission be sought for therapy to begin?
- Will the therapist give an outline, or a detailed account, of therapeutic work in sessions?
- Does the carer have control over the frequency of sessions and when they will terminate?
- Can the therapist deal directly and solely with the young person?

Depending on the psychological healthiness, functioning, and availability of the carer, and on the quality of the child's attachment relationships, it may be important to engage carers in the therapeutic process. This is particularly the case when working with young children because of the child's need for a consistent attachment figure during and between therapeutic sessions. Many of the initial goals of working with carers parallel those of the treatment process with children. Establishing rapport and engaging carers can be facilitated by the therapist listening attentively and empathizing with worries that the carer presents as a result of the child's abuse.

It is helpful to anticipate that the carer will have feelings and concerns about engaging the child in treatment. Carers may think that being in treatment will upset the child, believing that it is less disruptive to forget what has happened and for the child to 'move on' from the abuse experience. Educating carers about the therapeutic process and the benefits for the child is desirable in such cases.

Engaging carers in the aims of the therapy, in the process (when, how many sessions, what type of therapy), and liaison with other relevant professionals such as teachers, is highly beneficial. It is helpful for the therapist to acquire base-line information about the child's behaviour and personality, both before, during and after the abuse. Some information may be subjective, but there will also be objective criteria to help therapist and carer monitor the child's progress. Telling the carer that what happens in the therapy room will be in part confidential arouses insecurity in some people. They may feel threatened, particularly if they have not provided positive or appropriate parenting, or may feel inadequate as a carer and project those feelings onto the therapist. Fears about exposure of family secrets, whether related or unrelated to the abuse, may also cause the carer to feel reluctant for the child to enter and remain in treatment. Such projections should be addressed through the therapist being supportive, non-judgemental, and reassuring.

A child says:

'First of all I didn't want my mum to know about these things. But she had to. She was mad, but then felt sorry this had happened to me. Sometimes she would blow up, and sometimes we didn't get on at all. Then the social worker talked about a therapist person. I wasn't sure, but then I thought it might be a good idea to have someone to talk to (though I didn't know what I'd say). The social worker said we would meet, to see whether I thought seeing the therapist might be a good idea. I don't like meetings with lots of grown-ups, but this wasn't too bad. I knew my mum and the social worker, and the therapist was friendly and knew how to talk to kids. She didn't just talk, 'cos she had some puppets with her that I really liked and she let me work them. She showed me pictures of her 'den' where kids go – a sort of playroom – and a place for mum to have coffee and wait. We decided I would go four times, and that if I liked it I could go another four times. I didn't want to go in school time 'cos the other kids are nosey and would want to know about it. It was important that I didn't miss swimming on Tuesdays. The therapist was careful that we got the best time for me. Not like the police and doctor, when I had to go when *they* wanted. Yes, I thought I'd try this therapy. The social worker said that she would meet with mum. The therapist wouldn't talk to mum until we all came together in four weeks' time, but if there were any important messages for mum the therapist and I would talk, and she could tell the social worker. They also said they would have to tell the police if I said that anyone else had been hurting me or touching my private parts'.

The child's history

In the initial interview(s) with the carers, one of the objectives is to obtain a comprehensive history of the child including:

1   A brief description of the child's birth, infancy and early years.
2   The child's and carers' current family situation, including the child's relationship with immediate carers.
3   A history of serious illness and hospitalizations.
4   How the child coped with significant loss or separations.
5   Unusual features in the child's development.
6   Information regarding the child's functioning at home, at school, and other significant settings.
7   Other traumas the child or family have experienced, and whether the family is currently undergoing significant problems in addition to the abuse. How has the child or family coped in the past, and how do they currently cope when problems arise?
8   Details of the sexual abuse, how it came to light, how the child behaved during the abuse and afterwards. The carers' feelings and responses towards the abuse and the abuser.
9   The carer's understanding of what has happened to the alleged abuser(s).
10   The carer's own history of abuse as a child.

The child's symptoms (see also Chapters 8 and 9)

Speaking with the carer should provide useful information and insight about the child. Explore the carer's perception of the child's current feelings, functioning, and symptoms. What changes have there been in the child's attitudes and behaviour? Is the child engaging in destructive or self-destructive acts? If so, it is important to assess danger to the child and others. Suicidal ideation needs to be taken seriously. Children *do* attempt suicide and some succeed. It is difficult to assess how common suicidal attempts are due to the nature of the attempts. Many child suicides are probably reported as accidental deaths, and more will be said about the assessment of suicidal risk in Chapter 8. If the symptoms are severe, hospitalization may be necessary.

Is the child displaying symptoms that disturb or disrupt the carer? Some children exhibit phobias or other abnormal behaviours. Can carers and family members tolerate and understand the child's feelings and behaviour? It is often necessary to help the carer to comprehend disruptive symptomology in the context of the abuse.

Some families have difficulty accepting the child's behaviours and engage in denial regarding the effects of the abuse. Let carers know that it may take time for the behaviour to change. If appropriate, support the carer, give suggestions about how to cope with and set limits or boundaries around disruptive behaviours. If role reversal has occurred in the family and the child is performing a parental role, the child may not be allowed to have or exhibit negative feelings and symptoms. The child may always need to be 'fine' in order to take care of, or not burden, the carer, and the child's wellbeing may be sacrificed to maintain the parental or family *status quo*.

Providing education about the effects of the sexual abuse can be reassuring. Normalizing the child's feelings and symptoms is a valuable place to start. In addition, normalizing and supporting the carers' reactions and feelings provides much-needed relief to carers as well.

Assessment of parenting skills

Assessing the level of parenting skills gives information on the quality of the child–carer relationship, on the carer's understanding of the child's developmental needs and psychological response to the abuse, and on the carer's ability to work in partnership with the therapist. The following are significant questions:

1 Does the carer need support in order to be emotionally available to the child?
2 Does the carer have a reasonable understanding of the child's needs?
3 What kind of support does the carer require? Is the carer burdened by unresolved issues which erupt when with the therapist? Does the topic of conversation continuously shift from the child's feelings and functioning to the carer's functioning?
4 Are the carers needy, dysfunctional or traumatized by the child's abuse? If so, they should be encouraged to seek therapy for themselves, preferably from a different therapist. If the carer only requires additional support, a group for carers of abused children may be appropriate.

If the abuse has happened in the family home, social services and the legal system prefer to remove the alleged perpetrator rather than the child, though this is not always possible. The perpetrator's removal can raise concerns about the remaining carer's ability within the home, and the degree to which the perpetrator can be kept away from the child to prevent re-victimization and intimidation.

How much the carer will be included in the treatment process is a judgement for child and therapist. An interesting position is raised by the Gillick case (Gillick v. West Norfolk Area Health Authority (1985) quoted in Daniels and Jenkins (2000: 16–18)). In this case, the judgement argued that 'competent' children with mature minds can make their own decisions about treatment and level of confidentiality. Daniels and Jenkins note that limited confidentiality, when the child knows that carers will be informed about the therapy and some of its content, has hindered some children's progress. Some able young people have prospered in therapy despite vetoing the involvement or knowledge of their parents.

In general, it will be therapeutic for the child to experience the therapist as a person who respects, supports, and nurtures the carer. Establishing the child's realization that there are people in the environment who are responsive is an important piece of work in its own right.

There is usually liaison with the carer during the child's treatment process. The best scenario is for the family worker (or therapist) to meet with the carer for separate one-to-one sessions, probably monthly. The child should know the nature of these meetings. If information is to be shared, the therapist needs to discuss it with the child, obtaining the child's understanding and consent. In some cases, it may be better to help the child to disclose the material. Talking about the upcoming meetings with the child helps to prevent feelings of jealousy or concerns about confidential information being exposed.

Typical carer responses

There are a variety of ways in which adults respond to the abuse of a child in their care. The child is perceptive and will be influenced by the carer's reactions and beliefs about the abuse, even if not explicitly discussed. For this reason, it is always important to address their reactions and beliefs.

The most common responses involve feelings of anger, inadequacy, or failure. Most people consider that parents/carers should protect their child from harm, feeling they have failed if they have not done so. Others may respond negatively or critically, increasing the carer's feelings of self-blame or failure. Hence most carers suffer a temporary lowering of self-esteem as a result of the child's victimization. They may be concerned about others' reactions if or when they find out about the abuse. These feeling may be projected onto the therapist and may interfere with the therapeutic alliance if not addressed.

Carers may experience guilt if they are not able to respond to the child in a nurturing fashion in the aftermath of the victimization, and may resent the extra demands the child places on them. If there are siblings, the carer may worry that too much attention is being given to the abused child. Carers may feel a sense of guilt if they have allowed the child to be exposed to the abuser, even if unaware that the abuse was occurring. In some cases, the carer may have been neglectful or have had poor judgement.

The carer who is a sexual abuse survivor may deny or have repressed all abuse memories. The child may even have been exposed to the carer's own abuser. If so, carers may feel tremendous guilt and, due to their own denial or feelings of loyalty to the abuser, convince the child to recant the abuse. If the carer is a survivor, the child's abuse may trigger an intense emotional response due to the adult's denial, and unresolved issues may surface. As a result, carers can become emotionally incapacitated, finding it difficult to respond adequately to the child. Furthermore, their own unresolved issues may be projected onto the child in an attempt to obtain mastery, and they may experience increased difficulty in maintaining objectivity. In some cases, the carer may deny the adverse effects the sexual abuse is having on the child. If carers have repressed or denied the effects of their own victimization, they may desire to do the same with the child and may remove the child from treatment.

Powerlessness and anger are other typical reactions. Carers may believe that they should have known about the abuse and stopped it. They often feel angry towards the abuser, but are not sure what to do with their anger. Sometimes the anger is displaced or directed to the child who may be blamed for not revealing the abuse or for not trying to prevent it. In some cases, the child may be accused of being seductive or encouraging the abuse, particularly if the perpetrator is the partner, spouse, or close friend of the carer.

Most carers have natural fears about the effects of the abuse on the child. If symptoms are present, they may fear that the child will never be the same again. Inadvertently, they may reinforce the child's self-perception as being 'damaged goods'.

The carer may be hyper-vigilant and overprotective about the child's safety, which children often experience as another form of punishment and further evidence that they are bad and cannot be trusted. There may be increased conflict as a result of the restrictions placed on the child's activities.

Sadness and feelings of loss are other common reactions. The child's emotions and behaviour may distress the carer. The child may be tearful, depressed, or withdrawn, eliciting similar feelings in the carer who becomes protective and is worried that therapy will stir up feelings and intensify the child's pain. The therapist needs to be aware of this dynamic and help carers to understand why therapy will be beneficial.

There may be concerns related to the child's current and future sexuality. The child has lost a sense of innocence and has been sexualized prematurely. There may be additional worries if the child is acting out sexually or is engaging in inappropriate or offensive behaviour (see Chapter 9). Some carers experience homophobia if victim and perpetrator are both male. They worry that the child has latent homosexual tendencies or will become homosexual due to the abuse. Let them know that there is no significant evidence to support this view. Male victims may also feel this way and it can be detrimental to the child if this belief is unintentionally reinforced by the carer.

In some instances, carers experience the child's relationship with the therapist as threatening, particularly if they are insecure and do not have a positive relationship with the child. Jealousy is another possible reaction. Carers, if needy themselves, may resent the child receiving so much attention and support. This can be addressed by including them in the treatment process, giving them additional time, or referring them to another therapist. Any referral needs to be made sensitively so that the therapist's action is not interpreted as rejection.

Anticipating possible reactions and intervening promptly may prevent a child being removed from treatment. Being sensitive and responsive to the carer also facilitates the development of a positive alliance, which is highly desirable when working with young children. Unfortunately, it is not always possible to engage the carer in the treatment process. Failure to do so should not necessarily be considered bad practice on the part of the therapist, but it could affect the quality of the therapeutic relationship with the child.

The following two examples illustrate two different experiences of the therapeutic process. The first shows an unsuccessful attempt to engage a parent and the second demonstrates a successful outcome.

Case 1

Referred by the police, Janet brought her daughter Lynn, aged ten, for treatment after she was sexually abused by a maternal uncle. Lynn had told a sibling who then informed the mother. Janet had also been sexually abused by a close relative when she was young, and reacted to Lynn's abuse very angrily. Janet was narcissistic and tended to view the abuse as something 'bad' that had happened to 'her' rather than something that was primarily Lynn's misfortune. She viewed herself as a victim in every aspect of life. Lynn was depressed and often in tears, but her mother was unresponsive, self-absorbed, and reluctant to bring her daughter for therapy.

In addition, the mother felt depressed because her husband had been in poor health over the last six months. She felt overburdened with concerns and somewhat hostile to the therapist, whom she viewed as an intruder. She was defensive about having often left her daughter with her uncle even though Lynn had protested each time.

The mother insisted on coming to Lynn's first three therapy sessions, tending to monopolize the conversation. Although it was difficult, the therapist began to establish a positive relationship with the girl. The mother's narcissism prevented her from letting Lynn be the focus for long, and she would turn the conversation back to herself and her own issues. When the therapist commented that it would be beneficial to see Lynn for a session on her own, the mother agreed, but abruptly dropped out of treatment and did not return the therapist's phone calls or respond to the follow-up letter.

Case 2

Diana brought her daughter Kate, aged ten, for treatment after being abused by her biological father. Diana had left her husband six months previously, and had taken her son, aged six, with her. Kate had been her husband's 'favourite little girl' and Diana had left her daughter with him when she moved. The husband had been aggressive towards Diana in the past, forcing her to engage in perverted sexual acts. However, she convinced herself that he would take adequate care of Kate.

Three months after Diana left and was applying for a divorce, the father began sexually abusing Kate. Diana continued to see Kate several times weekly, speaking to her frequently on the telephone. After a further three months, Kate disclosed the sexual abuse to her mother. At this time, Kate was depressed, often in tears, and performing poorly in school. Diana reported the incident to the police and the father was arrested.

During the initial meeting with the therapist, Diana was anxious and tearful. She had poor self-esteem and was concerned about how the therapist would view her. Diana felt guilty and ashamed for leaving Kate with the father. She was sad regarding her daughter's victimization and appeared to be extremely needy herself. She felt powerless with regard to her husband and her own victimization by him. In addition, Diana was undergoing a good deal of stress at work, had little money, and felt isolated. She had poor parenting skills and was not sure how best to support Kate. It was evident that she was over burdened and depressed before Kate disclosed her abuse.

The therapist was able successfully to contain and comfort Diana during the initial meeting, the therapist's acceptance and compassion helping Diana to begin the establishment of a positive alliance. It was apparent that Diana was very needy, with unresolved issues relating to the abuse she had experienced at the hands of Kate's father. The therapist offered her a referral to another therapist in the agency, which she gratefully accepted. Meanwhile, the therapist continued working with her on strengthening her parenting skills. She also helped her to understand and support Kate through the therapeutic process.

Diana engaged in her own therapy for a period lasting more than two years, becoming more confident and better able to function. Kate's treatment lasted 15 months and she improved considerably. Diana and Kate developed a positive and healthy mother–daughter bond that had not existed previously.

Carer functioning and responsiveness

Assessment of carer availability and responsiveness needs to be an ongoing process. The following questions should be considered:

- What level of support are carers/family members able to provide?
- How responsive are carers/family members to the child?
- And most importantly, is the child safe and protected from further victimization?

Do not assume that because the abuse was extrafamilial the child is now safe. Some carers expose a child to further abuse. They may need assistance in establishing how to keep the child as safe as possible. It is very important to ascertain whether the carer unwillingly or willingly exposed the child to harm. Sometimes the abuser is a friend of the family who befriends the child and takes on surrogate carer responsibilities because the carers are emotionally or otherwise unavailable. The family often does not question the relationship and may be indifferent to it. The friend may have had unrestricted access to the child, who is often courted before being victimized. If a family member is the perpetrator, it is important to ensure that the carer keeps the perpetrator away from the child. A court order or legal backing should reinforce this.

The therapist's ongoing relationship with the carers

Part of the planning for the child's therapy should include a continuing scheduled relationship between the carer and the therapist, either directly or via the carer's or child's worker. Therapists may wish to state that, in general, they do not want to talk about the child and the content of the therapy session at the beginning or end of the child's sessions, as this is the child's time and it is not in the child's best interest for adult agendas to intervene. A separate time can be scheduled to discuss any concerns or the progress of therapy.

Unless there is a time-limited therapeutic contract, the therapist will wish to involve the carer as well as the child in determining when therapy should finish, and at this and intermediate stages the therapist may provide the carer with an assessment of the child's future needs.

The social worker's role

The social worker, or child protection worker, often has designated responsibility for the child and family, and is usually the intermediary between child, carers and therapist. One social worker described this as follows:

'My job is to do the best I can for the child. Sometimes this is easy if the carer supports what seems to be in the child's best interests, but it inevitably becomes complicated if the carer's needs get in the way such as when the sexual abuse trauma is minimized, or the abused child is scapegoated and becomes the recipient of the family's difficulties. Disruption following most forms of sexual abuse is to be expected. If the child's behaviour and growth are within developmental norms, and provided the child lives in a stable family and is safe from further abuse, then time might be the healer. However, if the child's behaviour is distressing, and is causing problems in several areas such as in school, with the peer group, and at home, referral to a therapist might be helpful. I initially chat to the carer about the possibility of therapy and, if appropriate, might also have a word with the potential therapist. If we seem to agree that therapeutic work might be useful, I get the carer's and child's permission to give the therapist further information prior to a meeting between the carer(s), the therapist and myself. Or the therapist might prefer to meet the carer (perhaps the child too) before having the information. The therapist will want quite a bit of background history and I might be able to get permission to provide copies of reports. We will need to talk about how many times the therapist might work with the child, when and where, who will take the child to sessions, and who will pay for what. I may have to seek authorization or funding from a senior colleague before we can get much further.

'During the initial meetings we will also decide what my role should be. I will arrange to see the carer from time to time, both to try to help with some of the adult's problems, to discuss concerns about the child, and to pass on any messages about the child from the therapist. We usually plan to meet together after a few of the child's sessions to talk about how things are going. It is a great relief to me to have a therapist involved, as I know the child will get some attention, and I can focus on helping to improve the child's environment.'

Summary

A good working relationship with carers is an integral part of the treatment process, whenever possible. The therapist requires information about the child's history, current circumstances, symptoms, and the events that precipitated the referral for therapy. In turn, carers are allies in the therapeutic process. They welcome a careful understanding of the type of therapy, the targets that may be achieved to a greater or lesser extent, and ways they can co-operate such as regularly bringing the child to a planned sequence of sessions. If engaged in the therapeutic process, carers will be better able to support the child though any difficult stages in the therapy when painful feelings are being processed.

Carers may be involved in decision-making about the level of confidentiality in the child's therapy. They need to be clear to whom they should turn for feedback about the child's progress and needs, and to whom they should provide ongoing information about alterations in the child's circumstances so that the therapist is aware of significant changes in the child's life. Some carers are eager to co-operate. Others find it more difficult, their own needs, and perhaps fears about what the child could disclose, getting in the way. In any event, they often appreciate having help in their own right.

Exercise

Imagine how vulnerable you might feel if you were meeting with a therapist following your child's abuse.
Might you feel afraid that you will be: criticized? judged? blamed?
Might you be concerned and afraid that you will be judged and labelled as a negligent or bad parent?
Might you feel: worried? overwhelmed? confused? guilty? sad? powerless? enraged? traumatized yourself?
What would make you, as a carer, feel reassured, comfortable, and supported?
How can the therapist best facilitate this process?

7   Theoretical Considerations

A survivor writes:

It is a secret
much, much bigger
than me.
It is a snake
I am powerless.
It will strangle me.

A horrible beast,
my secret
and I,
feeding on me
devouring my spirit,
my words, and heart.

And when I grow up,
it will spit me all out
buried in saliva
unrecognizable.

Hallelujah,
at last I will be free
or will I?

Knowledge of theory is vital to the therapist's practice (Cramond, 1997). The therapist should try to keep abreast of current research and literature and its practice implications.

In this chapter we will look at the major contributions of two developmental theorists, Erik Erikson and Jean Piaget. Children are in an ongoing phase of development and adaptation to reality. In formulating a treatment plan, the therapist needs to have knowledge of the developmental perspective in order to offer an appropriate intervention. Therapeutic interventions need to be strongly geared towards addressing specific deficits in the child's developmental process.

We will also look at the importance of the attachment process. The emphasis on and importance of the attachment process has developed from the psychoanalytic/

psychodynamic tradition. Attachment is a term referring to children's capacity to attach to others in their environment. Much of this is based on the child's earliest experience with carers, and the quality of that experience. Children's style of attachment will also be manifested in their interactions and relationship with the therapist. Being victimized, particularly by a trusted other, will have detrimental effects on the child's attachment capacity. In this chapter several different attachment styles will be addressed (illustrated by case examples), including the following:

- The parentified child.
- The insecure-avoidant child.
- The compulsively-compliant child.
- The insecure-ambivalent child.

Much of the therapist's work with the child will involve the assessment of the child's attachment style. It will also involve helping the child to develop a more secure and healthy attachment, both with the therapist and with appropriate others in the child's environment.

Identification of the child's development

At what stage is the child developmentally and what are the current developmental tasks the child is facing? It is important to assess the child's functioning on a cognitive, psychological, emotional, and developmental level. Is the child functioning appropriately to its age, recognizing that there are large variations in normality? Therapists need to remember that it is normal for a child to regress to a prior level of development as a result of being traumatized.

> Psychological literature is permeated with models of development representing the varied perspective of numerous theorists. However, common to the models is the consensus that:
>
> - development is an interactive, creative, ever changing and dynamic process;
> - the parent is not the exclusive (or even the primary) source of the child's construction of reality or development of coping strategies; and
> - significant growth and change can occur at any stage of life. (Harper, 1993: 61)

Clinical implications are clear. Optimally, work done in therapy should free the child so that the child's intra-psychic energy can be spent working through and mastering normal developmental tasks, and in re-stimulating growth in areas of deficit, instead of investing energy in defending against and surviving the trauma of the abuse.

Two of the major contributors to developmental theory are Piaget (Wadsworth, 1984) and Eric Erikson (1959). Summaries of their background and theoretical framework follow.

Piaget's developmental theory

Jean Piaget was a developmental psychologist, primarily concerned with changes and cognitive functioning from birth through to adolescence. He also studied the development of affect (emotions, values, and feelings), which he viewed as being related to cognitive development and intelligence. Piaget believed that all behaviour has both affective and cognitive aspects. According to Piaget, this interplay is manifested and can be observed in children's moral concepts.

In the broadest terms, Piaget asserts that cognitive and intellectual changes are the outcome of the developmental process. He does not suggest that a child moves from one stage to another, but that cognitive development is a type of continuous flow. Each stage of development is built upon and integrated with previous stages, but the ages during which children develop are not fixed.

Piaget (1954) summarizes the stages of cognitive development as follows:

1 The stage of sensori-motor intelligence (0–2 years)
During this stage, behaviour is primarily motor. The child does not yet internally represent events and 'think' conceptually, though 'cognitive' development as seen as schemata are constructed.

2 Tshe stage of pre-operational thought (2–7 years)
This stage is characterized by the development of language and other forms of representation, and rapid conceptual development. Reasoning during this stage is pre-logical or semi-logical.

3 The stage of concrete operations (7–11 years)
During these years, the child develops the ability to apply thought to concrete problems.

4 The stage of formal operations (11–15 years)
During this stage, the child's cognitive structuring reaches its greatest level of development, and the child becomes able to apply logical reasoning to all classes of problems. (Piaget 1954; Wadsworth, 1984: 25)

Erikson's psychosocial theory

Erikson was trained in psychoanalytic theory. He theorized that childhood was divided into developmental stages that must be resolved before a child moves from one to the next. If the 'psychosocial crisis' of each stage is not resolved, then the child will be forced to encounter the crisis repeatedly during subsequent stages until it is resolved. He also believed that children who are traumatized often revert to an earlier stage of development (regression).

Erikson defined the first four stages of psychosocial development with both positive and negative outcomes (Erikson, 1977: 222–37). The first stage he defined as the stage of trust versus mistrust (0–1 years). During this stage, in the positive outcome, an infant who is nurtured, loved, touched, and cared for, will learn to feel secure, and learn to trust in the environment. Conversely, in the negative outcome, the infant who does not receive the appropriate nurturing and affection, whose needs and desires are neglected or ignored, will become anxious and fearful. This child learns to mistrust the environment.

Erikson defined the second stage as that of autonomy versus shame (1–3 years). During this period, in the positive outcome, the child begins to learn self-control. The child also begins to learn control of the environment. These tasks lead to an increased sense of self-worth and pride in the child. In the negative outcome, the child does not begin to achieve autonomy. The child learns and continues to be dependent and controlled by other people. The result is increased self-doubts and a lack of pride.

In the third stage, initiative versus guilt (3–6 years) in the positive outcome, the child receives approval and praise for developing skills. The child learns how to master the environment. The child's imagination becomes increasingly pronounced, and the child engages in self-initiated play. The child begins to play with others and can take the roles of both leader and follower in play. In the negative outcome of this phase, the child learns failure. The child is made fun of, teased, and ridiculed. The child is responded to punitively.

Erikson defines the fourth stage as that of industry versus inferiority (6–13 years). During this phase, in the positive outcome the child begins to master more intricate skills of life. The child learns how to interact with others and to play by rules. The child feels confident, learns self-discipline, and feels competent in his or her abilities. In the negative outcome of this phase, the child feels a lack of confidence, feels inadequate, and even inferior. The child experiences and may anticipate failure.

The importance of attachment and the therapeutic process

Therapists need a strong knowledge base and awareness of attachment in order to understand how the trauma of sexual abuse will affect the child and the attachment process, on an emotional, cognitive, and behavioural level. Child and carer can benefit greatly from learning about this process as well.

> Children and family members are empowered when they learn the dynamics of attachment and trauma. They become better able to understand and cope with their experience when they know how relationships form, what happens when overwhelming and life-threatening circumstances interfere with this formation process, and how thinking, feeling, behaviour, and relationships are affected by trauma. (James, 1994: 65)

It is also believed that there is a physiological component to attachment. 'Events that occur during the first three or four years of life ... are encoded through the basal area of the brain and, thus, are held within sensori-motor/emotional modalities' (van der Kolk, 1996 quoted in Wieland, 1998: 12). Therefore the memories are reflected in the child's behaviour and body sensations. After four years of age, memories are recorded through the hippocampus within verbal memory except when highly stressed when it returns to the basal memory.

Attachment is an overall term referring to the state and quality of an individual's attachments.

These can be divided into secure and insecure attachment. Like many psychodynamic terms, 'attachment' carries both experiential and theoretical overtones. To feel attached is to feel safe and secure. By contrast, an insecurely attached person may have a mixture of feelings towards their attachment figure: intense love and dependency, fear of rejection, irritability and vigilance. One may theorize that their lack of security has aroused a simultaneous wish to be close and the angry determination to punish their attachment figure for the minutest sign of abandonment. (Holmes, 1993: 67)

Attachment theorists place strong significance on the correlation between psychological well-being and a child having a secure attachment to a parental figure. Bowlby has shown that having accessibility to a parental figure(s) sustains children's feelings of security and uses the term 'attachment' to describe this relational bond.

A young child's experience of an encouraging, supportive and cooperative mother, and a little later father, gives him a sense of worth, a belief in the helpfulness of others, and a favourable model on which to build future relationships. Furthermore, by enabling him to explore his environment with confidence and to deal with it effectively, such experience also promotes his sense of competence. Thenceforward, provided family relationships continue favourably, not only do these early patterns of thought, feeling and behaviour persist, but personality becomes increasingly structured to operate in moderately controlled and resilient ways, and increasingly capable of continuing so despite adverse circumstances. (Bowlby, 1982: 378)

In secure and healthy attachment, the child will turn to the favoured carer for support, nurturing, and affection at periods of stress, anxiety, or insecurity, being comforted by the closeness and proximity of parental-type figures. The child is equally able to experience and explore the world without fear of losing parental approval or affection. The child feels able to trust others, and is able to internalize feelings of comfort and security. Such feelings are initially provided by the carer, before subsequently becoming accessible to and part of the child's psychological make-up.

Conversely, the child who is not contained, comforted, and soothed, experiences stress and anxiety, and is unable to explore the environment knowing that the carer will be emotionally available when needed. The developmental task of exploration, an initial and important developmental step in preparation for the separation/ individuation process, is thwarted before it has even begun.

Mothers or other caretakers who are not reliable and attentive need to be watched with a wary eye by the child. It matters to the infant whether or not the mother is listening, caring or responding. There is always an element of anxiety, for the child can never be certain that it will be loved or fed, comforted or stimulated, encouraged or played with. The mother is not in tune with her baby. Either signals are not received or they are read incorrectly. The child may be stimulated when she feels sleepy, given a bottle when he is not hungry. The infant has no feelings of being in charge. Unlike the securely attached child with an alert and sensitive parent, things happen to the insecurely attached child without anyone apparently taking any notice of the baby's feelings and wishes. (Howe, 1993: 52)

The child's attachment to carers establishes expectations and provides the blueprint for future intimate relationships. In addition, the child's style of attachment with central carers has strong implications both for the therapeutic relationship and the child's ability or inability to relate and connect with other people in his or her environment. According to Wieland (1998: 40), the child's relationship with the therapist mirrors the attachment relationship.

The therapist working with sexually abused children will almost inevitably encounter deficits and disturbances in the child's attachment relationships. The evaluation and treatment of attachment issues is an integral part of the therapeutic process. Even though the attachment process may not be presented as the focus of treatment, it will need to be addressed in order to promote healing and psychological growth.

Attachment theory provides an explanation of the difficulty with which those who have been, or are being, abused find in separating themselves from the abuser. Attachment behaviour is activated by threat: the attached cling to their attachment figure when threatened. If that figure is also the perpetrator of violence and/or sexual abuse a vicious circle is set up from which it is very difficult for a victim to extricate herself. Both separation and threat arouse unbearable feelings of panic and the need to cling even harder. (Holmes, 1993: 36)

If a child's carers are emotionally unavailable or inconsistent, the child will not have formed a secure attachment. As a result, the child often attaches in an anxiety ridden, disorganized, or avoidant way. The child who has not experienced secure attachments may also display an insecure ambivalent attachment style. Children may alternate between clingy or needy behaviour and detached or aggressive behaviour. The child frequently represses or disavows any desire or longing for the carer, as these feelings are too painful for the child to experience or express. In this way, the child protects himself, and feels more in control of the situation.

Children without a secure attachment may appear apathetic and unresponsive. They have not had the opportunity of emotionally connecting with others, and may find the experience to be largely foreign. The child does not appear to value contact or relationships, and may even devalue them. Such children are frequently perceived as continuously taking and never giving anything in return. Unfortunately, other children and adults may find interaction with these children to be unsatisfying, which only serves to keep the child isolated and reinforces the child's beliefs and behaviour.

Children with attachment disturbances become easily alarmed by feelings of intimacy that may be evoked by a responsive person with whom the child comes into contact. These feelings may be viewed as dangerous. 'Intimacy is commonly avoided by adult and child trauma survivors because the inherent emotional closeness leads to feelings of vulnerability and feelings of loss of control, and both of these feelings are intolerable to victims of violent abuse and other trauma. Intimacy represents a threat, not safety' (James, 1994: 15).

When the therapist begins to form a positive relationship with the child, the child may become fearful and react by disavowing any feelings or desire to connect emotionally. The child may become disinterested, anxious, aggressive, devalue the therapist, or even reject her. Subsequently, a positive attachment relationship may take a long time to develop.

Many children display an anxious attachment style by being needy, dependent, and demanding. To the therapist, these children appear never to get enough attention or affection to soothe or contain them. The therapist may experience the needs of such children as demanding and exhausting. It may be challenging for the therapist to set appropriate limits and boundaries as there may be a concern that doing so will be interpreted as a form of rejection.

The process of boundary-setting and limits needs to be done in a sensitive fashion, paying attention to the child's experience of what is being said and done, and why. For example, a child may have difficulty separating from the therapist at the end of sessions. This will need to be processed with the child, and the child may need extra time to prepare for the ending of sessions. It is beneficial to explore with the child how he experiences the end of the session, and explore any feeling of loss or insecurity evoked. The therapist should help the child to find a way to cope with these feelings in the interim until the next session.

Other children demonstrate an insecure-ambivalent attachment style. The child may vacillate between being clingy, possessive, and demanding to being non-responsive or disinterested during sessions, or from one session to the next. This can be perplexing for the therapist. These children experience confused and ambivalent feelings regarding attachment. This may also be indicative of the carer's inconsistent parenting, particularly regarding emotional availability. This dynamic causes great confusion and conflict within the child, which will be manifested in the relationship with the therapist.

Some children also display what is referred to as insecure-disorganized attachment.

> For the child whose early attachment experiences fit within the category of disorganized attachment … the sense of chaos is likely to be even greater. For the child who experiences early abandonment or neglect, the pull toward the perpetrator, a person who is attending to him, is particularly strong. Both love and hate become intensified. … Feelings come to represent chaos. (Wieland, 1998: 14)

Below are several case examples which exemplify children's presenting styles of attachment behaviour and their implications for the treatment process.

Case 1: The parentified child

Shelly, aged six, came in for treatment following her sexual victimization by an uncle. Shelly appeared psuedo-mature for her age and was quickly observed to be in a parentified role. Her father had died when she was aged four, and she had been put in the role of comforter and helper to her mother who was often depressed. Shelly was praised and valued by her mother for her maturity and helpfulness. Shelly had also helped to take care of her brother, two years her junior. She insisted that she did not need to come for treatment. During the first two sessions, she spoke of her mother's problems and difficulties instead of her own. Initially, Shelly was disinterested in and dismissive of the therapist, denying that the abuse had affected her in any way.

The therapist found it initially difficult to engage Shelly in treatment. However, during the third session she was able successfully to empathize with Shelly's concerns regarding her mother, and her fears regarding her mother's possible fragmentation if anything were to be wrong with or to upset Shelly. Together they made a list, which the therapist agreed to keep in her office, so Shelly would not have to carry the concerns about her mother around with her. The therapist also agreed to help Shelly's mother, by arranging a referral to another therapist in the setting, as well as bi-weekly adjunct meetings between the mother and herself.

Shelly was able to attach to the therapist, although the process was slow and inconsistent. Over time, the therapist's patience, availability, and concern for her well-being enabled her to engage in the relationship; Shelly began to enjoy the attention and positive regard of the therapist. During this period, Shelly's parentified and pseudo-mature self was also enacted with the therapist, who subsequently helped Shelly to understand why and what she was doing, and to let her know that it was safe to be a child during therapy sessions. At this point, Shelly re-learned how to play and to behave in an age-appropriate fashion. She was able to escape from her parentified role, first during therapy sessions, and subsequently at home.

In the middle phase of treatment, Shelly was able to seek out her mother for the comfort and affection that she herself had previously provided *for* her mother. The role reversal shifted; the mother was able to provide affection and comfort to her child. The abuse and loss of her father were addressed at this stage of treatment, as the positive relationship with the therapist needed to be in place before these central therapeutic issues could be processed. The mother was instrumental in this process as well. The final stage of treatment lasted an additional six months during which a healthy attachment was facilitated.

Case 2: The insecure/avoidant child

Peter, aged five, was seen for treatment following an abuse incident by an adolescent male. Peter was anxious and aggressive following the incident. He had always been prone to anxiety and aggression, according to his mother. The parents were recently divorced and the family had been highly dysfunctional. Peter had witnessed many incidents of domestic violence directed at his mother, and his efforts to gain affection and attention from his father had always been rebuked. He no longer had any contact with his father, and stated that he had no interest or affection for him.

Peter's mother had previously been too busy and overwhelmed by the relationship with his father to attend or respond adequately to her son. She had also denied the effect that witnessing her abuse had had on Peter. She was now trying to rectify the situation, but Peter responded to her overtures with disinterest, distrust, or aggression. His reaction evoked feelings of inadequacy and guilt in her. In addition, both her parents had died when she was young and she had no stable role model for parenting. The therapist worked with Peter's mother on an individual basis, realizing the importance of helping the mother to tolerate and deal with Peter's negative behaviour, as well as to help her learn parenting skills and to respond positively to Peter, even when he ignored or rejected her.

The therapist found Peter's behaviour difficult to contain. She began by establishing ground rules regarding what he could and could not do in the playroom. She also helped him to use the toys to express his anger and aggression. Peter was surprised by the therapist's acceptance and responsiveness to what he regarded as his inherent 'badness'. Peter usually pushed people away, including his peers and mother, by his acting out behaviour. It was a position of power on his part. He had identified with the aggressor in the form of his father and the adolescent offender. Peter could not conceptualize himself being a victim in any way and was secretly afraid of the destructiveness of his anger. He also believed he could make people disappear if he wanted them to, a recurring theme in his play for many months.

Over a six-month period, the therapist helped him to control his behaviour which had had many negative consequences for him, particularly in school. Peter started to engage in play with the therapist, and the rejecting and aggressive themes began to change and lessen. She helped Peter to realize and experience some of the underlying emotions, such as loss, sadness, helplessness and fear, that had been manifested in his outbursts of anger. Peter gradually engaged with and trusted the therapist, becoming able to express his vulnerability and neediness. His range of experienced and expressed emotions broadened considerably. When the therapist responded positively to him, he had initially backed away, but now became able to sustain longer periods of closeness and contact.

At the same time, Peter's mother also became emotionally more available, and the relationship between the two of them started to improve. Peter was seen over a period of two years during which his aggressive outbursts and anxiety became virtually non-existent, and during which he developed a positive and sustaining relationship (a secure attachment style) with both the therapist, his mother, his teacher, and his peers at school.

Case 3: The compulsively-compliant child

Mary, aged six, came into treatment following an incident of sexual abuse by her mother's male friend. Mary was quiet, presenting as a child who was eager to please; she was hyper-aware of what might be expected of her. Mary's mother had low self-esteem and was narcissistic. She had ambivalent feelings about Mary being engaged in treatment, and was concerned that the therapist might become aware of her inadequacies as a mother. She was afraid that Mary might come to prefer the therapist over herself. Mary was viewed as an extension of herself and necessary for the mother to regulate and maintain her self-esteem.

Mary was obviously a good and compliant girl. She was quiet, polite, and well-mannered. Her face and voice were practically devoid of expression. Mary was reluctant to engage in the treatment process as she sensed her mother's ambivalent feelings. Separating from her mother often took 10 to 15 minutes, and she appeared anxious for a good deal of the session thereafter. The therapist felt that the therapeutic connection she was attempting to form with the child was superficial after many sessions. The child remained stifled in her play. For example, Mary did not know what toys to play with, could not initiate a theme in the play, and needed the therapist to approve almost every action she took.

The child's development of self and any separation from the mother had always been responded to with withdrawal and/or hostility. The mother found it threatening for the child to develop her own sense of self; the child's attachment and connection to her mother were based on her ability to be compliant and always 'good'. The mother needed the child to regulate her own self-esteem, and to provide soothing and comfort for herself. Very slowly, with the therapist, the child was able to develop and express more of her self. She began to initiate play and to engage more deeply with the experience of play. She appeared to be more relaxed and to enjoy playing in a way she had not done previously. At this point, unfortunately, the mother stopped bringing Mary to therapy, the mother having become threatened by the therapist's positive relationship with Mary. The therapist felt that the mother was very invested in keeping her daughter in the 'good compliant' role, in order to prevent herself from fragmenting and/or addressing her own deficits. The therapist considered she had not assessed the situation thoroughly enough, believing that the matter might have turned out differently if she had engaged the mother more in the treatment process, and if she had been more aware of the mother's issues and how they might impact on her daughter's treatment.

Case 4: The insecure/ambivalent child

Katie, aged seven, engaged in treatment following her sexual abuse by her mother's boyfriend. Katie was easy to engage in the therapy process. In fact, she became instantly demanding, clingy, and possessive of the therapist. She began asking the therapist inappropriate questions about her personal life and other children who came to therapy, and demanded to sit right next to the therapist, and to follow her about the room on every occasion. Katie appeared anxious and eager to please. The experience of instant intimacy was disconcerting for the therapist, who was afraid that the child might experience boundary setting as rejection.

Katie was open in disclosing details about the abuse and intimate family details. She appeared needy and eager for instant affection and contact. However, later in the initial session, Katie became disinterested and withdrawn from the therapist. She avoided contact and began playing aggressively with the dolls, calling them names and handling them roughly, this behaviour lasting for ten minutes. Katie then stood very close to the therapist and asked her personal questions about her own family and other children she might see for therapy. At the end of the session, the child had a difficult and emotional time parting from the therapist. The therapist attempted to console her by assuring her that she would be there next week, but the child appeared uncertain and unhappy.

The mother, a single parent, had a similar experience of the child. She worked full-time and was chronically ill, and was often emotionally and physically unavailable because of these circumstances. She had previously felt overwhelmed and pursued by her daughter, and had been grateful when a male friend of hers, the abuser, began spending time with Katie. The mother resented that the parental role had fallen completely onto her shoulders and felt overburdened. The child's father had provided inconsistent parenting and had frequently disappointed the child whom he currently saw monthly. Katie's neediness and clingy behaviour, as well as ignoring and being aggressive to the mother, intensified after the sexual abuse began. Fortunately, the child disclosed the abuse after the second incident.

The therapist realized that she needed to set some boundaries with the child regarding physical space and closeness. She also helped the mother about setting time limits on being held, and reassuring the child that she was cared for even when there was no physical contact. The mother was also encouraged not to be punitive or punishing when the child rejected her, and to have some understanding about why the child was behaving in this way. The therapist addressed Katie's inappropriate questions by helping the child to see the underlying reasons why she was asking them. For example, was she asking about other children being seen for treatment because she was secretly wondering if she was special or of concern to the therapist? The therapist continuously reassured Katie that she was indeed special and important. The child was gradually able to take in this information and believe it, beginning to need less reassurance. Over time, Katie was progressively able to hold onto, and keep, an internalized image of the 'good enough' therapist to sustain her between sessions, and to realize that she would be there for her from one week to the next.

The mother became more competent about reassuring and containing her child. She no longer felt as overwhelmed by her daughter's neediness, understanding that her daughter's insecurities were a symptom of her mother's previous unavailability, her father's rejection of her, and her sexual victimization. The mother became more emotionally connected to her daughter, which reinforced her self-esteem as a good parent. Katie became more secure in her attachment both to the therapist and to her mother, and was able to be separate physically and mentally while still feeling connected emotionally.

Summary

In this chapter, we have looked at some theory that is important and relevant to the therapist who treats abused children. We briefly discussed the work of two developmental theorists, Erik Erikson and Jean Piaget. When planning therapeutic interventions, the developmental process needs to be taken into consideration, as well as any deficits in the child's development, noting that it is considered natural for the child who has been traumatized to regress to a previous level of development.

We also looked at the importance of the attachment process and its implications for treatment. Attachment theory is important in informing our practice. The term 'attachment' refers to the child's capacity to attach to others in his or her environment. A great deal of this capacity will be based on the child's earliest experience with carers, and will be manifested in the child's relationship with the therapist during treatment. Attachment theorists believe that there is a significant correlation between a child having a secure experience of attachment and developing psychological well-being. Finally, several different attachment styles were identified and case examples were given.

For the therapist working with abused children, treating attachment disturbances will almost inevitably be a central treatment consideration. Treating these disturbances requires sensitivity, patience, diligence, and perseverance. Change may take a good deal of time. Repetition of positive experiences is necessary for trust to develop and positive change to occur. Subsequently, the quality of the attachment relationship between the child and the therapist strongly influences the successfulness of the therapeutic outcome.

8   Common Symptomology

When he came into the room
I felt my body tighten

When he came near
my heart began to race

When he bent over me
I felt myself shake

When he climbed into the bed
I felt sick

When he began to touch me
I became a cloud, a star, the moon

That little girl lying there
trapped under that man

I don't know who she was
but she wasn't me

I became nature
I was free.

Many sexually abused children exhibit behavioural or emotional problems that may provide the first indicator that something is wrong, though Fergusson and Mullen (1999: 59) found that 'a substantial minority of children who are sexually abused do not show behavioral symptoms'. As might be expected, severity and duration of abuse, the child's history and personality, and family stability, affect the child's response. A few children try to hide what has happened using defence mechanisms such as minimization, repression, dissociation, or denial (Chapter 10). Girls tend to internalize feelings, and may become depressed and withdrawn. Boys are more likely to externalize their feelings, and may become angry, aggressive and act out. The level and severity of symptoms varies from child to child, and individual differences support the premise that there should be tailor-made therapeutic plans 'in accordance with the abuse history and past and current circumstances of each child' (Parton and Wattam, 1999: 110). This chapter addresses possible symptoms and therapeutic implications. All the therapeutic work in the world will not help to reduce children's troubled behaviour if they are not currently protected from abuse.

Carers and therapists might not recognize negative, adaptive behaviors the child employs to survive and to avoid pain. Negative, unexplainable, or strange behaviors are many times driven by direct and immediate fear or are automatic responses to situations the child associates with fear and prior trauma. The underlying fears and their survival value to the child, however, may not easily be identified because of the following:

- The behaviour does not appear to avoid pain or danger, since it is itself dangerous or distances the child from a carer who could provide protection and comfort.
- It is not obvious that the situation might engender fear in the child.
- The child is unable to give reasons for his behaviour. It is long past the time of the trauma, and the child usually behaves as if all is well.
- Parents and therapists block or minimize awareness of the child's fears in order to protect themselves emotionally. It is painful to witness how deeply fearful, terrorized, and damaged these children really are. (James, 1994: 78)

Somatic complaints and bodily concerns

Therapists generally agree that boys are more likely to experience somatic complaints following sexual abuse. This may reflect social acceptability of bodily complaints versus emotional and psychological ones. Headaches, stomach aches, sore throats, and fatigue are the most frequently reported somatic complaints, sore throats and stomach aches often being linked with the child having been forced to perform oral sex.

Sexually abused children frequently have tremendous concerns about their bodies which they may feel have been damaged; this can be particularly true if the sexual abuse was painful and involved force. Older children might worry about contracting sexually transmitted diseases and AIDS. Some children are encopretic or enuretic. Some young children fear that people know about their abuse just by looking at them. They may view their bodies as 'different' and permanently 'damaged'. They may feel increased shame and self-consciousness and project these feelings onto others.

Treatment implications

Ensure that the child has had a thorough medical examination to exclude, or get treatment for, physical problems and infections. In order to come to terms with what has happened to them, children need to express their feelings and concerns about their bodies. They often respond to encouragement, as they may feel embarrassed about how their bodies work. This is particularly relevant with younger children, but older children frequently are confused and have misinformation about bodily functions. Most children desire and need accurate information about how their bodies work. Encourage children to ask questions about bodily functions, changes, or possible ill effects of the abuse. The therapist can help children to express their concerns by speaking about what some other children's worries might be.

If appropriate, help the child to understand the correlation between the somatic complaint and the abuse. Usually children are unaware of the link. Normalize the child's symptoms, give reassurance, and let the child know that the complaints will lessen and go away with time. AIDS, infection, or physical damage need assessment, treatment and the prognosis verified. The child should have suitable factual information and support, with encouragement to express feelings about the abuse, the abuser, and future concerns.

Reassure the child who believes that 'everyone knows' about the abuse that this is not so. Inform the child that it is impossible to tell if someone has been sexually abused simply by *looking* at them. Groups can be effective in helping children to realize that victimization is not physically visible.

At one level sexual abuse is experienced as a physical trauma. Children up to the age of about four encode memories in the basal brain and are likely to act out physically or emotionally; older children may revert to bodily symptoms under stress, but have greater access to language and emotion (van der Kolk, 1996). Children may experience disgust towards their bodies and attempt to disown them. Many adult survivors dissociate from their bodily experience as a result of sexual abuse as children. Focusing on taking care of, and enjoying, the body can help prevent disowning and dissociative tendencies from developing. Encourage children to participate in physical activity and to have a positive awareness of their body. Warm, fragrant baths and attractive clean clothes are part of the process of helping children feel better about themselves.

If children experienced physiological pleasure as a result of the sexual activity, they may feel that they were betrayed by their own body. Educating and normalizing physiological and pleasurable response to the abuse will help the child accept the physiological response as a normal and natural reaction.

Sleep disturbances

Sleep disturbances are common. Children may experience a fear of sleep or an inability to fall asleep; this may be particularly true if the abuse occurred at night. Children often complain of disturbed sleep; they may wake up frequently throughout the night and be unable to fall back to sleep. They may think about the abuse at this time, and experience painful emotions or thoughts related to the abuse. Some children engage in excessive masturbation. Children may have difficulty waking up in the morning due to the poor quality of sleep, and may be fatigued throughout the day.

Children frequently have frightening dreams and nightmares. Some dreams involve the actual abuse experience or a variation on what happened. Other common themes reported by children are monsters, wild animals, or situations in which the child, or those close to the child, is/are in danger. The child may be reluctant to go to sleep for fear of bad dreams.

Treatment implications

Theoretical analysis of dream content has focused on the adaptive work of the ego and on the problem-solving nature of dreams. Dreams help to process internal and external experience. For example, in a nightmare or dream children may achieve mastery by taking control of a situation in which they were previously powerless. Dreams can provide useful diagnostic information about the issues and conflicts the child is currently facing, and can indicate the child's ego strength and functioning.

Dreams or nightmares can be used as a tool to facilitate drawings, acting out, poetry, or discussion. The therapist can help the child to understand the meaning and importance of dreams. Dreams, like play and art therapy, can provide a safe distance for exploration. The feelings and experiences of the child, related to dreams, can be discussed, leading to greater understanding for the child.

Encourage the child to bring dream material to sessions. Have the child work on the dream and what it means. What feelings do the dream images bring up in the child? Normalize the feelings and help the child to see the connection, if applicable, to the abuse situation.

There are several ways of working on the dreams. They can be talked about, or the child may wish to make a dream journal. Writing dreams down as soon as they occurred 'seemed to get them out of Kerry's head, to distance and diminish their power' (Carolin and Milner, 1999: 27–8). They can be acted out, made into pictures or paintings, written as stories, or tape recorded. Children can be encouraged to change the dream or ending of the dream in any way they desire. James suggests that children can be empowered to reduce the frightening elements by making them smaller, twitching their noses at them, picking them up or some such ploy (1989: 198). Using a gestalt technique, older children can name the objects or feelings in the dream, the child talking as if she were each of those things with the therapist reflecting inferences and making links.

David, aged six, had a recurring dream in which he was in a park being molested. In the dream, the abuser was a policeman and he handcuffed David. David was frightened by this nightmare which he had repeatedly over the first two months of treatment. During sessions, he made up stories related to his dream, and changed the ending to one in which the abuser had a heart attack and died because David was very strong and had pushed him.

David also drew pictures in which he became larger and the abuser smaller. In these pictures, David handcuffed the abuser and arrested him. David wrote angry letters to the abuser telling him that he hated him, and that he was not afraid of him any more.

David's nightmares began to lessen in intensity and frequency. Within a few weeks, he dreamt one night that he became a fire-breathing dragon, melting the handcuffs the abuser was trying to put on him. The abuser then ran away and the dragon chased him until he fell over a steep cliff. The dragon's fiery breath set fire to all the trees in the park. The original setting of his abuse as well as the abuser were destroyed by David, who appeared to feel much better after this particular dream. Although he continued to have occasional nightmares, David no longer presented it as a treatment issue.

Performance at school

It is common for the child victim's behaviour and performance at school to change. Attendance may become less frequent. The child may begin having somatic complaints while at school, which interfere with the completion and quality of school work. Frequently, an abused child finds difficulty in concentrating, and may appear to be lethargic, preoccupied, and distracted. Unfortunately, these students are more likely to go unnoticed or undiagnosed, and may be labelled as being lazy or daydreamers.

A student who was previously well-functioning in class may become disruptive and/or aggressive with other children. The behaviour can become severe and may interfere with teaching. The child is usually identifying with the aggressor, attempting mastery by victimizing others.

Sometimes a child exhibits depressive symptoms and becomes isolated from other classmates. He may be unusually quiet and subdued, making statements about not caring or feeling hopeless. Unfortunately, these students often go unnoticed or are not identified as having serious problems.

A child may begin to exhibit symptoms of learning difficulties or disabilities such as Attention Deficit Hyperactivity Disorder or Conduct Disorder. Over time, such children may be labelled or misdiagnosed owing to their behavioural symptoms. The child's victimization often interferes with his capacity for learning and may cause regression in academic functioning.

In some cases a child's performance improves, even becoming perfectionist (sublimation) in an attempt to compensate for the trauma. Children may become frustrated, or make self-critical statements if they do not do things exactly right. The child may receive positive approval and recognition and, as a result, become dependent upon having positive feedback to maintain self-esteem.

Treatment implications

It is important to note, but not pathologize, the child's deteriorating performance in school. Carers are often concerned when their child begins to do poorly, especially if previously a good scholar. Let carers know that this is a common symptom for abused children. Reassure them that, over time, the child should regain previous standards. Assist them in taking the pressure off the child to perform well in school, as this can be counterproductive. Children are often distressed by the deterioration in their schooling. Help the child to understand that this is related to the abuse, and assist the child to take the pressure off herself. If the child has become perfectionist, working with her on the abuse issues and helping her improve self-esteem should facilitate more realistic goal setting and increased self-acceptance. The child's perfectionist tendencies will decrease over time. Help the child to feel inherently worthwhile without having to excel in order to feel good.

If the child is acting out or being disruptive in class, the teacher may become angry and punitive, which frequently exacerbates the problem. It may be helpful, and in some cases necessary, to advocate for the child with the classroom teacher or other school personnel. A child spends a large portion of the day in school, and it is important that the child be supported and understood in this setting. Teachers are more likely to be sensitive and understanding towards the child if they are aware of the child's traumatization.

The child's symptoms and behaviour are best viewed and understood in the context of the abuse and former life experiences. Often, the classroom teacher will want to know how best to support the child. Many teachers feel uncomfortable about responding to, or speaking to, a sexually abused child, fearing that they will say the wrong thing. It may be necessary to reassure teachers that what they say is not nearly as important as how the child experiences what is said. It will be very helpful if the child understands that school personnel are sensitive, caring, and supportive.

It may be beneficial to explore with school staff limits and consequences regarding the child's negative or disruptive behaviour. Shared strategies make it easier for carers and therapists to work with such children and to help them understand the limits and consequences of their behaviour in the school setting.

It is important for the therapist to talk with the carers, and advisable to speak with the child, in order to gain consent to speak with school staff and to divulge personal details. If the child is on the child protection register it is likely that at least one member of the school staff will be aware of the child's situation. In some cases the abuse will have been initially reported by school personnel, who may already be providing support for the child.

Fear/anxiety and feelings of powerlessness

Following abuse, the child will be fearful even if the abuse has stopped. Children frequently become hypervigilant during the abuse and hyperaware of other people's feelings and actions. This hypervigilance is often developed as a means of survival to protect the self from harm and anticipate or prevent further abuse. The child victim experiences a chronic perception of danger that can be intensified if the abuser has made threats against the child or family members about what would happen if the abuse were to become known. The child may experience flashbacks of the trauma, or painful memories triggered by certain stimuli. Smells, words, visual cues, places, and sounds are common triggers, and the child may be confused about whether the abusive experience is happening at that moment.

Unfortunately, these feelings of powerlessness in relation to the abuse are invariably transferred. The child feels powerless in other aspects of life and may self-identify as a victim, becoming passive and withdrawn, or overcompensating through truancy, running away or becoming aggressive.

Treatment implications

Explore the child's fears and fantasies about the abuser. Were implicit or explicit threats made by the abuser if the abuse was ever disclosed? Normalize the child's feelings of increased anxiety and fear. Speak with the child about how safe she is, or feels at present. Is the child afraid of re-victimization?

Help to empower the child. What did the child do, if anything, to prevent victimization in the past? Commend the child for any attempts made. At the same time, make it clear that the perpetrator was responsible for the abusive behaviour, and that adults and older children should never engage in sexual activity with children.

What are the child's external and internal resources for safety? How is the child protected by the various systems involved? Discuss with the child what is being done and how she can best be protected.

If the perpetrator has been incarcerated, the child may have fears and fantasies about what might happen on release. Explore and discuss these fantasies with the child as well.

> James, aged seven, had disguises he insisted on wearing when he went near where he had been molested. This self-protection occurred even after the perpetrator's arrest. James continued wearing his disguises until the paedophile was convicted and incarcerated. At this point James assured his therapist that by the time the paedophile was released he would be grown up enough to beat him up if he ever came near him again. At this point, James stopped needing to wear the disguises to protect himself.

If old enough, it is advisable to educate the child in self-protection (Gil, 1991: 81; Peake, 1989). A word of caution: Do not expect the child necessarily to be able to tell carers or other adults, or to stop the abuse, if it recurs. Children may interpret the 'prevention' information as evidence that they had failed to prevent or stop the previous abuse. Let them know that it is hard for children to stand up against bigger people, but that if they know to whom to go, or whom to contact, they might be better able to keep themselves safe. Identifying potentially helpful people in the community and letting children know about freephone advice services may prove useful.

The following questions can be useful in helping a child to know what to do if revictimized:

- What might be some warning signs to be on the lookout for?
- Whom would the child tell?
- What would the child say?
- What might the child do?

Discussing potential situations, role plays, and talking to children about paying attention to their feelings and trusting their instincts can be helpful for the child in talking and learning about self-protection. Professionals in the area of self-protection education for children have mixed opinions about the level of success of this work. On the positive side, it offers self-protection strategies, helps to empower the child, and the child may thus feel less vulnerable. Realistically, it may still be difficult for the child to withstand sexual advances from older people.

Depression

Depression is another common symptom for children, but one that often goes unnoticed or undiagnosed (Zimmerman, 1988). In the past there has been a misconception on the part of some people that children do not get depressed. Children *do* suffer from depression, but it may manifest differently from adults. As a disorder it is often not diagnosed because children have difficulty describing it. Depression in children is frequently manifested in the form of increased irritability.

Common complaints and symptoms include the following:

1 Low energy level or fatigue.
2 Poor appetite or overeating, leading to significant weight loss or weight gain.
3 Insomnia or hypersomnia.
4 Low self-esteem.
5 Poor concentration.
6 Feelings of hopelesness, often expressed in children as not caring about anything anymore.
7 Emotional numbing and dissociation from self.
8 Increased irritability.
9 Isolation from family and friends; the child may desire to spend significantly more time alone and become more introverted.
10 Crying and tearfulness.
11 Increased self-punishing behaviour, or engagement in risky and dangerous or accident-prone behaviour.
12 Use of alcohol or drugs to self-medicate.
13 Suicidal ideation, expressed by speaking of wanting to escape or go away, and suicide attempts.

Treatment implications

Help children to identify the symptoms they are currently experiencing. Assess the level and severity of the symptoms or seek qualified help. Find out how long the symptoms have been present and whether they have changed. Has the child experienced any of the symptoms before? If so, what precipitated the symptoms and when did they go away?

In the interest of good practice, a psychiatric evaluation is recommended if the child's depression is severe. In addition, it is important to rule out physiological or neurological causes for symptomology. In severe cases, psychotropic medication may be prescribed.

Assess and take seriously suicidal ideation, or talk of plans to attempt suicide. When assessing suicidal risk, use the term 'killing yourself' when speaking to the child, because this is a graphic way of describing suicide that will be more meaningful for the child. Establish whether there has ever been a previous suicide attempt, and if so when, what caused it, and the method used. Find out if the child has a current plan for committing suicide, and if so, what it is.

It is difficult to establish a reliable estimate of the incidence of suicide in the under-15 age group. Some suicides are interpreted as accidental deaths, and many attempts lead to injury, illness, or disability. Younger children often choose less successful methods than older children and adults. The five most common methods for younger children are jumping from heights, self-poisoning, hanging, stabbing, and running into traffic (Pfeffer, 1984).

Some of the factors leading to increased risk of suicide include:

1   Physical and sexual abuse.
2   Severe depression, at the recovery stage when the child feels more energetic.
3   A previous suicide attempt.
4   A close friend or relative has died from suicide.
5   Children and adolescents who drink or take drugs.

The therapist who considers that the child is actively suicidal or at serious risk should, unless there is clear reason to believe that such an action would put the child at significant risk of further harm, inform the child that the therapist will have to speak to the child's carer. The therapist would discuss with the parents the child's risk of suicide, and recommend a referral to the GP. If the family is unwilling, the therapist will need to consider making a report to social services as a protective measure.

If the therapist believes that notifying the carers about the child's suicidal risk will place the child in greater jeopardy, the therapist may notify the family GP and make a report to social services as well. In severe cases, the child may need to be hospitalized or placed in a safe unit where a suicide attempt may be less likely.

Anger

Anger is often an expression of underlying feelings of sadness, loss, powerlessness, fear, and anxiety. It is often easier for a child to experience and act out anger, rather than to experience more painful underlying emotions. In any case, children have a natural tendency to 'act out feelings'.

Expression of appropriate anger is a healthy, necessary, and integral part of the healing process. The child has a right to feel and express anger about the abuse, towards the abuser, and about other injustices in life. Anger may be a self-assertive expression of the child's feelings that the abuse was not deserved. Often these feelings surface later in the treatment process as the child's self-esteem improves.

Many children do not know how to express anger appropriately. They may come from families where they have never seen productive expressions of anger and its resolution. In some families, it is normal for anger to be suppressed, disavowed, or repressed. The carers may never express anger directly or argue in front of the child. Instead the anger may be expressed in passive aggressive ways. Family members may deny having angry feelings, and there may be an atmosphere of increased tension and discomfort which family members dismiss or accept as normal. As a result, children may be left feeling confused and doubting their own perceptions.

In some families, children may be punished for directly expressing anger, and consequently believe that they are inherently 'bad' because of angry feelings. They may assume that any expression of anger is harmful. This belief often occurs at an unconscious level, causing the child to disavow and repress feelings of anger. Furthermore, a child's anger may be manifested in ways that the carers are not able to tolerate or accept, such as acting out, fighting with siblings, or being belligerent with carers. Often the child's anger about the abuse will be displaced onto those closest to them. Some abused children will be extremely angry at the carer, particularly if the carer exposed the child to the abuser, or was unable to offer adequate protection. These children may either not be able to, or not allowed to, express their anger, as this may evoke strong feelings of inadequacy, guilt, or an angry response. The carer who does not understand the underlying causes of the child's anger may respond in an unhelpful or punitive manner.

In addition, if children are in a role-reversal parentified position, they may feel they need to protect and take care of family members, and not burden them with negative feelings, behaviour, or problems. The child may view the carer as 'fragile' and be afraid that the adult will fragment if the child expresses anger. Children may be ashamed and fearful of their own anger, and fantasize about how powerful and destructive that anger will be if manifested. The anger may instead be turned inwards in the form of depression, or expressed in self-destructive behaviours.

Treatment implications

Normalize and support children in their anger. Help them to realize that expression of anger is a healthy and natural response to the trauma and hurt they have endured. It is equally important to help the child to experience and express the underlying feelings that are currently masked by the anger, such as powerlessness, fear, loss, sadness, and shame.

Children inevitably need help in accepting and finding appropriate ways to express anger. Some suggestions are:

- writing letters, which are not necessarily sent, to people with whom the child is angry;
- punching pillows or hitting soft objects;

- the empty chair technique (help the child to address the chair as they would the person; children may need the therapist to help, to make some suggestions, or to model the action);
- drawing pictures and tearing them up or burning them (find a safe place and beware smoke alarms!);
- doing an anger dance and stamping;
- engaging in some kind of exercise; and
- making up a story or play where the culprit is punished.

If the child is not allowed to show anger directly in the household, help the child to find acceptable ways of expressing angry feelings. Find out what the carer will tolerate. Let the carer know that children's anger is normal, and needs to be expressed and accepted to facilitate the healing process.

Children's anger directed towards the carer will probably elicit confusion in the children as they usually believe they cannot both experience or express anger towards their carers and love them at the same time. Help the child to understand ambivalent and conflicting feelings. Normalizing the child's feelings and comparing them with those of other children can be valuable. Children may feel guilty about negative comments they make. Help them with issues related to disloyalty. Finally, let them know that it is safe to express anger appropriately during therapy. Therapy sessions are an accepting place to talk about and show angry feelings, the therapist helping the child to feel safe and supported in the process.

Acting out or aggressive behaviour

Many times, a child who has been sexually abused will act out or engage in aggressive behaviour. The underlying feelings related to the abuse are usually suppressed or repressed. A child's behaviour reflects what is going on emotionally, and most children need help in labelling, experiencing, and expressing emotions.

The child's behaviour is usually an unconscious attempt to resolve an intra-psychic conflict. The child may experience acting out and aggressive behaviour as a way of feeling powerful and in control. The child may subsequently become addicted to the sensation experienced, and the behaviour may be reinforced.

In helping children acquire 'control' over their behaviour, it is important to consider the flip side of control: dyscontrol. In some instances, apparent dyscontrol of behaviour actually represents a form of control for a child. By going 'out of control', the child may in fact be 'taking control'. (It is important to state clearly that in other instances, the child is simply overwhelmed by acute internal and external stresses and triggers, and is unable to regulate his or her behaviour.) When dyscontrol is a strategy for control, the child often tests the therapist with out-of-control behaviour – either by directly challenging the rules and boundaries of the therapeutic space, or by playing out themes of dyscontrol with figures and stories. The therapist's task is not to take control back from the child (though this may be necessary temporarily), but to help the child gain self-control.

The nature and source of dyscontrol dictate the kinds of therapeutic interventions that may be employed. In instances where dyscontrol is serving a dynamic purpose (either by expressing a central conflict or by permitting the child an escape), apt psychodynamic interventions aimed at restoring appropriate control of symbolic reparative work with damaged self-concepts can produce rapid improvement. In instances where dyscontrol is long-standing, has a heavy overlay of meanings and behaviours, and is associated with biological dysregulation ..., acquisition of control proceeds in slow increments with intermittent relapses and regressions. (Putnam, 1997: 284–5)

Bringing acting out behaviours under control can be demanding for therapist and carer. This process may take time, and many practitioners may try to find a quick and expedient, short-term way to end a behaviour, such as aggression, especially if it disturbs the adult. The therapist may feel pressured by the carer to bring the behaviour under control quickly. It is unrealistic to expect immediate change. Disappointment and feelings of failure are often the outcome if the child's behaviour is expected to change rapidly or stop completely. Acting out behaviours should be understood as providing a function for the child that will most likely serve one or several of the following needs:

1   Identification with the aggressor who has committed a violent act against the child.
2   An expression of the child's self-hatred and desire for self-destruction.
3   An expression of underlying feelings of sadness, loss, guilt, anxiety, and powerlessness manifested in acting out behaviour.
4   A manifestation of the child's desire for attention.
5   A demonstration of the child's feelings experienced during the action.
6   A reinforcement of the child's sense of self as being bad, and the ensuing negative response of others as punishment for this badness.
7   An expression of the child's state of dissociation and numbness. Acting out can be a substitute for feeling. The child is unaware of affect and internal experience.
8   A desire to hurt others the way the child has been hurt.
9   A manifestation of the child's protest and cry for help.

The therapist should acquire a detailed picture of the acting-out or aggressive behaviours. This picture will allow an assessment of how the behaviour has become part of the child's make-up, and will identify the function(s) the behaviour may serve. It is essential to establish how dangerous the behaviour is to the child and others. If the behaviour is severe, it may be necessary to seek a psychiatric assessment and, in extreme cases, hospitalization.

Treatment implications

The treatment goal is to help the child express and identify feelings and to find healthier and more adaptive ways to get needs met. The initial aim is to establish realistic limits and boundaries regarding the inappropriate behaviour, which should help to lessen its intensity. Naming the underlying feelings may bring insight. If appropriate, help the child to see the function the behaviour serves, and place it in the context of the abuse. Once again, help the child to understand the negative consequences of the behaviour. Assist the child in dealing with shame and other repercussions experienced as a result of acting out. Work with the child to identify and express underlying emotions manifested in the behaviour, including sadness, loss, powerlessness, anxiety, guilt, and shame. Assist the child in finding healthier and more productive ways of dealing with these feelings.

If necessary, help people in the child's environment to understand how to respond to the negative behaviour by setting appropriate limits and boundaries. Are there rules and reasonable consequences for acting out within the family? Is there positive reinforcement for the child when behaving well?

Regression

Although regression may also be caused by other factors, some children respond to their abuse by behaving as though younger than their chronological age (Macaskill, 1991: 75–77). The child reverts to an earlier way of functioning either because it feels safer or because, feeling safe with the current carer, the child needs to re-experience or to regrow through an earlier developmental phase that was not satisfactorily accomplished at the time. In extreme cases, children may revert to babyhood or toddlerhood, in which case they may be placed in therapeutic communities or with specialist carers.

Treatment implications

Accept regression as a necessary phase for the child. Often the behaviour can be contained within the home; if it spills into school life, regression needs particular care and negotiation with staff, and may cause problems with the child's peers. Once the needs of that developmental stage have been experienced and met, the child's normal development will resume.

Low self-esteem and poor sense of self

Sexually abused children frequently have extremely low self-esteem. They may feel worthless, valued only as sexual objects because of their experience. Some children describe themselves as feeling 'invisible' because they have gone unnoticed and unprotected from the sexual abuse, particularly if the abuse was lengthy and ongoing. The child with low self-esteem frequently feels unworthy and undeserving of positive attention and affection.

Being the victim of sexual abuse seriously impairs the child's developing sense of self and identity. In order to cope with and survive the trauma, children often suppress or repress their emotions, their affective range becoming strongly limited. This serves to protect the child from painful affect, but makes the child numb, removed, and distant from past experiences which interferes both with the child's capacity to function and the child's development of a sense of self.

In clinical experience, adult survivors often describe themselves as feeling empty, going through the motions of life, of feeling nothing, of being unable to connect with reality in a meaningful way, and of being unable to experience their emotions. They have defended themselves from the abuse and the aftermath of the abuse, and paid a large price for it. As adults, they often find it difficult to reconnect with their feelings and experiences, and need help in developing a cohesive and stable sense of identity and positive self-esteem.

Treatment implications

Over time, during the course of therapy, the child's experience of being listened to, contained, supported, understood, respected, and valued will result in their feeling that they are worthy, and deserving, of such treatment. With the therapist, the child may experience unconditional acceptance and empathy. This process facilitates the child's own self-acceptance and self-compassion. Gradually, the child begins to feel worthy of attention, affection, and positive experiences.

Within the therapeutic realm, children can gain an understanding, awareness, and acceptance of their feelings. The child can work through the painful feelings related to the abuse, and as a result the child's affective range can be broadened. She may no longer need to be numb or dissociative as a way of defending against the trauma. Children may no longer be afraid to feel, or to trust, their own judgements, instincts, and perceptions. The child's sense of self and self-esteem can continue to develop and flourish.

Summary

Sexually abused children presented for therapy often display a combination of symptoms varying from the observable and quantifiable such as bodily problems, sleep disturbances, and school refusal, to the less tangible such as fear, depression, regression, and low self-esteem. Most children are unable to talk about their abusive experiences, and their bodies, actions, and emotions may be the first messengers. However, carers may find it difficult to read and accept the message.

It is important that somatic complaints are taken seriously. A thorough, yet sympathetic, medical examination should be performed and, if indicated, appropriate remedial action taken. The child will benefit from a cognitive understanding about what is happening to her body, and why, plus appropriate emotional support. Part of the healing process may include sex education to help the child put feelings and experiences in context.

Sleep disturbances, especially nightmares and night terrors, can be physically and emotionally traumatic for the child. Careful bedtime routines and helping the child to express and explore dreams and nightmares may help.

Deterioration in school performance may be another problem. The child's standard of work may change, often deteriorating but sometimes becoming obsessional. It may appear that the child is developing learning difficulties. The child may find it difficult to relate to peers and/or teachers. Liaison with appropriate teaching staff to assess the extent of the problems, and working out a strategy to help the child within school are essential. The carer may also benefit from assistance in supporting the child, and the child can be helped to see that changes and improvements are possible.

Fear, anxiety, and feelings of powerlessness often underpin children's bodily symptoms and acting out behaviour, and it is vital to address these issues. Helping the child to explore feelings about the abuser, the abusive act(s), and any threats made, may initially be distressing but can be done gently and supportively. Therapist and carer can accept the child's fears and fantasies, and help the child to find strategies to feel safe.

Childhood depression may go unnoticed, the depressed child commonly suffering from several physical and emotional symptoms. When assessing a child, a qualified psychiatric assessment should be sought if the therapist considers that depression is a possibility. Children engaging in self-harm, substance abuse, or suicidal ideation should similarly have a specialist psychiatric referral.

Anger and acting out behaviour, although part of childhood development, may have particular significance and severity in children who have been sexually abused. Child and carer can be helped by exploring the behaviours and their meanings, and given strategies to control and limit them.

Children usually present with a combination of problems, which may shift in intensity as therapy progresses. The therapist's understanding of the potential causes of symptoms helps formulation of the treatment programme.

Exercise

Imagine that you begin feeling and behaving differently, but are unsure why this is happening.

You feel tearful, irritable and depressed. You no longer enjoy being with family or friends, and spend most of your time alone in your room.

Your grades at school deteriorate because you can no longer concentrate. You feel irritable and angry. It feels good to vent these feelings at schoolmates. You begin being disruptive at school and start a few fights. You are told off and punished. You feel that you are bad, and that you will show others just how truly bad you can be.

You begin having difficulty falling asleep at night. You feel afraid, and have nightmares. Sometimes you wet your bed. It is difficult to eat. Your stomach hurts, you feel tired, you have headaches frequently. You find yourself crying a lot of the time for no obvious reason.

You feel ashamed and guilty. You believe that you are bad because you are holding a secret. If anyone finds out, they will think it is your fault. You feel that no one would believe you even if you did tell. Maybe others can tell that you have been molested by looking at you. You feel sick with anxiety and dread. Maybe this is what you deserve. Maybe this is how it will always be.

Just imagine how overwhelming and confusing it must be for the abused child. What does he or she understand about the symptoms experienced? Most children are unaware of the link between the symptoms and the abuse they have experienced. Instead the symptoms are often viewed, by the child, as further proof and punishsment for their inherent badness.

9 Sexualized Behaviour, Substance Abuse, and Eating Disorders

It was as if:
I felt as if the words sexually abused
were branded across my forehead.
I deliberately kept those I cared for
away, and wouldn't let anyone get close to me.
As if I had a contagious disease that I had to protect
others from catching. The worst part was that I felt so
terribly alone. To this day, I have difficulty letting people get close to me,
but I am trying, and I get a little better every day.

As discussed in Chapter 8, sexual abuse of a child often causes a cluster of problems, including fear, pain, terror, anger, powerlessness and, in some cases, physical damage. In more severe cases another level of symptomology can be triggered. The child may exhibit sexualized behaviour ranging from excessive self-stimulation to promiscuous activities. This can be hard for carers, teachers, therapists, and others in the child's environment. Other children may resort to substance abuse as a way either of exerting power or of shielding themselves from their feelings. The development of eating disorders, particularly when there has been oral abuse, is another possibility. This chapter focuses on these additional disorders because all therapists, although perhaps wanting to seek specialist help, should have some knowledge of these serious ramifications of sexual abuse.

Sexualized behaviour

Sexuality for pre-school children is a matter of curiosity and exploration. Children are inquisitive about their bodies and those of the opposite sex. Older children try to understand their bodies and remain curious about sexuality and intercourse, love, marriage, and sexual organs. This curiosity is only one of many interests that normal children experience and explore.

Concerns arise when the child focuses on sexuality to a greater degree than is age appropriate, which is often the case when a child has been sexually abused. Such children become sexualized prematurely, often engaging in inappropriate and undue self-stimulation, sexual aggression, gender confusion, and blurred sexual boundaries leading to (attempted) intercourse. The child may experience anger, shame, fear, anxiety, excitement, or sexual arousal. The child may use force, or develop compulsive behaviour while engaging in sexualized behaviour. Finkelhor and Browne (1985) use the term 'traumatic sexualization'. 'The behaviour most consistently shown to distinguish between children who have been sexually abused and children who have not been sexually abused is increased sexualized behaviour' (Wieland, 1998: 153). Carers of children who have been sexually abused should always be alert to the possibility that the abused child could sexually abuse other children, especially siblings. Farmer and Pollock's research found that over two-thirds of sexually abused children in substitute family care showed sexual behaviour in the placement, with 50 per cent abusing another child at some stage (1998: 89, 90–1). An NSPCC research report based on 3000 respondents found, amongst other things, that the respondents were 'three times more likely to be seriously sexually abused – penetrated, subjected to oral sex or have pornographic photographs taken of them – by a brother or other male relative than by their father' (Cawson et al., 2000: quoted in Wellard, 2000: 10).

According to Johnson (1993a), there are several warning signals and guidelines when assessing a child's untoward sexual behaviour:

1 The child focuses on sexuality to a greater extent than on other aspects of the environment. Children's sexual interests should be in balance with their curiosity about, and exploration of, other parts of their lives.
2 The child has an ongoing compulsive interest in sexual, or sexually-related activities, and/or is more interested in engaging in sexual behaviours than in playing with friends, going to school, and doing other developmentally-appropriate activities.
3 The child engages in sexual behaviours with those who are much older or younger. Most school-age children interact sexually with children within a year or so of their own age. In general, the wider the age range between children engaging in sexual behaviours, the greater the concern.
4 The child continues to ask unfamiliar, or uninterested, children to engage in sexual activities. Healthy and natural sexual play usually occurs between friends and playmates.
5 The child, or group of children, bribes or emotionally and/or physically forces another child (children) of any age into sexual behaviours.
6 The child exhibits confusion or distorted ideas about the rights of others regarding sexual behaviours. The child may assert 'She wanted it' or 'I can touch him if I want to'.
7 The child tries to manipulate children or adults into touching his or her genitals, or causes physical harm to his own or others' genitals.
8 Other children repeatedly complain about the child's sexual behaviours, even after an adult has spoken to the child.
9 The child continues to behave sexually in front of adults who tell him to stop, or does not seem to comprehend admonitions to curtail overt sexual behaviours in public places.

10 The child appears anxious, tense, angry, or fearful when sexual topics arise in everyday life.

11 The child manifests a number of disturbing toileting behaviours: he plays with or smears faeces, urinates outside the toilet, uses excessive amounts of toilet paper, stuffs toilet bowls so that they overflow, and sniffs or steals underwear.

12 The child's drawings depict genitals as the predominant feature.

13 The child manually stimulates, or has oral or genital contact with, animals. These behaviours will vary in intensity and frequency, and need to be addressed by carers and in therapy. If the behaviours are severe and frequent, specialized treatment may be necessary.

Sexual activity outside the home

It is extremely distressing to carers, and to other children in the household, if the child becomes involved in casual sex, prostitution, and/or pornography. Education of the child involved about the risks of pornography or prostitution is essential (if the young person will listen). The therapist might try to help the child to explore the feelings that impel him or her to engage in prostitution. It may also represent a desire (on an unconscious level) to be in a position of control in deciding with whom to engage in sexual relations. The child may have an unconscious drive to live dangerously, may find excitement and acceptance, may feel valued, if only briefly, or may be drawn to prostitution because of family associations. Some youngsters do it for money or drugs, or to be part of the 'shock-horror' culture.

Treatment implications Children who abuse have twofold therapeutic and caring needs: those of a victim and those of a perpetrator (aggressor). Make links between the sexualized behaviour and the young person's abusive experiences. Formulate clear guidelines and give advice about 'normal' sexual behaviour and safety matters (making sure that vulnerable children are protected), and help the child to find alternate ways of obtaining sexual and personal gratification. Therapy can be an adjunct to consistent, understanding parenting. The child who becomes a sex offender and a risk to other children will need specialized treatment, and may have to be accommodated in specialist units.

Sexual acting out with peers, younger children, adults, animals, or objects

Children can develop inappropriate sexual constructs at a young age. Child victims may speak in sexual terms or talk inappropriately about sexual matters to other children. They may become interested in pornographic material, engage in compulsive masturbation, masturbate in front of other people, rub against or sexually touch children and adults, become exhibitionist, or try to remove other children's clothing. Children may try to engage other children, including younger siblings (and animals), in penetrative acts. Force is often used, sometimes inflicting physical damage.

Gil and Cavanagh Johnson (1993) identify the following as possible indicators that the child or young person is engaging in abusive sexual behaviours:

1 The age difference of the participants is greater than three years.
2 The perpetrating child is bigger than the molested child.
3 Differences in status or seniority.
4 Sexual behaviour that is outside the child's developmental stage.
5 When there is a sense of anxiety, fear and/or a high arousal level.

It is always important to take these issues seriously. Children subjected to sexual abuse, who have been treated more like objects than youngsters, with low self-esteem and lacking empathy, may become abusers. In a study, 50 per cent of adult sex offenders reported their first sexual offence in adolescence (Hollows and Armstrong, 1991: 11).

A child may act out sexually and engage in offending behaviour for many reasons:

1 Repetition compulsion: a desire to re-enact the trauma in order to resolve intra-psychic abuse-related issues.
2 Identification with the aggressor: an expression of the child's desire to be in a position of control. The child may also want to make another child feel the way they have felt as 'victim'.
3 Dissociation from the self or emotional numbing.
4 Premature sexualization: the child may need a way of expressing strongly sexualized feelings.
5 Behavioural modelling.

'The guidance document *Working Together Under the Children Act* (Department of Health, 1991) recommends that a comprehensive assessment should be undertaken in respect of any child who sexually abuses another' (Farmer and Pollock, 1998: 148). Practice wisdom advocates that it is important that abusing youngsters take responsibility for their abusive actions, and that they engage in a suitable treatment programme. One model is for youngsters to undertake group treatment for their abusive behaviour plus individual work on themselves as offender and victim (Crowe and Kettle, 1992). Children are unlikely voluntarily to disclose information related to their own sexualized or offending behaviour due to the shame and guilt they experience and the secrecy enjoined on them. The therapist may need to ask the child directly whether he has engaged in sexual activity, and let him know that sometimes children are tempted to engage in sexualized or offending behaviour as a result of being abused. Advise children that they should never coerce or force another child into sexual activity. If they feel like doing this, tell them they should speak to a trusted adult about these feelings.

It is hypothesized that there can be a correlation between being sexually victimized as a child, and engaging in sexually offending behaviour, though this is not to imply that all, or most, sexually abused children offend later in life. However, the therapist should always take seriously, and assess the extent and severity of, sexually offending behaviour. Young people who use sex aggressively could be a high risk to others and to themselves. Research shows that many of them have endured severe disruptions, parenting deficits, and traumatizing experiences (Skuse et al., 1996). It is not surprising that another research study postulated that sexually abused and abusing children are more disadvantaged than others in state care (Farmer and Pollock, 1998: 229). A research team at Great Ormond Street Children's Hospital, London, found that 'trauma, especially violence, is a key factor in the early lives of young abusers' (Hodges et al., 1994; Lanyado et al., 1995, quoted in Horne, 1999: 359). Children who are both sexual abuse victims and also sexual offenders may need a more robust form of treatment (Calder, 1999), though it is clear in *Working Together* (Department of Health, 1991) that young people who sexually abuse should initially be treated under child protection procedures.

Sexualized behaviour directed towards the therapist

Some sexually abused children appear to be pseudo-mature, behaving or dressing inappropriately for their age. They may ask personal, sexual, or other inappropriate questions and manifest sexualized behaviour towards the therapist. During sessions, a child may stand unnaturally close to, touch inappropriately, or masturbate in front of the therapist. Frequently, this is because the child has learned that such behaviour is appropriate when interacting with adults. The child may feel valued as a sexual object and such actions may have been rewarded in the past. Furthermore, as a consequence of the child's abuse, the child may now equate intimacy with sexualized behaviour, and may believe that this behaviour is expected when in a close relationship with an adult. Alternatively, children may be testing the boundaries of the relationship, attempting to discover if the therapist will respond sexually to their overtures. Safety and trust are central issues in this situation. The child may test the therapist several times before realizing and accepting that the therapist will not respond sexually.

Such behaviours towards the therapist can evoke discomfort and confusion, and may be disturbing. The therapist may feel guilty if sexually aroused in response to the child's sexualized behaviour. The therapist should prepare for this and respond appropriately if the situation arises, as outlined below.

Treatment implications Sex education is part of the therapeutic process. The therapist will need to explore, assess, and set appropriate boundaries for the child's sexualized behaviour. The therapist should tell children that they do not need to act in a sexual way for the therapist to appreciate and like them.

The therapist can define the relationship and therapy process in terms of a 'safe' place for the child, taking the opportunity to educate the child about appropriate and inappropriate touching. The child needs to be reassured that nothing sexual will occur between therapist and child. At this point, the therapist can reiterate that adults should never touch a child in sexual ways and should know that such behaviour is wrong. Let children know that you value them for themselves, and that they do not need to do anything specifically to please you.

It is a mistake to ignore the behaviour in the hope that it will go away. This will cause confusion and may feel dishonest to the child. The child may also view the therapist's silence as acquiescence. Furthermore, the behaviour will most likely recur until it is addressed. Respond to and address the behaviour every time it happens in the treatment process.

It is important to discuss the behaviour in the context of the child's relationship with other adults in their environment, in order to help the child understand what is appropriate and what is inappropriate. Let the child know that other people may find their sexualized behaviour to be confusing and unacceptable.

Normalize the behaviour in the context of the abuse in order to alleviate any shame or rejection the child may feel; the child may experience the therapist's boundary setting as a rejection. Let the child know that this is not the case. Inform the child that other children often feel and act in a sexualized fashion when they have been abused. Tell them that when a child is sexually abused, it causes confusion, and may lead to sexual behaviours that are inappropriate.

Additional issues for male victims of sexual abuse

Male children may suffer additional stigma and shame as a result of sexual abuse. Boys often believe that they are not *allowed* to be victims. Being sexually abused can increase a boy's self-doubts about his developing masculinity.

In addition, males often believe that they should have been able to fight off the abuser; males are more frequently victims of force and threats. The sexual abuse may be viewed as proof, to themselves, that they are physically and emotionally weak. Being abused by a female may increase their confusion. Male victims may believe or have been told that they were supposed to enjoy the sexual acts, and that they should feel fortunate that they had sexual experience at such a young age.

Boys may suffer from homophobia if the abuser was male. Carers may reinforce this belief and be concerned as well. The child could end up projecting this fear onto other male children, calling them names or accusing them of being gay or effeminate. The child may display violent or aggressive behaviour towards other boys in order to prove his masculinity, or in an effort to compensate for his own insecurities. The male child may also develop sexual identity confusion, believing that he is homosexual and that this is why he was molested by another male. Alternatively, he may believe that he is destined to become a homosexual because of the abuse. This issue can be exacerbated if the boy had pleasurable physiological responses to the abuse. The therapist should normalize the child's physiological response to the abuse.

As stated earlier, male children are more prone to act out and express anger, and may need additional help in identifying, experiencing, and expressing underlying emotions. Boys are more likely to believe that expressing emotions is a sign of weakness, and that crying is not masculine. These beliefs need to be questioned and gently challenged by the therapist. The male child may need permission and help in broadening his range of expressed affect in order to recover from the trauma.

Use of alcohol or drugs

The child victim may begin to use alcohol or illicit drugs to self-medicate and keep away painful affect or depression. Based on the current literature, there is a strong correlation between being the victim of sexual abuse and subsequent alcohol or drug usage. Although most substance abuse begins in adolescence or adulthood, drinking and drug taking sometimes start in childhood. According to Rutherford (1988), each year over 1000 children were admitted to hospital for acute intoxication. Yet there are few treatment resources available for children who suffer from alcohol or drug abuse. It is now considered that 16–24-year-olds are the heaviest drinkers in the population, and these adolescents and young adults probably begin drinking at significantly younger ages. Young people have been targeted by the marketing of designer drinks and alcopops, which are appealing to young drinkers.

Treatment implications   It is important to assess whether a child is drinking or using drugs, and if so, to what extent. Addiction problems can begin at a young age. In these cases, the child's behaviour is often hidden from family members, or is known about but minimized or denied as problematic. It is important to assess the severity and frequency of drinking or drug usage. Help the child to understand the behaviour in the context of the function it serves, and help the child to find more appropriate ways to cope with the trauma.

Development of eating disorders

Although there has been a recent thrust to reverse the trend, in many western cultures thinness has been highly valued, and female children are taught at increasingly young ages that it is best to be thin; dieting and concern about weight has started very young. Although all forms of anorexia can be devastating, prepubertal dieting may be particularly dangerous; children have less stored fat, and dieting and/or starvation can delay or interfere with secondary sexual development. Derogatory comments about the body or weight, calorie counting, dieting, and compulsive exercising may be indicative of the child heading towards an eating disorder later in life. Although having other causes, eating disorders are strongly linked with physical and sexual abuse, sexually abused children being more predisposed than those who are not. The therapist should be watchful for symptoms that develop. Eating disorders occur in both females and males, although they are more prevalent in females.

Eating disorders (anorexia nervosa, bulimia, obesity) are often manifested for several reasons:

1   The young person eats as a way of coping with or defending against painful affect. The eating disorder may help the child to block out feelings. The individual is usually unaware of internal experience or affect.

2 It is the young person's attempt to have some control over her life. She becomes obsessed with controlling the intake of food and body weight, and desperately tries to control that aspect of her life. This compulsive focus keeps intra-psychic energy away from the abuse and painful affects related to it. The eating disorder becomes an obsession and a 'way of life' for the sufferer, and is difficult to relinquish.
3 It is an expression of rage turned inwards and a way of punishing or destroying the self.
4 It often suggests a symbiotic union with a parent and a desire to remain 'mummy's or daddy's little girl', and illustrates the conflicts during the beginning of the separation/individuation phase of development.
5 The young woman does not want to mature sexually, and is distressed at sexual maturation.
6 She gains weight or becomes obese in order to keep a safe and intimate distance from the opposite sex.
7 The young person believes that if she loses enough weight, the abuse will stop.
8 It can be a powerful protest against what has been or is being done to the girl.
9 It can be a cry for help.

Treatment implications   The therapist should be watchful for indications that the child is dieting or using food as a way of coping with or defending against the trauma. Asking questions about eating habits, food, and bodily perception should be helpful in assessing developing symptoms related to potential eating dysfunctions or disorders.

Summary

Children's inappropriate sexualized behaviour is often of great concern. Such children may be targeted by unscrupulous people for further inappropriate sexual activity, or the children themselves may become abusers and incite other children to sexual behaviours. Consternation arises when children behave seductively with adults. In extreme cases, children who act out violently and persistently can be a great risk to themselves and to others. Some will become involved in prostitution and pornography. Sexualized children may behave inappropriately with their carers and therapists. These problems have to be appropriately tackled by acknowledging the various feelings involved though discussion, sex education, and establishing behavioural guidelines. Sexual abuse and sexual activities may also involve the child in substance abuse and drugs. Eating disorders are another concomitant danger of sexual abuse. The therapist confronting these symptoms in a sexually abused child may, in severe cases, wish to seek the advice of an expert in these disorders.

10   The Child's Coping Styles and Defence Mechanisms

Written by a survivor:

Fairy (Scary) Tales
Sometimes, at night, when I leave my body,
I imagine that I, too, could go
to the land of
fairytales.
A shocking revelation.

Snow White
was a simpleton.
Didn't she realise
7 dwarfs are too much
for one little girl?

Little Bo Peep
molested.
Confidence lost,
simply put,
she lost the sheep,
and is that why?

Jack and Jill
ran up the hill
in an awful hurry.
One might ask,
were they simply
thirsty?

Rapunzel,
beware,
don't let down your hair.
Sleeping Beauty was awakened
by her stepfather,
long before
a prince came.

No longer
will I go there,
and I,
I ask myself,
is no one safe
in the world of fairy tales?

A therapist speaks: 'The children I worked with were remarkable. I was constantly impressed by their courage and capacity to survive what had been severe trauma. How each child coped and responded to the trauma varied greatly. It seemed that much of it was due to their genetic makeup and personality. How the child was responded to following the trauma, and how nurturing the family was, remains a significant element in the process.'

'The child's functioning prior to the abuse was also often indicative of how long treatment might take. Assessing the symptoms the child presented, and the coping styles and defence mechanisms the child used, was an invaluable part of the treatment process. I feel that my training and experience doing this work only served to increase the respect I felt for the children, and I was amazed at the resilience and fortitude of the human spirit and psyche.'

This chapter discusses the anxiety a child experiences when abused. The child sexual abuse accommodation syndrome, and hypervigilance, are two ways in which the child tries to deal with, make sense of, and have control of the trauma. These occur on an unconscious level, and can be highly detrimental to the child. In order to cope with and survive anxiety, the child relies on coping styles and defence mechanisms. These are described in some detail. Short clinical vignettes are given, and the reader is asked which coping style or defence mechanism the child is employing. Respecting defence mechanisms and coping styles is advocated as they are important in protecting the child from overwhelming anxiety and/or possible fragmentation.

Information regarding the diagnosis of post traumatic stress disorder is given, with details specifically about children. Finally the defence mechanism of dissociation, and the extreme form of dissociation (multiple personality disorder (MPD), or dissociative identity disorder (DID)) are discussed in some detail, and illustrated with case material.

The child sexual abuse accommodation syndrome

Roland Summit (1983) has described how the sexually abused child, in secrecy, helplessness, and entrapment, begins psychologically to adapt over time to what is an unliveable situation. The abusive interaction may continue over a long period, continuously threatening the child's physical and psychological integrity. The child's life and traumatic experience turned, through the process of accommodation, into a seemingly normal event. Basic psychological structures develop which allow psychic survival at the cost of severely altered perceptions of external and emotional reality.

> She may discover altered states of consciousness to shut off pain or to dissociate from his or her body, as if looking on from a distance at the child suffering the abuse. Unfortunately, the same mechanisms, which allow psychic survival, become handicaps to healthy and adaptive psychological integration and functioning as an adult. (Summit, 1983: 185)

Hypervigilance

Children who have been sexually abused almost always experience a sense of chronic stress, anxiety, and fear. Frequently, the sexually abused child becomes *hypervigilant* in an effort to cope with and survive the overpowering nature of the experience. The child becomes hyper-aware of dangers in the environment, even at times when they are not present.

The child also becomes hyper-aware of other people's feelings and actions in an effort to protect herself, and to avoid further abuse. This difficulty relating to self-reference is referred to in the literature as 'other-directedness':

> This concept refers to the fact that many survivors of severe child abuse experienced invasion, exploitation, sudden and unpredictable violence, and betrayal or abandonment during large portions of childhood and adolescence. The abuse victim quickly learns that safety is predicated upon hypervigilance. She or he may become adept at reading the slightest nuance in the abuser's demeanour or behaviour, since rapid and accurate assessment of that person's psychological or emotional state may allow the victim either to avoid an abuse episode or to placate/satisfy the perpetrator before a more aversive event transpires. The child's proficiency at meeting the needs and/or avoiding the violence of the abuser, however, exacts a psychological price – the sustained attention she or he must pay to environmental threats inevitably pulls energy and focus away from the developmental task of self-awareness. At a time when loved and well-treated children are becoming acquainted with self-celebrating a developing sense of discovery, autonomy, and fledgling impressions of self-efficacy – the abuse victim is absorbed in the daily task of psychological and physical survival.

> Thus the defensive requirement of other-directedness implies an equivalent lack of self-awareness. As a result, the survivor may be exquisitely attuned to the experience of others, but relatively unaware of his/her own needs, issues, or dynamics. Such individuals have a difficult time moving beyond a reactive survival mode later in life, and experience considerable difficulties at times when self-awareness, self-soothing, and self-confidence are called for. (Briere, 1989: 45–6)

The increased hypervigilance the child experiences gives the child an illusion of power and control which may be difficult to relinquish. If these issues are left unaddressed during the therapy process, it is highly likely that the child will remain hyper-sensitive and hyper-responsible for other people's emotions and perceptions, and largely cut off from her own. As a result, the child will be unable to develop a stable and cohesive sense of self, or self reference.

Anxiety

Anxiety can be defined as an unpleasant feeling of apprehension, usually accompanied by physiological symptoms such as sweaty palms, tightness of the chest, inhibited breathing, or a rapid heartbeat. Anxiety is a message that alerts the child to deal with a threat of some kind. Whether an event is threatening or not depends on the nature of the event as well as the internal and external resources of the child. How the child perceives the event also has a significant influence.

Feelings of anxiety usually lead to action intended to lessen or eliminate the stress as quickly and efficiently as possible. The child may use a deliberate or conscious method (coping style), or the child can utilize an unconscious method (defence mechanism). A defence mechanism can be adaptive or destructive depending on the consequences and how frequently it is used. For example, repression can be used adaptively, enabling the child to forget about a difficult situation and to enjoy something pleasurable. On the other hand, use of repression as a defence mechanism can be destructive when it is utilized frequently and as the only way to survive or cope with anxiety.

The use of dissociation as a defence mechanism can also be adaptive or destructive. Overwhelming and intense affect can be blocked from the child's awareness. It can be protective in that it enables the child to survive intense trauma. Unfortunately, children who use this defence mechanism frequently experience difficulty when attempting to get in touch with their emotions. They may experience numbness and a disconnection from themselves instead of more normal reactions.

When the child does reconnect with feeling, these feelings can be powerful and overwhelming, and the child may not have developed ways of experiencing and expressing these feeling that are adaptive or psychologically healthy. Therapy provides an opportunity and a safe place to go through this process.

Part of the therapist's work involves assessing which coping styles and defence mechanisms the child employs, and the frequency with which they are used. The therapist may help the child to broaden her array of available coping styles and defence mechanisms. As the child proceeds throughout therapy, she should have less need of defence mechanisms. In the meantime, coping styles and defence mechanisms should not be viewed as resistance, but instead be respected as protective and necessary for the child's emotional and psychological wellbeing.

Defence mechanisms and coping styles

The following is a partial list of defence mechanisms relevant to children as described in the Diagnostic and Statistical Manual of Mental Disorders, DSM IV TR (American Psychiatric Association, 2000: 811–13):

acting out   The individual deals with emotional conflict or internal or external stressors by actions rather than reflections or feelings. This definition is broader than the original concept of the acting out of transference feelings or wishes during psychotherapy and is intended to include behaviour arising both within and outside the transference relationship. Defensive acting out is not synonymous with 'bad behaviour' because it requires evidence that the behaviour is related to emotional conflicts.

affiliation   The individual deals with emotional conflict or internal or external stressors by turning to others for help or support. This involves sharing problems with others but does not imply trying to make someone else responsible for them.

altruism   The individual deals with emotional conflict or internal or external stressors by dedication to meeting the needs of others. Unlike the self-sacrifice sometimes characteristic of reaction formation, the individual receives gratification either vicariously or from the response of others.

autistic fantasy   The individual deals with emotional conflict or internal or external stressors by excessive daydreaming as a substitute for human relationships, more effective action, or problem solving.

denial   The individual deals with emotional conflict or internal or external stressors by refusing to acknowledge some painful aspect of external reality or subjective experience that would be apparent to others. The term *psychotic denial* is used when there is gross impairment in reality testing.

devaluation   The individual deals with emotional conflict or internal or external stressors by attributing exaggerated negative qualities to self or others.

displacement   The individual deals with emotional conflict or internal or external stressors by transferring a feeling about, or a response to, one object onto another (usually less threatening) substitute object.

dissociation   The individual deals with emotional conflict or internal or external stressors with a breakdown in the usually integrated functions of consciousness, memory, perception of self or the environment, or sensory/motor behaviour.

idealization   The individual deals with emotional conflict or internal or external stressors by attributing exaggerated positive qualities to others.

isolation of affect   The individual deals with emotional conflict or internal or external stressors by separation of ideas from the feelings originally associated with them. The individual loses touch with the feelings associated with a given idea (e.g., a traumatic event) while remaining aware of the cognitive elements of it (e.g., descriptive details).

omnipotence   The individual deals with emotional conflict or internal or external stressors by feeling or acting as if he or she possesses special powers or abilities and is superior to others.

passive aggression   The individual deals with emotional conflict or internal or external stressors by indirectly and unassertively expressing aggression toward others. There is a facade of overt compliance masking covert resistance, resentment, or hostility. Passive aggression often occurs in response to demands for independent action or performance or the lack of gratification of dependent wishes but may be adaptive for individuals in subordinate positions who have no other way to express assertiveness more overtly.

projection   The individual deals with emotional conflict or internal or external stressors by falsely attributing to another his or her own unacceptable feelings, impulses, or thoughts.

projective identification   As in projection, the individual deals with emotional conflict or internal or external stressors by falsely attributing to another his or her own unacceptable feelings, impulses, or thoughts. Unlike simple projection, the individual does not fully disavow what is projected. Instead, the individual remains aware of his or her own affects or impulses but misattributes them as justifiable reactions to the other person. Not infrequently, the individual induces the very feelings in others that were first mistakenly believed to be there, making it difficult to clarify who did what to whom first.

repression   The individual deals with emotional conflict or internal or external stressors by expelling disturbing wishes, thoughts, or experiences from conscious awareness. The feeling component may remain conscious, detached from its associated ideas.

splitting   The individual deals with emotional conflict or internal or external stressors by compartmentalizing opposite affect states and failing to integrate the positive and negative qualities of the self or others into cohesive images. Because ambivalent affects cannot be experienced simultaneously, more balanced views and expectations of self or others are excluded from emotional awareness. Self and object images tend to alternate between polar opposites: exclusively loving, powerful, worthy, nurturant, and kind – or exclusively bad, hateful, angry, destructive, rejecting, or worthless.

sublimation   The individual deals with emotional conflict or internal or external stressors by channelling potentially maladaptive feelings or impulses into socially acceptable behaviour (e.g., contact sports to channel angry impulses).

suppression   The individual deals with emotional conflict or internal or external stressors by intentionally avoiding thinking about disturbing problems, wishes, feelings, or experiences.

undoing   The individual deals with emotional conflict or internal or external stressors by words or behaviour designed to negate or to make amends symbolically for unacceptable thoughts, feelings, or actions.

The diagnosis of post traumatic stress disorder (PTSD)

'Children and young people who have experienced an extremely disturbing and life-threatening event such as a disaster, accident or violent crime may develop post-traumatic stress disorder (PTSD) … PTSD usually follows from incidents which invoke intense fear, terror and helplessness' (Turkel and Eth, 1990 quoted in Sharp and Cowie, 1998: 26). Sharp and Cowie (1998: 27) go on to say that 'In children and young people the symptoms vary with developmental phase', and they draw up the table shown on p. 120.

Effects of PTSD on children and young people

Pre-school children	Primary aged children	Adolescents
• Withdrawn • Subdued • Mute • Regression • Increased dependence on care-takers • Re-enacting traumatic incident through play	• Concentration difficulties • Deterioration of performance in school • Confusion over the sequence of events • Preoccupation with the small details of the incident • Psychosomatic symptoms • Sleep disturbance • Bed wetting • Immature behaviour • Repetitive questioning about the incident • Rude, irritable, provocative • Withdrawn and clingy • Re-enactment of the incident or imagined traumatic incidents	• Hyper-vigilant • Recurring thoughts and dreams about the incident • Depression • Helplessness • Anxiety • Survival guilt • Rebellious and antisocial • Drug or alcohol abuse • Sexual behaviour • Truancy • Suicidal thoughts and behaviour

Source: Sharp and Cowie, 1998: 28.

The child victim will often exhibit symptoms that meet the criteria for a diagnosis of PTSD, as categorized in the DSM IV TR (American Psychiatric Association, 2000: 467–68). The diagnostic criteria are as follows:

A.   The person has been exposed to a traumatic event in which both of the following were present:

(1) the person experienced, witnessed, or was confronted with an event or events that involved actual or threatened death or serious injury, or a threat to the personal integrity of self or others
(2) the person's response involved intense fear, helplessness, or horror. **Note**: In children, this may be expressed instead by disorganized or agitated behaviour

B.   The traumatic event is persistently re-experienced in one (or more) of the following ways:

(1) recurrent and intrusive distressing recollections of the event, including images, thoughts, or perceptions. **Note**: In young children, repetitive play may occur in which themes or aspects of the trauma are expressed.
(2) recurrent distressing dreams of the event. **Note**: In children, there may be frightening dreams without recognizable content.
(3) acting or feeling as if the traumatic event were recurring (includes a sense of reliving the experience, illusions, hallucinations, and dissociative flashback episodes, including those that occur on awakening or when intoxicated). **Note**: In young children, trauma-specific re-enactment may occur.
(4) intense psychological distress at exposure to internal or external cues that symbolize or resemble an aspect of the traumatic event.
(5) physiological reactivity on exposure to internal or external cues that symbolize or resemble an aspect of the traumatic event.

C. Persistent avoidance of stimuli associated with the trauma and numbing of general responsiveness (not present before the trauma), as indicated by three (or more) of the following:

(1) efforts to avoid thoughts, feelings, or conversations associated with the trauma
(2) efforts to avoid activities, places, or people that arouse recollections of the trauma
(3) inability to recall an important aspect of the trauma
(4) markedly diminished interest or participation in significant activities
(5) feelings of detachment or estrangement from others
(6) restricted range of affect (e.g., unable to have loving feelings)
(7) sense of a foreshortened future (e.g., does not expect to have a career, marriage, children, or a normal life span)

D. Persistent symptoms of increased arousal (not present before the trauma), as indicated by two (or more) of the following:

(1) difficulty falling or staying asleep
(2) irritability or outbursts of anger
(3) difficulty concentrating
(4) hypervigilance
(5) exaggerated startle response

Treatment implications

The therapist should try to determine whether the child suffers from any of the symptoms described above. Many child victims of sexual abuse meet the necessary criteria for a diagnosis of PTSD.

It is important to assess how many coping mechanisms and defences a child employs. In addition, it is helpful to assess how much the current coping mechanisms and defences are interfering with the child's acceptance and resolution of the trauma. How much do these psychological mechanisms inhibit or interfere with developmental tasks the child is currently facing?

Over time and with the therapist's help, the child will begin to experience less anxiety, and will develop a broader range of coping mechanisms, defences, and internal and external resources. As children process the trauma and other conflicting issues, they have less need of the more primitive coping mechanisms such as repression, dissociation, and acting out. The therapist can also help the child to find more functional and adaptive ways of coping with anxiety.

Dissociation

According to Putnam:

> Dissociation is a psychophysiological process that alters a person's thoughts, feelings or actions, so that for a certain period of time certain information is not associated or integrated with other information as it is normally or logically ... this process, which is manifest along a continuum of severity, produces a range of clinical and behavioural phenomena involving alterations in memory and identity. (1993: 40)

Dissociation can best be viewed along a continuum from very mild to extreme, as in individuals with multiple personality disorder (MPD), now also known as dissociative identity disorder (DID). It is a primitive defence that indicates a breakdown of the integrative functions of the self. It can be a breakdown in consciousness, memory, functioning or perception of the environment or the self, and is a psychological survival strategy. Research on post traumatic dissociation in the subsequent development of PTSD (Putnam, 1997: 75), and on the existence of many maladaptive forms of dissociation, demonstrates that there is a high price to pay for dissociative defences as noted previously by Roland Summit (1983: 185).

An example of this is the way sexual abuse survivors frequently describe their experience of sexual abuse as one of dissociation, of not feeling anything, of not being there, or of leaving their bodies ... floating and being somewhere else. Many children describe their recollection of the abuse experience as analogous to recalling a nightmare. In each case reality is tenuous, in part because of the child's natural tendency to disassociate in order to protect the self from experiencing the trauma. Common analogies that children use to describe the event include feeling as if they were drowning, falling, or leaving their bodies and floating near the ceiling.

According to Putnam, 'Dissociative children and adolescents may present with severe behavioural problems, with psychotic-like symptoms, with affective symptoms, with compulsive self-injurious or violent antisocial behaviour, or with florid disassociative symptoms. The differential diagnosis of children and adolescents presenting with significant behavioural problems should include pathological dissociation' (1997: 213).

Dissociation is a strong factor in causing the child to engage in self-destructive or self-harming behaviour in present or later life. Self-mutilation is frequently associated with the use of dissociation as a central defence mechanism and is strongly linked with sexual abuse. It is most frequently experienced by adolescent and adult survivors, although children may also engage in related activities such as head banging, pulling out hair, engaging in risky behaviour, deliberately injuring themselves, or other forms of self-harm.

The individual may engage in this behaviour to stop flashbacks or painful affect coming into consciousness. Self-harm may be a way of feeling physical pain, as a confirmation of being alive, or of distracting awareness from intra-psychic pain to what may be experienced as more tolerable, physical pain. This behaviour is also used as a way of gaining control, of self-soothing (releasing tension and anxiety) or as a powerful and disturbing way of expressing rage at oneself or others.

The role of sexual abuse in the formulation of MPD and DID

Severe and ongoing physical and sexual abuse are linked to the development of multiple personality disorder (MPD) or dissociative identity disorder (DID) through several mechanisms. According to Putnam:

> The first is a disruption of the developmental tasks of a consolidation of self across behavioural states and the acquisition of control over the modulation of states. The

recurring trauma (generally child abuse) instead creates a situation in which it is adaptive for the child to heighten the separation between behavioural states, in order to compartmentalize overwhelming affects and memories generated by the trauma. In particular, children may use their enhanced disassociative capacity to escape from the trauma by specifically entering into disassociative states. Disassociative states of consciousness have long been recognized as adaptive responses to acute trauma, because they provide: (1) escape from the constraints of reality; (2) containment of traumatic memories and affects outside of normal conscious awareness; (3) alteration or detachment of sense of self (so that the trauma happens to someone else or to a depersonalized self); and (4) analgesia. (1989: 53)

Child victims of sexual abuse who develop MPD or DID do not develop an integrated identity. Instead they create multiple selves with multiple functions through a series of dissociative states that are created and strengthened over time. These states are consolidated and become *alter* personalities. An alter personality is not a separate person. The alter personalities have differing values from each other, and from the primary personality. They serve different roles/functions, and switch control over the individual's behaviour. Each claims some level of amnesia and/or disinterest for the other alters (Putnam, 1989: 103–30). In the context of the abuse the child has suffered, this development is a powerful and complex survival strategy, becoming a way of life that frequently goes undiagnosed until adulthood, if at all.

The following case shows some of the difficulties in correctly diagnosing the development of MPD or DID in childhood:

George, aged seven, was frequently very aggressive towards other children in his class. Following one incident, where he had stabbed another child with a pencil, he was referred to the school counsellor for weekly sessions. There were also concerns about neglect, as he often came to school hungry, dishevelled, and smelling of urine. George was late to school almost daily, and was frequently absent.

The social worker at the school was concerned and confused by George's demeanour and behaviour during sessions. Often he appeared to be spaced out and did not hear her, or respond to things she said. George seemed not to remember previous sessions with her. He described himself as a different person each day; he spoke of being a monster, a pirate, or a villain from a television show, and often talked of his 'friends' who went everywhere with him. The social worker asked him if they were imaginary friends, but he insisted they were 'real'. The social worker felt that this information indicated that he had an active imagination and that he needed his various friends in order to feel secure. Overall, she dismissed the child's strange behaviour as being caused by his anxiety due to the dysfunctional household. The possibility that the boy might be developing MPD/DID never occurred to her.

A neglect report was filed with social services at this time, due to the mother's inability to respond to requests made by the school. The mother, Sarah, was very dysfunctional, and the other two siblings also suffered from many problems. Sarah was open about the difficulties in the household. She reported being completely overwhelmed, and having difficulty taking care of and controlling the children. She also reported that the father was physically abusive to her. Sarah insisted that though the children witnessed her abuse by the father, he was not physically abusive to the children.

Over time it became apparent that the children were being physically abused by the father, and were also sexually abusing each other. The children reported the physical abuse and the mother reported the sibling sexual abuse. It was believed that at least one of the children had been sexually abused by an adult, and was then acting out the abuse on the siblings. The abuser may have been the father, who had undergone severe physical and sexual abuse himself.

During a holiday break from school, George reported trying to kill himself by running into traffic. He was slightly injured. George openly discussed his suicide attempt with his mother and social worker. Following this incident, the children were removed from the home and hospitalized in a specialized treatment programme that had expertise in the evaluation and treatment of MPD/DID.

During the assessment phase, it was discovered that George, his brother and older sister were in the process of developing MPD/DID. Sarah, the mother, who had been a victim of severe physical abuse for most of her life, was similarly diagnosed. The mother and three children received specialized intensive treatment over two years. The hospital staff reported to the social worker that they had never worked with such a severely disturbed family. The treatment with the children was moderately successful and was ongoing over the next two years. The mother was unable to make sufficient improvement, and the children were subsequently placed in foster homes.

MPD or DID is much less common in children than in adults. In children, the differences between personalities are quite subtle. In addition, the number of personalities is fewer. Symptoms of depression and somatic complaints are less common in children, but the symptoms of amnesia and inner voices are similar to adults. Perhaps most significantly, therapy with children with this diagnosis is usually brief and marked by steady improvement.

In adults, therapy may last anywhere from two to over ten years before there is significant improvement, but in children therapy may last only a few months. Kluft (1985) believes that the shorter therapy time is due to the lack of narcissistic investment in the separate personalities. This dynamic highlights the importance of accurate assessment and the need for specialized treatment for any child who is developing or has developed this disorder.

Normal children naturally peak in dissociation at age five or six. Dissociative tendencies lessen at about age eleven. At age nine or ten, children may conceal dissociation. The child may experience flashbacks or intrusive images and thoughts. As a result, the child may shut down affect to protect the self, or may suffer from amnesia.

When conducting treatment, if a child seems dissociative, it is important to assess the level of dissociation. James gives some useful indicators:

- spontaneous trance states, when the child 'spaces out' or stares off into space
- use of another name
- a claim not to be himself or a claim of dual indentity (sic)
- referring (sic) to self as 'we'
- change in ability to perform tasks
- denial of behaviour that has been observed by others
- changes in vision, handwriting, style of dress
- drastic changes in behaviour, unexplained outbursts, disorientation
- hearing voices
- loss of time
- drawing self as multiple persons
- describing self as 'unreal at times, feels like an alien [a mild form of this is not uncommon in typical adolescent experience]
- describing surroundings as becoming altered, feels remote from his environment
- getting lost coming home from school or from friend's house. (1989: 104–5)

Many dissociative tendencies can be reflected in a child's art work. Children who are strongly dissociative frequently draw pictures that are fragmented, damaged, or bizarre, an unconscious representation of the self. The child may lose awareness while drawing, change techniques, and/or draw pictures that are vastly different from those drawn previously. Technique changes can also represent an attempt to self-soothe, or be an affective discharge on the child's part.

Other questions that might indicate severe dissociation include the following:

- Does the child seem to change her demeanour and personality from session to session? The child may go from being shy to outgoing, or from being gentle to aggressive.
- Does the child relate to the therapist in a different fashion from session to session?
- Is the child unresponsive and in her own world?
- Does the child forget things either in or between sessions?
- Does the child appear confused and forgetful about day-to-day things?
- Does the child describe experiences in which she does not remember being there?

All these dynamics can be natural, and it is therefore important to assess the degree to which what is discussed or observed is normal or abnormal. The more extremely the child displays these behaviours noted above, the more likely it is that the child is suffering from dissociation or MPD/DID. It is often helpful to speak with carers about assessing possible symptoms. Has the carer noticed any of the above symptoms?

The possibility of these developments in a child who has been physically or sexually abused should always be considered and assessed. If the child shows evidence of MPD/DID, specialized training for the therapist, or a referral for specialist treatment, is indicated.

Summary

In this chapter, we discussed Summit's child sexual abuse accommodation syndrome, which describes how the child adapts psychologically to an unliveable situation – that of being abused. The effects and the toll it takes on the child were briefly examined. We next looked at Briere's writings regarding 'hypervigilance'. The child's hypervigilance gives the child an illusion of power and control, which often makes it difficult to relinquish.

The child's defensive position of other-directedness exacts a price, and takes the child's energy away from awareness of and development of self, and a subsequent development of self-reference. The child becomes incredibly attuned to the needs and affect of others, and largely ignores or is unaware of her own needs and affect.

Anxiety was looked at, and the actions designed to lessen or eliminate these feelings were identified as coping styles (conscious method), and defence mechanisms (unconscious method). Defences were defined as adaptive or destructive depending on the nature and frequency with which they are used. Part of the therapist's work will involve assessing which coping styles and defence mechanisms the child utilizes, and in helping the child to broaden her array of available coping styles and defences. These should always be respected as protective and necessary for the child's psychological well-being.

Next PTSD (post traumatic stress disorder) was discussed, and criteria (from the DSM IV) were given to make the diagnosis, as well as information pertaining to the specific effects of PTSD on children.

Dissociation was described as being along a continuum from mild to severe; the severe form being defined as MPD (multiple personality disorder) or DID (dissociative identity disorder). Dissociation is considered to be a protective, yet primitive defence. MPD/DID was briefly examined including the process by which it occurs, and how it is manifested, and a case example given.

Lastly some diagnostic indicators were given to assess dissociation and MPD/DID. It is crucial that children be assessed, and the correct diagnosis be given as they require specialized knowledge and treatment. Often they go undiagnosed until adulthood (if ever diagnosed correctly at all), when MPD/DID is much harder to treat. Kluft (1985) states that children benefit from a shorter treatment period as they do not have the same narcissistic investment in the separate personalities, as do adults.

Exercise

Read the following case examples and define which coping styles or defence mechanism the child is utilizing. There may be more than one answer. The answers can be found in Appendix 1.

Vignette A

Following his abuse, Wayne, aged eight, becomes aggressive in the playground and disruptive in the classroom. These behaviours develop rather suddenly and escalate rapidly. At home, he is sullen, irritable, and argumentative with his younger brothers.

Vignette B

Rachael, age nine, tells the therapist that her stepmother fondling her wasn't 'a big deal'. She says that it really hasn't affected her. She says that her current apathy and depression are completely unrelated to the abuse.

Vignette C

Anne, age 11, is reluctant to join the therapy group for sexually abused girls. She feels disdain towards the group members, although she has never met them. She believes that the members would have little to offer her as they are all victims themselves. She states that they would most likely be losers and that associating with them would certainly make her worse, not better.

Vignette D

Edmund, age ten, becomes numb (cut off from his feelings), and lethargic following his abuse. He was previously expressive and extraverted, but is rapidly becoming more introverted. He has lost interest in the usual activities he had previously enjoyed. His teachers describe him as being forgetful and unable to concentrate. He often appears distracted and 'spaced out'.

Vignette E

Amber, age nine, following her abuse, begins to tease her sister, which frequently results in tears. Amber tells her mother that she is just having fun and her sister is over-reacting. She also sometimes accidentally misplaces or breaks her sister's toys. Amber is frequently late for school and often forgets to do her homework or breaks things that are needed at school.

Vignette F

Elizabeth appears to have been relatively unaffected by her abuse, according to her mother. In fact, her performance at school has improved, and, at home, she is even more helpful and considerate to her mother and sisters than she was before the abuse.

Vignette G

Susie, aged ten, was abused by her biological father. A year after the abuse, her mother begins dating. Susie often calls her mother a 'slut' and asks her inappropriate questions about the intimacy of her relationship with the new man. Her mother has been very careful and discreet about beginning to date again. Susie's mother is confused and upset about her daughter's insinuations.

Vignette H

Tom, aged six, refuses to talk about the abuse. Whenever the trauma comes into his awareness (consciousness), he quickly thinks about something else, or switches activities. He often tells himself that it never really happened ... that it was a bad dream. He keeps himself very busy, and switches activities constantly to avoid thinking about the abuse.

11 Tools of the Therapeutic Process

A child speaks: 'There's this play place. It's magic and I can be whatever I want. Sometimes it's a ship at sea, sometimes it's a forest with lots of monsters. Sometimes it's scary and sometimes I feel all afraid. Other times I'm big and strong and have lots of adventures. It's all kinds of things. Sometimes I get angry with Bill, my therapist, but he plays with me. He doesn't barge in like lots of grown-ups who play with kids; it's *my* game and I can tell him. I can paint and splodge. Sand and water are fab. Sometimes I feel little and afraid, but I can still feel safe and Bill says how I'm feeling when even I don't always know how it is. Sometimes we talk and Bill helps explain the muddles. He says it's OK to be angry and I have a special punching cushion. I get mad sometimes when we have to finish, 'cos I could go on for ever and ever. Bill doesn't change. Most grown-ups get grumpy and mad and don't know what to do, but Bill stays the same. He's sort of safe and knows how kids feel when they're in a mess. I wish I could see Bill for ever and ever, but he says when I grow up a bit more and feel a bit better there'll probably be other things I want to do. Yeh! Like travel to the moon, go to Disney World, play for Man. United!'

There are three major strands to the child's healing. The first is that the child should be safe and adequately parented. The second is that direct, focused work may be required around topics such as the abuse, sex education, prevention work, and life story work. The third is the important task of helping the inner person of the child to heal from the trauma imposed by the abuse, losses, and life experience. Therapeutic play (Carroll, 1997) or directive/focused play can be used for specific areas, but there is an important role for child-centred, or non-directive, therapy (West, 1996; Wilson et al., 1992). The foremost aim is to help restore the child to age-appropriate equilibrium within a stabilized family setting. Change is unlikely unless the child can talk about the abuse and feels safe and nurtured, with carers who offer support through acting out behaviours. '*The best outcomes in terms of behaviour were for those young people who had been helped to explore their difficult experiences and feelings **both** in a therapeutic relationship **and** in their everyday lives*' (authors' italics) (Farmer and Pollock, 1998: 182).

This chapter discusses some of the process of therapeutic sessions in individual therapy and group treatment.

Is the child able to verbalize feelings about the abuse?

Many children do not want, or are unable, to talk about the abuse:

- The child may be too young and without adequate vocabulary to recount the abuse experience.
- If abuse occurred at a pre-verbal stage of development it is, initially, more likely to be acted out.
- The child wishes to minimize or deny the abuse or its effects.
- The child represses or disavows feelings about the abuse.
- It is too painful for the child to discuss the abuse.
- The child is afraid of what the therapist, or other people, will think (a projection of shame, guilt, badness, and so on).
- The child does not want to upset others by speaking about the abuse.
- The child is afraid what the abuser might do if abusive details are revealed.

When deciding which therapeutic technique will be most appropriate, there are several considerations:

1   What is the child's age (chronological, emotional, developmental)?
2   Which creative activities does the child enjoy?
3   Which process will best facilitate working through the issues?

Techniques used

Therapy attempts to engage the child at unconscious as well as conscious levels (Donovan and McIntyre, 1990), helping the child to express the inexpressible and to rehearse new ways of being. Young children have immature language and conceptual development. Many abused children have speech difficulties; others may be selectively mute, having been 'silenced' by their abuser or suffering from dissociation and post traumatic stress (Chapter 10). Sitting and talking to the child is not necessarily the best way forward.

Depending on age and developmental level, most children express themselves through play (Gil, 1991) or other creative activity. Therapeutic sessions can be structured, with the therapist suggesting exercises designed to highlight specific topics. Or the child may use the materials freely (within parameters of safety and decorum) without a pre-set agenda, involving the therapist (or not) as the child chooses. Alternatively, part of the session can be structured with the therapist suggesting the activity, and part of it child-centred with the child taking the lead. The therapist aims to harness the child's imagination and understanding in structured work, using materials to explore topics such as the abusive experience, feelings, self-concept, loss, changes in the child's life, keeping safe, or sex education. Some therapists use art work (painting, drawing, modelling, collage) (Dalley, 1984; Dalley et al., 1987; Giles and Mendelson, 1999; Gilroy and Lee, 1995; Kramer, 1971; Silverstone, 1997), drama (role plays, drama therapy techniques) (Bannister, 1997; Jennings, 1995; Winn, 1994), story telling (books, making up stories, making up endings from story stems, taking it in turns to tell the tale) (Gersie, 1991; Gersie and King, 1990) and poetry. Other media are dance, movement and music (Heal and Wigram, 1993; Oldfield, 1999; Payne, 1992; Stanton-Jones, 1992; Wigram et al., 1995). Worksheets (Geldard and Geldard, 1997) including sentence completion and drawings are another tool for focused work. Sample worksheets are included in Appendix 2.

Therapists should be competent with the type of therapy on offer, and make the experience enjoyable for the child. The therapeutic session may be the only place where children can truly relax and be themselves. If they feel safe, children may begin to reveal all aspects of personality and emotional range, expressing, and trying to resolve, intra-psychic issues and conflicts. It is beneficial to have verbal discussion of the central issues as well, if feasible.

Why are creative methods effective?

For most children, play and creative techniques are natural methods of communication, and a way of working through issues that does not rely on the spoken word. Creative methods are usually enjoyable. They provide containment of emotion, enabling concrete expression of experience and feelings plus a natural distance and safety from the trauma. Unconscious material can be uncovered more easily. Being creative is often cathartic for the abused child, and activities can also be continued at home. For example, the therapist may suggest that the child write a journal and bring it to sessions, or draw a dream diary. These can be kinds of transitional objects and help to contain the child between sessions. The integration of several techniques is often the most beneficial way to use creative therapies (Naitove, 1982).

When using creative methods, the emphasis should be on the creative process and not on the product itself. This will help to alleviate the child's insecurities about not being able to draw well or produce a good story. Children's feelings regarding their self-worth are often played out in creative activities. The child may make self-derogatory comments during the creative process, be perfectionist and throw pictures away because there is some error, or the picture is 'not good enough'. As children's self-esteem improves and they begin to experience more self-acceptance, this behaviour will lessen and optimally will stop.

The therapist should avoid making judgements about the product, accepting unconditionally the child's creations. Consistent acceptance helps children become less punitive and more accepting of themselves and the created work. Acceptance is especially important when the work contains shocking or violent themes. If disapproval is expressed, the children may censor themselves in future.

The creative process in itself can be a good release of emotion and offer a cathartic outlet for the child. It also provides an effective vehicle for communicating important unconscious material regarding intra-psychic issues and conflicts for the child. Undertaking creative activities can help the child become aware of and express feelings previously unavailable or unacceptable.

The following example illustrates how artwork was successfully used:

Gregory, aged six, was referred by his teacher for counselling because he was extremely quiet. She felt that he might be depressed. Gregory was indeed very quiet and withdrawn, and avoided eye contact during the initial session. He appeared confused about why he had been sent to the therapist, stating that there were 'no problems' and 'nothing was wrong'. He appeared defensive and afraid.

The therapist attempted to speak with him for a while and then decided it would be most advantageous, due to his discomfort with conversing, to move to artwork. Gregory brightened. He did not have any ideas about what he would like to draw, so the therapist suggested a picture of something that made him happy followed by something that made him sad.

Gregory was meticulous and took time to complete his drawing. He appeared self-conscious so the therapist avoided watching him. After about ten minutes, Gregory presented his picture to her. She asked him to tell her about it. She could see that it was a picture of a house. Gregory told her that it was his house and it was on fire. There was clearly a figure in it, which he identified as himself. The therapist noticed the figure had been drawn with no arms. (It is quite common for a child to represent feelings of powerlessness by drawing a picture of themselves without certain body parts.) She asked if there was anyone else in the house with him and he stated no. She asked what happened next. He replied that the house had burnt down.

The therapist was confused, and confirmed that indeed this was a picture that represented happiness to him. She enquired what had happened to Gregory during the fire. Had he escaped? He said he had climbed out of the window, and smiled. She asked him to explain what was going on outside the house, as there was clearly a picture of the sun and a tree. He told her that his father was outside in the sunshine. Gregory proceeded to draw a picture of his father, who was drawn very large relative to the Gregory figure. Gregory said he was cross with his dad for being outside when he wanted him to stay in the house.

The therapist was alarmed by Gregory's picture, and her feelings were validated. Social Services was currently involved with the family. It turned out that Gregory had been neglected and left alone in the house frequently. He had also been sexually abused by his father. Gregory was seen by the therapist over the remaining school year, and for the next year as well. He was placed in a foster home and adopted by his grandmother. His father was convicted and had no further contact with Gregory.

Much of the therapeutic process involved artwork, stories, and puppets, which Gregory preferred rather than talking about what had happened. The therapist's interpretations to Gregory remained in the metaphor of the medium Gregory was using. He began working on art projects at his foster home and bringing them to sessions. Gregory became proud of his creativity, and his self-esteem improved through completing these projects which was an enjoyable and satisfying process for him.

Child-centred therapy

Child-centred, or non-directive, therapy is based on the work of Virginia Axline (1964, 1969) and Carl Rogers (1951). Who can forget the immortal *Dibs* (Axline, 1964)? Axline viewed play as a natural medium of expression and communication for children, and play and creative activities as essential components of a child's development, maturation, and self-actualization. They permit a process of self-discovery, an exploration of how the world works, and play is often the first step in relating to others. When used therapeutically, it provides an opportunity for children to 'play out' feelings and problems.

Child-centred therapy is based on the premise that, given a supportive environment, children have within themselves the capacity and ability to solve inner problems, and to develop positively. Development of the self is taken to mean achieving personal potential and leading a satisfying, productive life, a self founded on understanding and self-acceptance. Children have a right to self-determination and are encouraged to take responsibility for themselves.

In the therapy room, the therapist is sensitive to what the child is feeling and doing through the process of play. The therapist may reflect these feelings to the child to increase acceptance and self-understanding. By accepting and understanding the child, without judgement, the therapist encourages the child to explore and express herself in a deeper and more significant fashion. Within safe boundaries, the child may feel free to share thoughts and feelings that were previously repressed or denied because they were deemed unacceptable. The play process can be used to strengthen a child's understanding and insight.

Often this insight is developed within the metaphor of the child's play or imaginative experience. The skilled therapist may reflect on or interpret some of the child's feelings and actions; if interpretations refer to important emotional content and are made clearly but not insistently, the child often understands and develops a stronger self-observing ego. If appropriate, the therapist can ask the child if she has ever felt the way the character in the play has, and elaborate in more detail on this information. It is important to stay in the metaphor if the child so wishes.

Children often show a remarkable capacity for insight. According to Klein (1981), this insight is explained by the fact that the connections between conscious and unconscious are closer in young children than in adults, and infantile repressions are less powerful.

The following example illustrates the play therapy process:

Frank, aged six, initially presented as a quiet and subdued child who had been sexually abused by his aunt and uncle. Frank was reluctant to speak about the abuse. Instead, he often used the dolls and dolls' house to act out the sexual abuse. In his play, the little boy would be victimized by two dolls representing the aunt and uncle. After the aunt and uncle dolls left, the little boy cried himself to sleep, replicating Frank's experience.

The therapist spoke to Frank, within the context of his play, about how the little boy doll felt scared, powerless, and saddened by what had happened. Frank had previously had a close relationship with his uncle and aunt. He felt confused, betrayed, and saddened by his loss of them. He had not initially disclosed the abuse because his mother was close to her brother, and he did not want to spoil their relationship.

Frank's father had abandoned the family when Frank was three years old. Since then, Frank had attempted to take care of and felt responsible for his mother. He did not wish to cause her any trouble, as he had an underlying fear that she might fragment, and he would subsequently be left with no one. During the sessions, Frank played this scenario out with the dolls. The mother doll would walk into the room while the aunt and uncle dolls were there. Sometimes the mother protected the boy, but at other times the mother doll left the room, distressed, going into her bedroom to cry. The therapist interpreted that the boy doll must have been sad, confused, and cross when the mother did not respond to or protect him.

Frank was resentful, and angry, about having to be responsible and compliant; he was not supposed to have, or express, angry feelings. His anger was internalized in the form of depression. Frank's mother reinforced this by rewarding him for being good. She was unaware of Frank's fear about her possible fragmentation, and his fear that she might need to go away. He acted this scenario out, with the mother figure being taken to hospital because her son had been sexually abused. Frank's feelings of insecurity and vulnerability were naturally intensified by the abuse he had suffered from his aunt and uncle.

By the fourth month of treatment, he began experimenting with his anger, using the dolls and dolls' house. At first, he pretended that his aunt and uncle were injured by violent acts of nature, such as hurricanes or tornadoes. Next, he had the little boy doll use weapons to injure the aunt and uncle. Finally Frank used the doll's fists to tear apart the aunt and uncle dolls that were left begging for mercy. He had the mother doll enter the room and witness his strength.

During this phase, Frank often scanned the therapist's face to make sure his behaviour was acceptable. The therapist reassured him that it was all right, and that his feelings were a normal response to being hurt. He gradually began to talk about his feelings without using the anonymity of the doll family.

Frank also started to express angry feelings at home. The therapist worked with the mother to help her to tolerate this, and to encourage his appropriate expression of anger. He also began to show anger about his father's abandonment. Much of the work ended up focusing on this significant loss which had never been addressed.

Frank was seen over a seven-month period. Most of the processing and resolution of the abuse occurred through the play, facilitated by the empathic and sensitive interpretations of the therapist. Frank made significant progress.

Guidelines for assessing and observing the child during play

A child experiences himself through the experience of play. It is a natural medium of expression for the child. Unconscious issues will be likely to surface, and can be addressed in the play metaphor or more directly if appropriate. The following guidelines will assist the therapist in her interaction, assessment and observation of the child during play.

The child's relationship style

How the child relates and responds to the therapist provides valuable information during the assessment and treatment process. It also gives information about the child's capacity to respond to others. Answering the following questions is useful:

- How does the child interact with the therapist?
- How does the child greet the therapist, or respond to the therapist's greeting?
- Is the child eager or anxious to separate from the carer? During the first few sessions the child may naturally be a bit cautious before engaging with the therapist. Alternatively, the child may instantly bond and reveal inappropriately intimate things.
- How does the child deal with proximity to others? Does the child stand inappropriately close or initiate physical contact?
- Is the child overly friendly or overly eager to please?
- Does the child have appropriate boundaries?
- Does the child show an interest in interacting with the therapist, or is the child disinterested and detached?
- Does the child appear to be needy and desperate for attention? Does he act as if the therapist were his closest friend after one session? Is the child clingy or pseudo independent/mature?

- Does the child ask questions of the therapist and, if so, how personal are they? What is the child really asking and what is the underlying intent?
- Does the child engage the therapist in play during the sessions, or does he exclude the therapist?
- When the therapist plays with the child, how is the therapist treated? Does the child try to control the therapist?
- If playing a game, does the child always need to win, and does he cheat or change the rules? This process should be commented upon non-judgementally or the child may look upon the therapist as being dishonest.

The answers to these questions provide diagnostic information. The dynamics reflect the child's feelings about himself, and about how he relates to and bonds with others in the outside world. As time goes on, the therapist should note that the child's behaviour becomes healthier and more appropriate.

The child's mood and emotional range

It is important to assess the child's mood, noting how it develops and changes during the session. Often this will be manifested physically by the child's facial expressions, body language, eye contact or lack of it and energy level. How does the child look physically, and what is the child's body language? Countertransference feelings evoked in the therapist can be a good indicator of how the child has been feeling during the session. If at the end of the session the therapist feels depleted, sad, or depressed, this can indicate how the child is feeling. On the other hand, some children leave the therapist feeling energetic or exhausted.

What is the child's expressed range of affect? Does the child appear to experience many emotions during the session, or is the child restricted emotionally? Can she elaborate or talk about emotions? Do her emotions shift rapidly and is she able to sustain them? If the child displays only one central affect during the session such as anger or sadness, this can indicate that the child experiences and expresses a narrow emotional range. Are the emotions shown consistent with the situation? Or is the child laughing and smiling while pretending to be violent or destructive? Is the child crying or sad while discussing a situation which would normally be considered positive? What is the context in which the emotion is being displayed and does it appear within the normal range of development, keeping in mind that a more elaborate range of emotions is expectable in older children.

If a child begins experiencing anxiety related to the play or interaction with the therapist, what does she do? Does she suddenly switch the topic of conversation or the theme of the play? Does she make frequent trips to the toilet? It is helpful to notice these transitions and to assess what may have precipitated these changes. Was the material particularly salient for the child or emotionally painful? What caused her to become anxious or afraid? How disorganized or fragmented the child becomes is also a diagnostic indicator of the child's general functioning and ego strength. The therapist should note these issues.

If the child appears distressed, the therapist may feel compelled to reassure or comfort her. It is often helpful to wait a little and to see how the child responds.

Is she able to calm, soothe, or contain herself, and to what extent? Waiting before responding can provide important diagnostic information, and gives children the message that they are capable of comforting themselves. How quickly and how much the therapist needs to intervene varies from child to child.

The child's use of the therapy room

The child's use of the environment provides important diagnostic information. The therapist should consider the following questions:

- How does the child use the environment?
- Does the child's behaviour seem age appropriate?
- How does the child make use of the space?
- How does the child react to or handle the materials/toys? Does she appear reluctant to play or use certain things? Does she take care of materials/toys, or does she throw them around?
- Does the child appear comfortable in the room? Is she apprehensive, or nervous? Does the child take the initiative and engage in activities for herself or does she wait for the therapist to initiate play?
- Can the child provide structure for herself? This dynamic is symbolic of the child's internal sense of structure.
- Is the child able to integrate activities and make use of different materials? For example, will she take the lion from the box and build a cage for it with the bricks or add members of the family to the scene? This is diagnostic of the child's own intra-psychic integration. A child who is fragmented tends to move from object to object, without attempting to integrate them, compared with a more centred child with a greater attention span. This is also to some extent dependent on age and developmental level.
- Does the child play with the same toys and utilize the same themes every session? This may represent a need for structure and be indicative of insecurity in the child, or it could indicate that the child is 'stuck' for some reason. Perhaps the child is on the brink of bringing out painful material, or the therapist is obstructing the child's expression.

Themes in the play

The central themes in the child's play are related, directly or indirectly, to the intra-psychic conflicts the child is facing. The therapist should be watchful for themes that occur frequently. Some useful questions to ask are:

- What is the child trying to communicate or resolve through the thematic play?
- Is there a central theme or issue that occurs within the session from week to week, and does it change or develop?
- Do the themes seem developmentally appropriate for the child's age? Does the child use imagination within the normal range for the child's age?

- What role does the child take? Does she experiment or is the play set and somewhat rigid?
- Is there a sequence of issues presented?
- How do the play and themes affect the child emotionally?
- Is the play repetitive?
- Does the play seem productive or destructive?

Themes are significant and indicative of the child's intra-psychic issues and attempts at mastery. Note the example below:

Six-year-old Beatrice came into the session and began playing with the doll family. At first she appeared calm and was acting out normal daily activities. Then it was suddenly bedtime. The daddy doll came into the little girl doll's bedroom and got into bed with her. At this point, Beatrice became visibly upset and walked away from the dolls' house. She began shuffling through her folder and then knocked over the crayons. She picked up a pencil and pretended to stab one of the rag dolls, while telling the doll that she was very bad. The child returned to the dolls' house and announced that it was morning, and that the daddy had died and needed to be taken to hospital to see if he could be fixed. She then commented that the little girl was sad that the daddy was dead and that she wasn't sure if she wanted the doctors to 'fix' him. Beatrice sat next to the therapist.

The therapist observed the child's interaction with the character in the dolls' house and made comments relating to how the little girl was feeling, staying in the child's game. When Beatrice became upset and spilt the crayons, the therapist focused on the child feeling out of control, rather than on what was upsetting her. She also commented that the little girl seemed angry at the rag doll. The therapist asked the child what the rag doll had done to be so bad. Beatrice shrugged. The therapist commented that sometimes kids feel upset and mad, and may feel like spilling things or doing physical things. The therapist's sensitive tone and observation helped Beatrice to feel understood. The therapist asked if she was all right now? Beatrice nodded and appeared to calm down, replacing the rag doll in the chair.

Beatrice was able to return to the playhouse to finish the game, acting out the scenario many times, the ending changing on each occasion. Sometimes the girl doll screamed at the daddy and sent him out of the room. Other times she pretended to be asleep, or began crying when the father doll entered the room.

Beatrice had been sexually abused by her father for three months, during which he would come into her bed at night and fondle her. During the day, the father was affectionate and behaved appropriately. The child was confused, having ambivalent feelings towards her father and her mother, who had initially denied the abuse. The child no longer had contact with her father and sometimes had nightmares or fantasized that he was dead. She missed him, and experienced difficulty in accepting and integrating the abuse. She didn't like directly speaking about the abuse, but was proficient in using the dolls to express her feelings. The therapist stayed in the 'doll' metaphor, as she respected the child's desire and need to do so.

Themes will relate to the child's life history, for example experiences of family, school, and social life, including major changes and significant events such as hospitalizations, birth, and loss of significant people or pets. Themes specifically connected to sexual abuse could include trust and mistrust (Erikson, 1977), powerlessness, betrayal and self-blame, poor ego functioning, reliving the abusive experience (see post traumatic stress disorder, Chapter 10), eroticization, stigmatization, destructiveness, attachment disorder, and dissociation (James, 1989).

The ending of the session

The ending of sessions can evoke many feelings in a child, which the therapist should notice and comment upon. The child may have difficulty separating from the therapist. Helpful questions include:

- How does the child experience the endings of sessions?
- Is the child sad and distressed near the end of sessions?
- Does the child disavow sad feelings and disconnect emotionally from the therapist?
- Does the child bring up emotional issues towards the end of the session in order to prolong the ending? The therapist should comment on the child's feelings about the ending of the session, acknowledging that saying goodbye may be difficult or painful. It is helpful to explore what the ending means for the child.
- Does the child have difficulty putting toys and materials away?
- Does she disclose fantasies about seeing the therapist more regularly, or out of the therapy setting? Does the child have difficulty accepting the limitations of the relationship? Intense feelings of neediness may be aroused, feelings that may have been repressed or disavowed. The therapist may need to explore and acknowledge the child's fantasies and feelings relating to the therapeutic relationship. This should be handled delicately so as not to arouse shame or remorse in the child. The child who frequently feels disappointed by the limitations of the relationship will hopefully not interpret the therapist's explanation of boundaries as indifference or rejection.

Often a child wants to leave something with the therapist such as a picture, or alternatively to take home an object from the therapy room. It is helpful if the therapist interprets to the child that the child is important, and will remain in the therapist's thoughts. The child can be reassured that the therapist will be there for the child next session. It is important to try and find out what the underlying issue or message is that the child may be attempting to communicate to the therapist.

Separation and individuation as well as unresolved loss issues can be stirred up at the end of sessions. It is helpful to gauge how a child will react to the ending of the session, and to anticipate and normalize any reactions the child has. It is important that the child be given adequate warning about the ending, with sufficient time to prepare and process feelings evoked by the ending.

Individual therapy or group treatment?

Many sexually abused children can benefit from group therapy (Johnson, 1993b; Mandell et al., 1989: 10). Groups are a natural medium for children (Dwivedi, 1993). Some children such as those who are 'out of control' and acting out sexually or otherwise, and very withdrawn children, would firstly be better in individual treatment.

Benefits of the group process

The group framework discussed below is in large part based on the work of Yalom (1995).

A child can benefit from hearing about the experiences of other children. Group members may provide examples of how other children have reacted to and coped with abuse. As a result, new perspectives and understanding can be gained, and the child's array of coping mechanisms broadened. Children have the opportunity to observe different stages of the healing process and this can encourage and help them to anticipate what the future may hold.

> When the group has successfully sorted out some of the issues of power and control, it is freed to develop trust, cohesion, and a degree of intimacy. The group begins to be important to the members, relationships matter, and emotional investment in 'our group' develops. Group culture emerges. (Brown, 1992: 106)

The group members provide a new support system for the child, facilitating the child's social skills. The importance of peer relationships and the development of social skills are significant accomplishments and developmental tasks. In the group, children may engage in new friendships, feel accepted and supported by peers, which serves to increase their self-esteem. Ideally, these new skills can then be transferred and utilized in the outside world.

The group can also facilitate the exploration of feelings and beliefs related to the abuse. Individual children may subsequently become more aware of, and accepting of, their feelings and beliefs. Some children feel less threatened in a group, feeling more comfortable relating to peers, particularly those who have had similar experiences. Trust, intimacy, and relationship issues surface between the group members and group leaders, and can therefore be addressed.

The group as an interacting system

> A group is a dynamic interacting system in which each individual's role and behaviour is in varying degrees a function of the group-as-a-whole and of group process, as well as an individual characteristic. As a group develops, the roles get shared among the members. Sometimes an individual finds a role which enables her both to contribute to, and to benefit from, the group in a way suiting her personal resources and needs. At other times people get 'stuck' in problematic roles which may be dysfunctional for them, and also for the group. (Brown, 1992: 123)

Examples of these roles are as follows:

- The scapegoat
- The victim
- The distracter
- The monopolizing member
- The critical one
- The passive/non-contributing member
- The disrupter
- The martyr
- The joker
- The needy member

A child may identify with a certain role, or the group may unconsciously put that role on a group member. The underlying assumption in this process is that each individual child's role has a purpose for the group as a whole.

The therapist(s) need to decide how best to process and resolve problematic roles or behaviours on the part of the child or the group as a whole. The therapists may choose to speak to the child directly or to all the children in the group as a whole. For example:

> 'The rest of you are being very quiet and letting Hannah do all the talking. Why do you think that is happening?'

> 'Andy, when things are getting serious, it seems you have a need to be funny. I'm wondering why that is?'

The first step is to acknowledge and explore members' feelings about what is happening. Look at the process by which the behaviour or situation came about, and explore the children's needs and motivations that may have precipitated the behaviour and situation. This process encourages the entire group to take responsibility for the problem, and for alleviating it. This needs to be done in an age-appropriate fashion, making sure that the children understand the process. The younger the children are, the more active a role the therapist will need to assume in this process.

When forming a group, it is important to consider the following behavioural attributes of the group members:

- ability to communicate;
- degree of disturbance;

- motivitation to work or join in group activity; and
- ability to relate to others. (Benson, 1987: 25)

Things to work out in advance

When starting a group for abused children there are many elements to consider. West (1996: 140) provides a framework listing some of the central considerations:

- Who will run the group?
- How will children be recruited, and how will they be transported to group sessions?
- Will it be an open or closed group?
- What is the theoretical base of the group?
- How many sessions will there be?
- What will be the times, dates, and place of sessions?
- What will be the format of the sessions?
- What materials are required?
- What will be the group rules?
- What level of confidentiality will apply to group members and the group process?
- What follow-up arrangements will be made?
- How will the group be recorded?
- What methods will be used to evaluate the group?
- What level of feedback about individual children will be given to referrers/ carers/school?
- Can children in the group also have individual therapy?
- What contingency arrangements will be made for children who still need help when the group is finished, or for children who should be referred out while the group is active?
- What are the arrangements for the group workers' own consultation/ supervision?
- What is the role and purpose of a carer's group?

It is also helpful to establish guidelines for a positive and cohesive group experience. These can be suggested, developed, and discussed within the group. We suggest the following should be included:

1 Children should understand why they are participating in the group.
2 Children should listen to one another.
3 Each child should feel valued.
4 Children should attend the group regularly.
5 Children should interact positively and respect each other.
6 Group goals should be defined.
7 Children should feel empowered within the group.
8 The children should be sensitive and empathic to one another.
9 The group members should feel safe to explore and process abuse related issues.

A familiar format of group sessions may help children to feel safe, for example a predictable way of opening the group, a group activity, non-directive play, and a closing procedure (Kaduson and Schaefer, 2000: 274).

When doing therapeutic group work with sexually abused children, Howard recommends working on a multi-dimensional level, including a psychotherapeutic, psychoeducational, and skills development component.

> Psychotherapy addresses the psychological damage which results from sexually abusive experiences. The recognition of both positive and negative feelings towards the perpetrator are expressed by the participants via the therapist working directly with the group process. A psychoeducational approach, concentrating on sex-education and self-protection, enhances the child's knowledge base. The exploration and understanding of facts and information is vital and should not be seen as secondary to other therapeutic aspects. It is lack of information and knowledge which makes children easy targets for abusers. (1993: 222)

Information will help to empower the child and to correct misconceptions about bodily functions and sexuality. These beliefs are often on an unconscious level so repetition and working on different levels may be necessary. It can be useful to have an *ask anything box* where children can ask anonymous questions (in order to prevent self-consciousness), and discussion can ensue.

It is empowering for the child to receive information and suggestions about self-protection. Guidelines for discussion and exercises are as follows:

- Ways to protect yourself.
- Who would you tell if you felt threatened or were being abused?
- What might you say?
- How might you feel?
- What might you do?

Work with the children on paying attention to their feelings, instincts, and perceptions regarding their personal safety. What might be warning and danger signs? Work as a group to identify these. Help children to establish ownership of their bodies. How do they feel about touching? What feels OK to them? What doesn't feel OK? Help them to identify and develop a sense of what is appropriate and feels safe for them.

At the same time, be careful not to imply that the child is responsible for the abuse, either in the past or if it recurs in the future. Children may interpret self-protection information as evidence that they could, or should, have taken action. The child may be courted or forced into sexual activity at some point in the future, and be unable to take action. It is unfair and counterproductive to set the child up for failure.

The group as family

A group can serve as a new family for child victims. Sibling and parental transferences are likely and can be explored. The group models a family where, ideally, feelings can be expressed, explored, accepted, and worked through in a *safe* place without fear of minimization, denial, rejection, or other negative repercussions. The child can therefore learn about family dynamics and relationships, and feel understood, accepted, and valued by group members and therapist(s). Holmes addresses the importance of affiliation in the group therapy process:

> Affiliation to group members helps demoralized patients feel that they are of some value and importance, and to overcome isolation. Attachment in group therapy is to the group 'matrix' (derived from the word for mother, that holds its members securely and allows for exploration and affective processing). (1993: 173)

The central issues related to each child's abuse can be addressed verbally and through individual and group exercises involving toys, play, games, drama, art work, stories, writing, puppetry, and group exercises and projects. Visualization and relaxation exercises can also be useful. Role plays can be beneficial as they facilitate increased energy and spontaneity. They also can enhance under-standing, awareness, and creativity. During the process, they can be stopped to explore feelings, options, and solutions. The roles can be changed to obtain different perspectives, and to involve more group members. Role plays can be highly cathartic.

Together, the therapist and children in the group can examine and work through central symptoms and issues that they are currently facing, and help the members to understand that they are related to the abuse rather than due to some inherent flaw or badness in the children.

Gradually over time, the children are able to externalize the blame and respon-sibility they inevitably feel. Subsequently, the children feel a greater sense of altruism and empathy for each other and, as a result, increased self-compassion and self-acceptance.

The following example brings together many of the facets of group therapy:

Victoria, aged 11, had been sexually abused by her father over of period of three years. The abuse had been disclosed by her following her father's death. Victoria had an unhappy and conflictual relationship with her mother, who was emotionally unavailable due to her own emotional difficulties. Victoria alternated between depression and acting out in the form of aggressive behaviour. She had been expelled from school several times for fighting other girls, before the disclosure of her abuse.

Victoria was seen in individual treatment for ten sessions and was then referred for group therapy. The therapist felt that she would benefit from the group experience, partially because she was reluctant to speak with adults and she desired more contact with her peers. Victoria also spoke of being lonely, and had very poor social skills.

Victoria was very quiet for the first few months of treatment. When she spoke, she often expressed 'denial' about having any issues or symptoms related to the abuse. She was often disdainful towards other members. The group had several well-functioning members who addressed her defensiveness in a non-threatening way, and were empathic and kind to her. Victoria's hostility lessened considerably as a result. Victoria felt accepted and supported by group members, but still continued to be wary, keeping them at a distance.

Soon after, Victoria's hostility began to diminish. During one particular session Victoria was observed to comfort another girl who was a new member. Victoria suddenly became aware that she could contribute and offer something to other group members. She slowly began to realize that she had some similar feelings and experiences, and she began to engage with and contribute to the group. Victoria became adept at comforting others in ways that she desired to be comforted herself.

Victoria clearly tended to focus exclusively on other group members as a way of avoiding her own issues and feelings. Over time Victoria became aware of this dynamic and was able to accept more responsibility for her own healing process. She also began to develop more authentic relationships with other members. Victoria became able to accept and internalize positive comments made about her by other members of the group. Gradually, she was much more accepting of others and of herself.

The social skills she learned in the group were manifested in her relationships with peers at school, where she began to establish friendships as well. Victoria continued in the group for an additional six months and made considerable progress.

A carer group

It may be beneficial to involve carers in the work that is being done (Kaduson and Schaefer, 2000: 271). One way of accomplishing this is to establish a support group for carers. This involvement also facilitates the carers' engagement and investment in the process. In addition, they frequently need information and support in understanding the child's symptoms, in learning how to address the child's sexual abuse, and in understanding the healing process.

They can benefit from hearing about other carers' experiences, and realize that they, other family members, and the abused child are not alone. In such a setting, stigma and shame can be reduced. Carers usually feel responsible or to blame even if this is not the case; they are often afraid that others will be judgemental and blame them for the child's abuse. In addition, they may feel that they should have *known* about what was happening even if there was no indication; or they may feel guilty because they exposed the child to the abuser, and may even have encouraged the relationship. The carers, as a group, can be empowered as how best to protect their children, and how to prevent further victimization. It can be valuable if the carers are members of a support group for all the above reasons.

A carer speaks:

'It's like this. I bring Sam once a week to see his therapist, Bill. It was explained at the beginning what would happen. He would go with Bill into the playroom where there are lots of toys. I had a look – it's lovely. Most of the time Bill would let Sam do what he wants, but sometimes he has a few special things for him to do, like card games, paintings, and puzzles. We worked out what we want to do to make life better for Sam, and sometimes Bill asks me how Sam is getting on. He doesn't tell me much about what goes on in the playroom; Sam sometimes shows me something, or tells me of something he particularly liked. But I know that Bill will tell me of anything really important. At first I wasn't sure that just playing would help, but it seems to. And in Sam's paintings I've seen some of his feelings that I didn't know before. He's not as angry as he was, nor is he as shy, and he gets on better with the other kids. I think everyone that's been abused like Sam should have the chance of therapy. It's not always easy, though. Sometimes Sam gets upset and is a bit naughty, but that's because he is dealing with upsetting things in the past, and it works out all right in the end. I go to the carers' group, which helps a lot. We're told a bit about what is going on in the children's groups, but we also decide on things we want to talk about and do for ourselves, because most of us are finding life difficult.'

A social worker speaks:

'I was really pleased that Bill agreed to meet Sam and his mum, and that they wanted Sam to have therapy with Bill. I know that Bill works mostly in a child-centred way, using toys, and that he sometimes focuses on specific issues like anger and the abuse. He found out what Sam liked doing – painting, games, and puzzles – and uses these. Sometimes he and Sam do worksheets. Bill gave some worksheets to Sam's mother, which she enjoyed doing. With other children Bill might do acting, and has a lovely collection of musical instruments. At our last review meeting, we decided that Sam's sessions with Bill are helping him, and we have arranged for Sam to have another six sessions, if he agrees. At the same time Sam's mother has been in a group with other carers whose kids have been sexually abused. She found this very useful, and I have noticed her grow in self-confidence, and in her ability to parent Sam.'

Summary

In this chapter we have identified some of the processes that take place in the therapy room between therapist and child. Major areas of work tend to be psychotherapeutic and psychoeducational, often including assisting the child to explore facts and feelings relating to the abuse, helping the child to feel safe, and encouraging the child's self-esteem. For children not with their natural parents, life story work and future plans will also be important.

Some children are able to talk about these issues; others find play a more congenial medium, playing out symbolic themes relating to their abuse and life situation; other children may cut off, or dissociate, from traumatic events. The therapist's task, whilst respecting the child's defences, is to facilitate the child to express feelings and to help the child feel better about herself. Some of the work may be done directively, with the therapist introducing topics and ideas through creative media such as worksheets, stories, drawings, and books; some of the work may be non-directive with the child deciding on the play and activities. A good knowledge of child development and of children's reactions to stress helps the therapist to find the most suitable ways of working with the child. A case example demonstrates that play and creative techniques are often the child's preferred methods of communication, aided by the therapist's understanding of, and ability to communicate in, the language of symbolism and metaphor.

As well as being a participant in the therapy session, the therapist is an observer and assessor. Things the therapist takes into account include how the child responds to him or her, the child's ability to express emotions, the way in which the child uses the therapy room, and how the child deals with the ending of the session. All this provides important indicators of the child's level of functioning and relationship with others. A second case example highlights the relevance of the therapist's ability to identify and work with the themes that the child brings to the sessions, the themes normally highlighting things that are important to the child.

We then discuss the use of group work in child therapy. Groups are a natural medium for many children (Dwivedi, 1993). However, severely traumatized children, those who act out sexually or otherwise, and very withdrawn children, may initially be better placed in individual treatment. Groups can be useful to facilitate peer relationships, social skills, and age-appropriate development, and to reduce the isolation that many individual sexually-abused children experience. The group also provides the opportunity to work at family-related issues.

Group therapists need to be aware of the processes that can manifest in a therapy group. Careful planning is essential, involving carers and referrers as well as the children. A case example demonstrates many of the issues pertaining to group therapy with a sexually abused child. The children's carers often have significant needs, and a concurrent group for carers can be a vital part of the overall therapy.

A carer and a social worker speak about their experiences of having a sexually abused child in therapy.

Some examples of worksheets taken from the book by Spinal-Robinson and Easton Wickham (1992a) can be found in Appendix 2.

Exercise

Use your non-dominant hand to do the following:

• Draw a self-portrait of yourself as a child.
• Write a few paragraphs describing yourself and your experience of childhood.

This should help to get more in touch with your inner child. Is it easy or hard for you to connect with that part of yourself? Ponder the following:

• What feelings could you or couldn't you express as a child?
• What did you use to express yourself?
• How and what did you like to play with?
• Do you remember certain themes in your play?
• What did you play with when you were upset, distressed, or angry?
• How did you communicate and work through issues or difficulties?
• What did you use for comfort?

Can you recall your play, and what it was like for you as a child?
As a therapist, are you relaxed and uninhibited when you play with a child?
Do you still play?

---

12   Liaison with Agencies and Services: Professional Work within Child Protection Procedures and Courts

A therapist's response to working with severely abused children:

The child is hurt, wounded, troubled
Staring eyes, a gentle watchfulness
Or frenzied, stubborn activity evoke concern.
We feel compassion towards the body that has been
      neglected
      penetrated
      abused
How can so-called grown-ups behave this way?

We feel concern towards a soul that has received such a
      hostile reception in a dangerous world.
We know that better experiences, better feelings are possible.
We feel dreadful within ourselves as if, in a sense, we have
      been part of this inhumanity to a little child.
But we have something better to offer, some healing
      understanding, helping experience that will enable the
      child to express, and maybe overcome, distress and trauma.

Without that help the child may be locked in, becoming a
      non-being for ever.

We are important.

Children live in systems: families, whether their own or those provided by others; schools; youth groups, and so on. Abused children may also be involved in the child protection, care, and legal systems. These systems are highly complex (Furniss, 1991; Reder et al., 1993, Reder and Duncan, 1999), and in order to understand how to liaise with them and ensure the best help for troubled children, therapists need to comprehend the relevant legal and policy frameworks.

The testimony of abused young people makes horrifying and salutary reading (Reder et al., 1993; Sereny, 1999; Waterhouse, 2000). Sometimes it is the child who asks for help and starts to reveal the abuse perpetrated by a carer, neighbour, or maybe even a 'professional' (such as teacher, nursery worker, doctor, health visitor, or social worker). If the child tells other children about the abuse, an adult is often subsequently informed, setting a train of events in motion. What might this be like from the child's perspective? It behoves child therapists to understand child protection procedures so that they have some knowledge of the processes to which children have been subjected, and can make professional representations in appropriate places.

An important series of research studies (Department of Health, 1995a) contains significant messages for all who work in the field of promoting and safeguarding children's welfare. Importantly, some of the studies' findings were that the voices of children were still getting lost in well-meaning professionals' attempts to protect them. This message was delivered by the Rt. Hon. Dame Elizabeth Butler-Sloss (1988) almost a decade earlier in reviewing events in Cleveland. She reminded us that a child is a person, not an object. Whilst exploring some of the issues of multi-professional working of particular relevance to child therapists, this chapter demonstrates a commitment to maintaining a focus on children's needs as *people* with rights enshrined in law.

Child protection procedures: a brief overview

Following the death of Maria Colwell the government issued to local authorities a circular which led to the establishment of Area Review Committees (DHSS, 1974). These committees (now renamed Area Child Protection Committees (ACPCs)) were responsible for establishing multi-agency child protection procedures for the investigation and joint planning by local agencies when suspicions of child abuse came to light.

These child protection procedures, incorporating multi-agency child protection case conferences with the possibility of registering children's names on child protection registers, have continued, with revised multi-agency practice guidelines being issued to agencies working with children and families. The most recent (Department of Health et al., 1999) reflects the influence of an important series of research studies which reviewed, 20 years since their inception, families' and professionals' views on the child protection procedures (Department of Health, 1995b).

Some of the key findings from these studies were that services for children and families had become preoccupied with *child protection* rather than *support*. Many research participants comprising children, carers, and professionals, felt that the 'procedures' had become oppressive and counterproductive in that they erected barriers to trust and co-operation between professionals and the children and families whom they were trying to help.

These findings have had a major impact on the restructuring of services for children and families (Department of Health, 2000; Little, 1997). There is an increasing emphasis on multi-agency services, incorporating the statutory, voluntary, and private sector working together to assess and support children's needs. Hopefully, this is done before families become subject to severe pressures which may impact on their parenting ability and even lead to their harming their children.

This refocusing of services by central government is reflected in policy documents issued to local authorities and the health service (Department of Health, 1998a, 1998b, 1998c). For example, the Quality Protects programme (Depatment of Health, 1998a) established objectives for children and family services. The service objectives are much broader than the protection of children living in the community. They also incorporate meeting the needs of children in care, children needing adoption, and those leaving care. To meet the objectives, social services departments have to demonstrate that they are working closely with other statutory services, such as health and education, as well as the voluntary and independent sectors.

Legislation, principles, and codes of practice

Therapists and allied professionals have a duty to ensure that they have a good working knowledge of the Children Act (England and Wales) 1989 (Children Act, 1989), and the principles underpinning it (Allen, 2000; Ryan, 1998; White et al., 1995).

These principles, established in social work practice, are that:

- the child's welfare is paramount;
- there should be a minimum delay in deciding issues regarding the child's upbringing; and
- courts should not make an order unless satisfied that it is better for the child to do so. (White et al., 1995: 11)

These principles are informed by the 'welfare checklist' contained in section 1(3) of the Children Act 1989. This list, establishing factors to be taken into account when courts make decisions concerning children's welfare, includes the wishes and feelings of the child; the child's physical, emotional, and educational needs; the likely effect of any change made to the child's circumstances; the ability of parents, or other relevant people, to meet the child's needs; and the likely impact on the child of harm suffered or likely to be suffered.

The Children Act 1989 established the important principle that in applying for a care order under s.31 of the Act, authorities should try to ensure that children's needs are met. Local authorities not only have to satisfy the court that a child has suffered significant harm by its carers (or may be likely to suffer it) but that an order is *necessary* to prevent harm. This requirement heralded an important shift in emphasis in terms of the most appropriate context for children's upbringing, that is, even when children are known to have suffered significant harm from their carers (and may suffer it again), the expectation is that professionals will work with children and their families in their family context, if at all possible, to bring about positive change for the child.

This emphasis on *the family* is echoed in an important new concept within the Children Act 1989: *parental responsibility*. As stated by Jackson (1989) (cited in Bridge et al., 1990: 13) '... like the welfare principle ... the idea of parental responsibility runs through the Bill like a golden thread ...'. This concept emphasizes parents' (both mothers and fathers if married, and unmarried fathers via a court order) ongoing involvement with their children. This involvement requires agencies (social services departments, guardians *ad litem*, courts) to consult parents regarding decisions concerning their children. The rights of parents to remain involved in decision making affecting their children continues even when courts have made a care order conferring 'parental responsibility' on social services departments. Under previous child care legislation, 'parental rights' passed to the local authority with the making of a 'Care Order'. The only order which now 'cancels' 'parental responsibility' is an adoption order.

Parents have the right to be consulted by agency professionals throughout *child protection procedures* and child protection case conferences. Parental rights concerning *contact* with their children (unless a social services department obtains a court order to vary or terminate contact on the grounds that it is causing or is likely to cause the child 'significant harm' (s.34 CA1989)), can cause conflict between professionals trying to work together. This is understandable when some professionals are working closely with children to help them recover from painful experiences caused by the people whom the child should be able to trust most. Ongoing contact with such individuals can contribute to the child's distress.

Also important is a knowledge of the UN Convention on the Rights of the Child (1989), to which the UK subscribes, and the Human Rights Act 1998. The UN Convention on the Rights of the Child (1989) urges that the 'best interests of the child' should be considered (Article 3.1), enjoins nations to take 'all appropriate legislative, administrative, social and educational measures to protect the child from all forms of abuse or exploitation, including sexual abuse' (Article 19.1), and exhorts countries to institute effective measures (Article 19.2) and 'to protect children from all forms of sexual exploitation and sexual abuse' (Article 34).

Safeguarding children

The emphasis of the Children Act 1989 is clearly one of minimum intervention. Social workers should only take such action as is absolutely necessary, removing children from their families or foster carers to safeguard their welfare as a last resort, and shall return children home as soon as it is safe (s.44 (5)(b) CA1989). In cases of extreme parental non co-operation, an Emergency Protection Order (EPO) can be applied for through the courts which gives the local authority temporary parental responsibility with the custodial carer (ss.44, 45, 48 CA1989). The child may be removed from home for a maximum of eight days, parents being able to challenge the order after 72 hours. In severe cases, if circumstances warrant, the local authority might apply for an interim Care Order (s.38 CA1989). If investigations reveal that the child is at risk from another person living in the child's household, the preferred course of action is for that person to be encouraged or compelled to leave the household (s.2 (5) CA1989). Children who have been removed for their own safety can usually be returned home if the perpetrator of the abuse moves out.

Section 31 of the Children Act 1989 authorizes the local authority to apply to court for a care or supervision order. As highlighted earlier, a care order gives joint parental responsibility to the local authority. The local authority may then decide that the child's needs will be met, at least for the time being, only if the child lives somewhere other than with the current carers. Adhering to one of the Act's guiding principles that children should remain in their family if at all possible, the local authority has a duty to try to place the child with alternative family members. However, if this is not possible, then the child has to enter local authority 'care'.

Again, as emphasized under the Act's guiding principles, courts have to consider whether an order is necessary in order to promote and safeguard a child's welfare. If possible, the courts will decide that the local authority should continue to work with the family 'voluntarily', either whilst the child remains at home or alternatively that the child should be 'accommodated', with the parents' permission, by the local authority under s.20 of the Children Act 1989. The child *accommodated* (s.20 CA1989) or *in care* (s.31 CA1989) becomes a 'Looked After Child' and as such becomes subject to regular reviews. Most local authorities have adopted the 'Looking After Children Assessment and Review' framework developed by Ward (1995).

A court can only make a supervision or care order under S.31 Children Act 1989 if it is satisfied of certain criteria on the evidence presented by the local authority and an independent professional appointed by the court (a guardian *ad litem*). These criteria include the meeting of a 'significant harm' threshold; that the harm, or likelihood of harm, is attributable to the care given by the parent; or that the child is beyond parental control.

Significant harm is defined in ss.31(9)(b) and (10) of the Children Act 1989: 'harm' means ill-treatment or the impairment of health or development; 'development' means physical, intellectual, emotional, social, or behavioural development; 'health' means physical or mental health; and 'ill treatment' includes sexual abuse and forms of ill-treatment that are not physical. If the significant harm suffered, or likely to be suffered, by a child relates to health or development, this has to be 'compared with that which could be reasonably expected of a similar child'.

As highlighted already, under current government policies, assessing children's needs under s.17 Children Act 1989 is now emphasized. However, if there is a 'reasonable cause to suspect that a child … is suffering, or is likely to suffer, significant harm' the local authority is required to make enquiries to enable them to decide whether any action is needed to 'safeguard or promote the child's welfare'. This duty is contained in s.47 Children Act 1989. The enquiry may be undertaken by a social worker, usually employed by a local authority, or by an NSPCC officer, along with a police officer or other professional considered appropriate. The enquiry may lead to the police referring the 'case' to the Crown Prosecution Service which decides whether to charge within the criminal justice system the person believed to have harmed the child. Evidence, however firm, that the perpetrator can be identified does not mean that a criminal charge will be made or that the matter will be referred to a criminal court.

Investigating suspected 'significant harm': collecting possible 'evidence'

A key factor in deciding whether to pursue criminal procedures or to convene a case conference within child protection procedures is whether this is necessary in order to protect the child or other children, and the likely impact of such courses of action on the child. We know, for example, that despite carefully gathered evidence, including videotaped evidence from children subject to alleged sexual abuse, most alleged perpetrators of sexual abuse are found not guilty by criminal courts (Westcott and Jones, 1997). Indeed, despite the introduction of *The Memorandum of Good Practice on Video Recorded Interviews with Child Witnesses for Criminal Proceedings* (Home Office and DoH, 1992) designed to make children's testimony in court less stressful, only one in four videos are actually used by the court (Westcott and Jones, 1997).

The video interview

The original purpose of making the ordeal of appearing in court to give evidence in criminal proceedings less stressful for children already abused has not been fully realized by the introduction of the *Memorandum of Good Practice on Video Recorded Interviews with Child Witnesses for Criminal Proceedings* (Home Office and DoH, 1992). The intention is that the video should be shown to the Crown Prosecution Service and the child spared the ordeal of giving evidence in chief in the court setting and within sight of the alleged abuser. The child's evidence should be pre-recorded; eventually it is the intention that cross-examination will also be pre-recorded, but in the meantime it is recommended that it should take place on a live television link (Home Office and DoH, 1992). The 'video interview' is undertaken by trained personnel, following a prescribed format (Home Office and DoH, 1992).

The forensic medical examination

A forensic medical examination may be required to provide evidence for possible criminal proceedings. The child may also need help with medical symptoms. If there has been penetration the child may have related bleeding or laceration. Penetration may include the insertion of foreign objects, and the vagina or anus may be unusually stretched as a result of the abuse. There may be bruising or visible damage to the body. The child may complain of burning while urinating, or pain in the vaginal, rectal, or throat area. If the sexual abuse is very recent, semen may still be present, and may be revealed by examination of vaginal, anal, or oral swabs. The child may be infected, for example with AIDS, syphilis, herpes virus infection, or gonorrhoea. Children may suffer from bacterial infections such as yeast (candida) or trichomonas, as well as urinary tract infections. However, these conditions do not always indicate sexual abuse. If the female child has reached the age of sexual maturity there is the possibility of pregnancy or miscarriage.

Frequently, a child does not display clear-cut physical changes or damage to the body following sexual abuse. The absence or presence of physical evidence is an important factor in the investigation, but it is not beneficial or therapeutic to rely upon the results of the physical examination to prove or disprove that sexual abuse has taken place. In fact, the majority of cases do not involve direct medical evidence.

If the investigating professionals consider it important that the child should be medically examined, it is necessary to obtain both parental and, when the child is old enough, the child's consent for a medical examination to take place. If parents are unwilling, the child protection service may apply to the court for an Emergency Protection Order or an Assessment Order (ss.43, 44, 45 CA1989) and order a medical examination. The 'paramountcy principle' that this is in the best interests of the child needs to be clearly argued by the local authority.

There are arguments for saying that a comprehensive medical examination should take place whenever sexual abuse is suspected. Some professionals consider that a physical examination is re-traumatizing and ask why children should be subjected to one if they are only disclosing fondling. Yet not submitting a child to a physical examination can lead to evidence being lost. In addition, it is important to realize that often a child does not initially disclose the full extent of the sexual abuse. As well as possibly providing evidence of sexual abuse, a physical examination can identify any medical problems that may need treatment. Additionally, it can provide information and reassurance to the family. A comprehensive medical evaluation can help to address the child's concerns, fears, and self-perception of being 'damaged goods' (Porter et al., 1982: 109). Children may have strange ideas about what has happened or will happen to their bodies as a result of being abused.

The following case illustrates how the medical examination helped to unravel a child's misconceptions related to bodily functioning:

Gina, aged eight, believed that she was pregnant as a result of her sexual abuse. She dieted compulsively in order not to gain weight and attract attention to her stomach, which she believed was significantly larger following her abuse. Two years later, Gina could not understand why she had not had a baby. She did not realise that she was not at the age where she would normally be capable of conception. She believed that she must have had an abortion while she was sleeping, or that she had given birth to the baby, and it had subsequently been taken away from her. She often searched her stomach for a scar that would reveal where the baby had been removed. She believed that she would never be able to become pregnant in the future. For several years, she was confused about this situation, and believed that the birth or abortion was due to her damaged body, and had been punishment for her inherent 'badness'.

When Gina reached puberty, she became fearful, disliking the changes her body was undergoing. She became obsessed with her weight and sexual development. Gina feared that she would attract the attention of males, and that she would be sexually abused again. She restricted her food intake, becoming anorexic. Gina was hospitalized, during which time her sexual victimization was finally disclosed. After hospitalization, Gina engaged in individual therapy on an outpatient basis. She was seen over a period of two years, and the treatment outcome was only moderately successful.

The child's view of the process

If abuse is suspected, the child will realize that grown-ups are concerned. The child may not be believed and may sense that some adults are shocked, even angry. Someone the child does not know may want to conduct an 'interview' (a grown-up word) – maybe more than one interview – probably in an unfamiliar place with strangers. Perhaps there are a few toys in the room, but there will be sounds, smells and feelings that make this an odd experience. Whilst the 'interview' about the child's world and the alleged abuse is happening, the most important people in the child's life such as carers, teachers, or nursery staff, possibly brothers and sisters, friends and relatives, will also be 'interviewed'. What happens to these people? What do they talk about? If an alleged perpetrator lives with the family, the child may be taken to live somewhere else. Or the perpetrator might be taken away. Either way the family is upset and life is not the same.

By this stage the child may be confused about the many things that are happening. What *is* a social worker or a child protection officer? Children in the playground say that social workers take children away and lock them in dungeons. Why should the police be involved? And as for courts. What is a court? Solicitors and counsel are as much mumbo-jumbo as are therapists and psychiatrists. Carers may not know much about these things either.

On top of all this the child may have a medical examination. Children may be touched and examined in a way that brings back feelings and memories of the trauma. The child may have to attend a 'video interview' which feels strange and icky. The child does not know what is expected, and to have people watching is scary. The video interview is a particularly tricky experience for children who have been abused on camera.

If the alleged perpetrator is arrested, the child should be informed, and may experience a strong response about what has happened. Will the alleged perpetrator be 'locked up' for life? Will the perpetrator be angry at the child for what has happened? The child should be made aware that the perpetrator might not necessarily be punished by the legal system. If unconvicted – and this is often the outcome in criminal prosecutions for 'sexual abuse' – children usually interpret this as evidence of not being believed, or of the child's own responsibility for the abuse.

The child as a court witness

The child giving evidence needs to be prepared for court (NSPCC, 1993). Understandably child and carers have many questions or concerns. A child may be extremely anxious about the potential outcome if the perpetrator has had a significant role in the child's life. In some cases the child feels pressured by the perpetrator or a misguided carer to recant the disclosure.

As the court date approaches, the child should meet with relevant legal personnel and be prepared for possible questions and cross-examination. A visit to the courtrooms may be made including familiarization with audio-visual equipment. The child needs to be able to understand the process as much as possible, and to feel comfortable and supported. In some courts, only the court usher will be allowed to sit with the child in the 'video link' room. The child protection worker and therapist strive to help to normalize the child's feelings of fear and anxiety, and to assist the child to anticipate and cope with the stress inherent in the situation of being a court witness. It is common for the child to experience flashbacks, dreams, nightmares, and painful emotions. The child will most likely regress, and symptoms may re-emerge or intensify. The child may feel again as if the victimization has recently occurred, and may fear that any progress has been lost. Helping child and carer to anticipate and understand what is happening is reassuring and comforting. A close working relationship between the various involved professionals such as therapist, social worker, police, crown prosecution solicitors and barristers, and court ushers is essential.

It has been acknowledged that courts are traditionally intimidating, using legalistic procedures and antiquated dress, and there is a strong move to make them more child-friendly. The use of videotaped evidence and videolinks for cross-examination should become more uniform across the country. The expectation that children should undergo a forensic medical examination, give evidence, and be submitted to adult rules of cross-examination in the presence of the abuser and many strangers, could be viewed as an abuse of vulnerable young people.

The therapist's roles in the legal setting

Legal requirements are important when working with sexually abused children. Balancing legal requirements and the child's needs can be challenging. Although therapists are primarily concerned with the child's physical and emotional safety, well-being, and emotional healing, they also have a duty to report alleged abuse to the child protection agency or police to ensure that the child is protected.

Children are not always happy to have their abuse brought to light and this contributes to making abuse cases complicated and time consuming, and imposes heavy demands on the therapist and other social care professionals.

The therapist as an expert witness

When employed as an expert witness in criminal proceedings, or undertaking therapy pending a trial, or if making a professional assessment, the therapist should ascertain from the Crown Prosecution Service and defence counsel the exact nature of the work that is required, such as the purpose and timescale of the intervention, and whether written records and/or videotapes of sessions will be required by the court. The therapist must not be seen to contaminate potential evidence by coaching the child or 'putting ideas into her/his head'. When working with children in this situation, therapists will carefully ask open-ended questions, avoid leading questions, give the child time to form his/her thoughts, and document what the child does and says using the child's language when-ever possible; this should include comments or questions that may have elicited the child's response. It behoves the therapist to be cautious about discussing details of the abuse with the child, as the defence may use this as evidence that the therapist has 'rehearsed' the evidence with the child in such a way as to make the child's account unreliable. The therapist needs to keep accurate and careful records.

The therapist's records can be obtained by the court via a court order or witness summons, and the defence may subpoena the therapist's records as part of the legal procedure. When records are requested, the therapist can seek legal advice and approach the judge via a barrister to ask that access to such records be restricted (Daniels and Jenkins, 2000: 103). Therapist and child need to be clear that the normal rules of confidentiality do not apply, and that the material of the session can be made available to people concerned with the court case (even to the alleged perpetrator).

If becoming aware during the work that the abuse was more extensive or more severe than initially reported, the therapist should contact the child's designated worker and other appropriate authorities, as this new information may have a bearing on decision making in the legal process and, possibly, conviction of the alleged abuser. In such an eventuality, the therapist needs to let the child and family know that the information will be passed on, helping them to process feelings they may have about this.

Sometimes therapists are commissioned by legal advisors to appear as expert witnesses in civil or criminal court proceedings. Experts are seen as having appropriate knowledge and experience (for example in child development, normal and abnormal child behaviour, children's reaction to stress and trauma), in addition to the expert's related professional field. As well as providing facts, the expert witness can offer hypotheses and opinions based on professional expertise.

The therapist may be asked to testify about the alleged abuse, the behavioural and emotional effects the victimization has had on the child, and the child's relationship or attachment to a parent or carer. For the therapist preparing to testify, the following suggestions are helpful (Mealor and Ackert, 1989; Plotnikoff and Woolfson, 1996):

Important preparations
1 Meet with your legal representative.
2 Review your credentials so that you can intelligently discuss your professional qualifications.
3 Be sure you understand the purpose of having been called to court so you have at least a general idea of the scope of your testimony.
4 If you are going to testify concerning records, make sure you are thoroughly familiar with them.
5 Re-read your own and other people's statements.
6 If the evidence that you are to give involves facts or circumstances which have occurred at some time in the past, be sure you have taken the time to refresh your memory.

Giving evidence
1 Dress appropriately and be on time.
2 Read the oath or non-religious affirmation in a firm, clear voice.
3 Give your name, job title, and qualifications.
4 Call the magistrate Sir or Madam. A High Court judge is addressed as My Lord or My Lady, and all other judges as Your Honour.
5 In the witness box, speak clearly and confidently, facing the bench and the jury.
6 Remember that the evidence will be important, maybe crucial.
7 Expect to be nervous. It is a normal reaction. Do not be afraid to admit the limits of knowledge. Witnesses will be more relaxed if they listen carefully to each question before answering, and limit their answer to what is requested. Under no circumstances advocate or lecture.
8 You will need to seek the Court's permission to refer to notes, which other legal representatives are also entitled to see.
9 Respond with direct answers and avoid speaking in professional jargon, especially if there is a jury. Be sincere and try to remain unfazed.
10 If called as an expert witness, an expert's opinion is expected, restricted to one's areas of expertise. Avoid exaggeration, as well as false modesty.
11 An expert would rarely object to a question, or ask a question of the judge. If an answer results in an incorrect impression, then simply say so and seek permission to clarify the point. If a mistake has been made, point it out and correct it.
12 Try not to worry about cross-examination by legal counsel. An expert witness is a professional, and should give evidence as such. Let the lawyers and the court worry about tangential matters.
13 Finally, be polite. Experts are expected to put their point of view and to answer questions, not to argue.

Therapists working with children awaiting appearance as court witnesses

Sometimes, if a long delay is anticipated before an alleged abuser comes to trial, a therapist may be asked by the court (or defence counsel) to undertake specified therapeutic work in the interim with the alleged victim. 'There is a strongly held but mistaken view among professionals that the child must not receive therapy until *after* they have completed giving evidence in court ...' in case of allegations by the defence that the child has been 'coached'. 'Even where the social services are fully convinced of the urgent need for therapy for the child, it is claimed in some cases that such therapy requires prior authorization by a reluctant Crown Prosecution Service' (Daniels and Jenkins, 2000: 102). However, this is not the case:

> Once the video recorded interview is complete, it should be possible for appropriate counselling and therapy to take place. It should become standard practice to inform the police and Crown Prosecution Service about the nature of any such therapy in each case. The defence may justifiably wish to know about both the nature and content of the therapy that has taken place before the child gives evidence in cross-examination. (Home Office/Department of Health 1992, para. 3.44 quoted in Daniels and Jenkins, 2000: 102)

Practice varies from area to area. General advice seems to be to approach the Crown Prosecution Service if it is considered that therapy might be beneficial. Child-centred play therapy may be more favourably considered (Ryan and Wilson, 1993) than group work or directive therapies where arguments of contamination are greater.

Children who disclose abuse

Therapists working with troubled children should always be alert to the possibility of abuse. Careful records of therapy sessions, clearly separating facts from opinions, should be kept. Even though this puts youngsters in a double-bind, they need to be told that there is limited confidentiality and that the therapist will have to inform the child protection worker or carer if it is suspected that the child has been, or is being, abused. Careful listening and observation, plus a detailed knowledge of the child's background and history of abuse, should help establish whether the child is 'playing out' former known abuse, or whether current or hitherto undisclosed 'old' abuse is being demonstrated.

If it is thought that the child is revealing 'new' abuse, child protection procedures will be considered, and the therapist should be prepared to be interviewed, and to give a statement. If additional abuse is suspected and the therapy is to continue during the investigation, the therapist is advised to get the agreement of appropriate personnel such as police, legal teams, and designated worker/social worker. A non-directive approach may minimize subsequent accusations of 'coaching' the child, or 'tainting' the evidence (Ryan and Wilson, 1996: 188–233; West, 1996: 132; Wilson et al., 1992: 218–24). It is important to realize that the therapeutic alliance can be damaged if the therapist strays into the roles of advocate and/or law enforcer (Daniels and Jenkins, 2000: 105).

Giving evidence about therapeutic involvement

Therapists will need to comment succinctly on:

• the purpose of the work, and the therapist's theoretical approach;
• the length of time the therapist has been working with the child;
• major themes, issues or outcomes of the work;
• changes in the child's behaviour and attitudes;
• details of, and surrounding, further disclosures; and
• the child's response to family and environment.

Recommendations may or may not be sought about the therapist's view on the family relationships or the child's future.

Child protection and court involvement: the effects on the child

Children and families often need support and advocacy throughout the legal and other official processes. The designated worker and child protection team do their best to prepare child and carers during the investigation and court proceedings (NSPCC, 1993). Although not having direct responsibility, the therapist may want to check that the child's needs are being met, and that he has been informed of the legal process and possible outcomes, and should explore how the child understands and perceives this.

Carers may also have a strong response to the legal process. Carers who have ambivalent feelings about the child's disclosure, or remain loyal to the alleged perpetrator, may feel powerless and angry as a result of official intervention. Furthermore, if the process is lengthy, carers may understandably feel frustrated and powerless. If it is decided that legal proceedings will not take place, the family is often left feeling confused, powerless, angry, and re-traumatized by the system and various individuals involved (Walton, 1996). The therapist may need to work with social workers and other professionals to ensure that the family is helped and supported by advocating on the child's behalf to help the family make their position and desires known.

Formal communication and report writing

Unless specializing in forensic work, court work will not usually be a major part of a therapist's caseload, but liaison with children's designated workers, social workers, and other professionals, as well as with carers, will be frequent. Contact needs to be maintained with the child's carers, either directly or through the child's designated worker or social worker. The therapist should be kept informed about major changes in the child's circumstances, behaviour, developmental, and educational attainment. The therapist may share the major themes of the therapeutic work with the child's designated worker and carer, and may suggest how the child can be helped in family, school, and social life to enable maximum potential.

With 'children in need' or 'looked after' (that is, 'accommodated' or in the care of the local authority), six-monthly review meetings, involving the relevant professionals, the child (if old enough to participate), and the child's carer(s), are an important opportunity to share progress and plan for the future.

Case conferences within child protection procedures can be held at any time if there have been significant concerns arising from the child protection plan, or if something unforeseen happens. For both of these meetings the therapist should present a brief, succinct report that will neither betray the child's confidences nor the detail of the session (apart from abuse allegations). Reports on the period under review could include:

- the purpose of and amount of contact the therapist has with child, carers, and relevant others;
- significant changes in the child's life;
- aims of the therapy sessions;
- major themes and outcomes of the therapeutic work;
- changes observed in the child's demeanour and emotional state within sessions;
- recommendations about ways in which carers, teachers, and so on can assist the child; and
- future therapeutic plans.

Therapists are urged to check the up-to-date requirements of the Data Protection Act 1998 that came into effect in 2000. Individuals, including children under the age of 18, have the right to see information held on them by agencies and departments, including factual information, opinions, and local authority plans for the individual, including existing and new paperwork, and electronic files. Local authorities can refuse access to records if the disclosure is considered likely to cause serious harm to the physical or mental health of the person concerned, or to another person identified in the records. The local authority decides whether the young person understands what it means to exercise this right. If the child is unable to, parents can request access to a young person's records. The local authority has the discretion to disclose personal information held on children and families to social services staff directly involved in a case or anyone who cares for the youngster. Data protection is a changing area, and therapists are urged to make sure they are up to date (Community Care, 2000: 4; Huber, 2000: 11).

Summary

As well as subscribing to their own professional codes of practice, therapists have legal and procedural responsibilities and obligations within the remit of legislation such as the Children Act 1989, and local authority child protection procedures formulated as a result of central government policies. Central government policies, and therefore local authority approaches, alter from time to time in the light of research findings and changes in legislation, and there are local variations in details of policy implementation and resource allocation.

Emphasis has been increasingly placed on inter-agency co-operation, a detailed and formal assessment of the child and family and, if need is established, on providing support to enable the child to develop properly and remain within the family. The Children Act 1989 established three major principles:

1 The child's welfare is paramount.
2 There should be minimum delay in deciding issues regarding the child's upbringing.
3 The court should only make an order under the Children Act 1989 if satisfied that an order would be in the child's best interests.

Parental responsibility is highlighted. Whenever possible, parents should participate in decisions about their child's welfare.

The emphasis of the Children Act 1989 is one of minimum intervention, but child protection procedures are laid down and implemented when assessment suggests that this would be appropriate. If criminal action against the alleged perpetrator(s) of child sexual abuse is considered, evidence is required that is suitable for a court of law. Evidence collection is difficult with, and for, children, who may be involved in a videotaped interview for submission to the Crown Prosecution Service and court, and a forensic medical examination. Giving evidence, either on video tape or live in the court, poses major problems for most children, who have to adhere to the strict laws of evidence required in an adult court. This is difficult for a child with immature linguistic and conceptual abilities. Appearing in court is daunting, and children will benefit from careful preparation about court procedures.

The therapist must be familiar with court procedures:

1 She may be called as an expert witness to give the court an assessment about the child and family and, if appropriate, the child's response to therapy.
2 Therapists asked to undertake therapeutic sessions with a child who is waiting to appear as a court witness should get clear directions from the Crown Prosecution Service and defence counsel about the type of work that is required, and whether case records and/or tapes of the sessions will be required by the court.
3 Therapists already undertaking therapy with children who have been sexually abused can be involved in child protection and court procedures if, during therapy, the child reveals additional abuse.

Therapists must communicate effectively, both orally and in writing, in formal settings, and need to be able to marshall thoughts for discussion both with carers, child, and officials.

Therapists involved in child protection procedures and legal matters are urged to ensure that they have had adequate training, and that their knowledge is up to date.

13 The Grieving Process and the Termination of Therapy

An adolescent survivor writes:

The invisible one

I was a child
unseen
nothing and
no one left
to call my own

my body
a receptacle of pain.
Why couldn't anyone see?
Why wouldn't anyone
help me?

Perhaps
it would have been better
if I really had
been invisible?

In this chapter we discuss the losses the abused child has undergone, how loss affects the child, and the importance of the grieving process. We also discuss the termination process of therapy including the following:

- primary considerations and tasks;
- the process and preparation for ending;
- countertransference issues;
- the reasons for termination;
- the child's feelings and reactions to ending treatment;
- evaluating the therapy process;
- maintaining therapeutic boundaries;
- the loss of the therapist and previous losses; and
- the final session.

The ending of treatment is a significant process, to be handled with great thought and sensitivity. It can be a highly productive and beneficial time. In this chapter, we provide guidelines for planning and proceeding with this treatment phase.

Losses and grieving

It is almost inevitable that a sexually abused child will have experienced many losses. Grieving for these losses is a crucial part of the therapeutic process. 'Loss plays a major role in many crisis situations, and the attendant reactions of confusion, anger, and desperation may be understood as mourning responses associated with the loss.' Webb emphasizes that a crisis assessment must include past as well as present losses since memories of past experiences of loss and bereavement are typically reawakened in current loss situations (Webb, 1999: 10). Unresolved loss issues are detrimental to the child and, if left unresolved, will certainly present problems for the child in his/her future. These feelings can be very strong and overwhelming when they do come into consciousness. Dealing with loss in the session and with the therapist, the child can be contained, comforted, and soothed. These feelings can be processed, bit by bit, in a way that is not too painful and overwhelming for the child.

Some of the central losses of an abused child may be loss of any of the following:

1   Trust.
2   Positive body awareness.
3   Self-esteem.
4   Innocence; the child was prematurely exposed to sexuality and lost the opportunity to choose his first sexual partner.
5   Choice and control.
6   Health (increased somatic complaints).
7   Feeling that he/she is normal and similar to other children.
8   Perception of safety; the child now views the world as dangerous.
9   Carer approval if there have been negative consequences of disclosure, or negative repercussions due to the child's symptomology.
10   The abuser; this may be significant if the abuser was a close and trusted individual or family member.
11   'What might have been' if the child had never been abused.

There may be additional losses related to the trauma. The therapist should explore this throughout the treatment process, being particularly watchful for areas where grief work is necessary. It is best done gradually, as it can be a lengthy process, and so that it is not experienced as overwhelming by the child.

According to Putnam, the bereavement process, for an abused child, can be even more complicated and difficult:

> For maltreated children, the issues of loss, grief, and bereavement are complicated and often atypical. The universal need of a grieving child to idealize a missing parent (or

other relative or friend) may conflict with memories of maltreatment. Indeed, the person is often not dead, just absent because of abandonment or the denial of visitation rights. There are few (if any) peers with similar experiences in whom the child can confide and with whom feelings can be shared. The missing person is often vilified by others (e.g., foster parents and caseworkers), who do not acknowledge the child's grief over the loss. Grief in a maltreated child also produces powerful countertransference feelings in therapists and caretakers. (1997: 289)

Treatment implications

The following ideas are largely based on the grief work described by Worden (1991) and adapted to work with children who have been sexually abused. According to Worden, the following symptoms are among many of the common manifestations of grief:

- Sadness
- Anger
- Loneliness
- Fatigue
- Helplessness
- Shock
- Yearning
- Numbness

All the above represent normal manifestations of grief or loss. However, feelings that exist for abnormally long periods of time and at excessive intensity may indicate a complicated grief reaction.

The grieving process takes time. The amount of time needed to work through the following stages, and achieve some degree of resolution, will vary from child to child, depending on the child's previous level of functioning, ego strength, external support, and how the child is responded to following the trauma. Children who are in well-functioning and nurturing families will be in a stronger position to recover more quickly.

As stated in Chapter 2, the central task of therapy is to help the child accept and integrate the trauma intrapsychically. The same can be said of the losses. The child may need help identifying and conceptualizing the process of grieving as related to the victimization. To many children, and even some adults, the concept of grief is often very narrow, so the therapist may need to broaden the definition of loss to encompass the trauma. The child needs to acknowledge and accept the losses and the grief as part of a normal and healthy process.

There are generally considered to be four central tasks in grief work. The first is to help children to understand and accept the reality, and subjective meaning, of the various losses they have experienced. The initial reaction to the trauma, and the accompanying losses, may be disbelief, minimization, or denial. Children may also feel numb or dissociative, blocking out the feelings related to the loss as a way of self-protection from both the trauma and subsequent losses related to the abuse.

The second central task in grief work is to experience the pain of grieving. This is best done gradually, in a way that is not too overwhelming for the child. The therapist can help to comfort and support the child throughout the process. It is important that the therapist accepts and encourages the child's grief, and does not avoid these losses in order to protect the child from emotional pain. For example, the therapist should not reassure the child inappropriately, or appear overly concerned or distressed by the child's pain. Countertransference feelings always need to be monitored. It is often distressing for the therapist to tolerate and accept a child's emotional pain, especially when feeling protective of the child and deeply empathic.

The child may also be grieving for what might have been if he had not been sexually abused, or had the abuser not betrayed him, and so the abuser could still be involved in the child's life. The impact of the abuse on the rest of the family, if there have been negative consequences as a result of the disclosure, is also significant in this process.

The therapist needs to help carers to understand the necessity of the grieving process, and to assist them in supporting the child. The family may or may not be able to tolerate the child's emotions. They will likely find this difficult or upsetting. In addition, the carers usually experience their own grief about the child's sexual victimization, and may also need help and support from the therapist. Unresolved losses from the past tend to surface for child, carer, and therapist.

The third central task is one of adjusting to the new situation and adapting to the changes. Children need to be told that grieving takes time, and that they are not alone. Child and family both have to accommodate and integrate the loss in their lives which involves accepting its reality and implications for the future.

The fourth and final task is acceptance of the loss, and the subsequent resolution process. This involves moving beyond the abuse experience. It involves the definition of the self as being more than a victim of sexual abuse. It involves a reinvestment of energy into the child's current and future life. Child and family should eventually be able to move beyond the trauma, and to heal from the losses that were previously so painful.

The therapist's understanding of the grief process and compassion for the child facilitates this grieving. The therapist helps the child work through this process, helping the child develop understanding, resolution, and self-compassion.

The termination phase of treatment: central considerations and tasks

The termination phase is an important part of treatment and needs to be thought about and negotiated sensitively. Ending the therapeutic relationship is of great significance to the child. The therapist is a real person in the child's life; therefore the loss of the therapist is a real loss to the child.

It is to be expected that it will be difficult for the therapist and the child to end their relationship. As stated earlier, anxieties related to separation and loss are often aroused in both.

Therefore, it is important that the therapist is aware of countertransference feelings that may be manifested in order to avoid painful feelings, and deny the inevitability and sadness of the ending. Therapists need to work through their own feelings, in order to be completely available to the child, and to be careful not to convey mixed or ambiguous messages to the child at this emotionally sensitive time. In summary, the therapist must give permission for the child to leave the relationship. This also holds true, to some extent, for the relationship between carer and therapist, particularly if there has been a strong partnership.

Reasons for termination

The termination phase of treatment occurs for many reasons, the ideal one being that the child's symptoms have lessened, or gone away completely. If the child is functioning more adaptively, she has taken on certain functions that the therapist had previously provided. The carer may also be supplying a healthier parenting style.

Over time there is hopefully evidence that the child has got better. Material brought into sessions may show the child to be functioning more appropriately, and the child may now be able to relate to the therapist in different ways. The child's self-esteem and sense of self should have been strengthened during the therapeutic process.

Positive changes in the child may be noted by other important adults, such as carers, teachers, and siblings. This may provide the impetus to end the therapy. Alternatively, termination may occur because children have completed as much work as is realistic, considering their developmental stage and/or age.

Termination may also take place because the family wishes to remove the child from treatment since the most obvious negative symptomology has been alleviated. The carer may not appreciate the need for the child to continue in treatment. With work remaining to be done, this can prove frustrating for child and therapist.

Other reasons for ending therapy include financial or time considerations. In some cases the family may leave the area. If the family has to end treatment prematurely, it can be especially difficult for child and therapist as this is beyond their control. These issues need to be addressed in the termination process as well.

The ending of therapy can also be precipitated by the therapist leaving the setting. This can increase the sense of rejection the child may feel, and the therapist should anticipate this reaction. In this case, the therapist is more prone to counter-transference feelings of guilt and shame for leaving the child before therapy is completed, which makes facing the implications harder.

Another reason for ending may be that the therapy process is not helpful to the child. In this case, it is beneficial if the therapist can try to determine why the treatment process has not worked, and so help the family to understand this situation without attributing blame.

The specific reason for termination is clearly crucial to the way the termination process is addressed. The therapist is advised to anticipate these various issues, as they affect each individual child. The termination process can provide an excellent opportunity to work through very significant issues, and can be a highly productive phase of treatment.

The child's feelings and experience

Simply raising the subject of termination is often enough to evoke feelings of anxiety, fear, sadness, rejection, loss, or anger in the child (and possibly the carer). Children may have strongly ambivalent feelings. On the one hand, they may feel relieved because the ending of treatment is an indication of improvement, especially when this is positively rewarded by family members. On the other hand, the child may feel guilty about his desire to leave the therapist.

It is also likely the child will feel rejected, afraid that he is no longer valued, and will be forgotten by the therapist. The therapist needs to reassure the child that he is indeed special, cared about, and valued, yet also to reinforce the message that he is ready to leave treatment.

West gives some strong guidelines for finishing play therapy:

- involve the child in the decision to terminate
  - fix a date
  - make sure carers, school and so on are aware of what you are doing
  - decide on how to 'countdown' with the child to prepare him or her for the reality of ending
  - remember that children are individuals who will have their own ideas about the best way of finishing. (1996: 109)

Because the therapist is aware of the potential impact of termination, there may be a tendency to collude in, and deny, the reality of the impending ending. The therapist needs to acknowledge its reality, helping the child explore and process her emotional reactions. This process may need to occur with the carer as well.

The therapy process can be lengthy, particularly if the child has experienced severe and lengthy abuse. If possible, the therapist should be sure to allow sufficient time for termination so that children can work through their feelings and any potential loss issues (present and past), either connected with, or which have been precipitated by, the end of treatment.

As West states, it is important to set a specific termination date or number of sessions, once the decision has been made to end treatment. By addressing the ending directly and sensitively, the therapist gives children adequate time to process their responses to it. A direct and honest approach also empowers the child. Many children have experienced painful or abrupt endings of relationships without having had time to prepare themselves psychologically and emotionally.

Denial of the ending is a common reaction in children as well as adults. For this reason it is important that the therapist discuss the final ending of therapy at every session, including a countdown of the sessions. This can be done in a playful, visual way. The child can help the therapist to decide what would be fun. For example, the child could colour in spots on a dalmation dog, or add parts to a picture, or write or tell a story, or build something that can be completed in the final session. Otherwise, the child may prefer to forget about, or not think about, the ending. The therapist has the responsibility for not letting this happen.

The therapist should acknowledge the difficulties inherent in the process, and may to some extent predict, and also normalize, the wide array of feelings that may be evoked in the child. This process encourages the child to own his or her feelings, to share his or her feelings, and helps to lessen any shame or confusion the child may experience.

Some children respond to the ending process by devaluing or minimizing the progress made in treatment, or the therapist's contribution to their healing. The child may also withdraw from the therapist, rejecting the therapist before being rejected. The therapist can respond by making an interpretation to the child about what they are doing, which may help the child to respond in a healthier fashion.

Evaluation of the process

An important piece of work related to termination involves reviewing the treatment process, separately, with child and carer. Important questions to consider include:

- What were the symptoms and intra-psychic issues the child was facing at the start of the process?
- Were there any specific goals set by child, carer, or therapist at the beginning of treatment?
- How were these goals negotiated and have they been achieved?
- What is the present state of the child and what improvements have the child and carer made?
- How has the child used the therapy process?

Another part of the evaluation process involves identifying any remaining goals and unfinished work, some of which may be left undone because of developmental considerations. For example, the child may be too young for a particular aspect of treatment to be appropriate. It is important to let carers know that different developmental stages may require future treatment, most commonly at puberty and adolescence. They should understand that this is not abnormal, nor is it an indication that the current treatment has not been successful.

If therapy has not progressed as well as was expected, feelings of disappointment on the part of the child or carer will likely be present. It is important to acknowledge and work through these feelings. The review with child and carer can look at what the desired outcome might have been, and whether it was realistic. In some cases, carers might wish the child to receive treatment at a later date. There may also be other options such as group treatment that have not been tried, and the therapist can explore these possibilities with them.

It is valuable to discuss with child and carer the kind of warning signs that indicate the need for future treatment. What might cause them to seek therapy again, and how would they feel about this possibility? It is useful to let them know if the therapist anticipates being available in the future. In order to avoid confusion and mixed messages, the therapist can reiterate that she feels the child is ready to terminate treatment now, even though possible options for the future are being discussed. Let them know that information about future treatment possibilities is given out as a matter of course.

The therapist needs to acknowledge and help the child (and carer) to deal with their fears and anxiety about losing the therapist. The child may feel unable to hold on to the positive changes without the therapist, and carers can share these concerns. Such feelings are normal, and do not mean the child is not ready to end treatment.

Normalizing regression and boundaries

It is important to anticipate that regression may occur, and symptoms may re-emerge briefly. These symptoms symbolize that the child still needs the therapist, and represents the child's anxiety about functioning independently. The child can be helped to understand the returned symptoms in the context of the impending separation/ending.

In addition, child or carer may express interest in maintaining a relationship with the therapist outside the treatment process; the carer may extend an invitation or speak of having a social relationship. At this time, the child may also express fantasies or hopes about a continuing relationship with the therapist.

This can be awkward. It is anti-therapeutic and unethical to maintain any relationship with the client after treatment has ended. These matters need to be handled sensitively, so as not to evoke feelings of rejection on the part of child or carer. The therapist can most effectively deal with these requests by discussing them in the context of professional boundaries and ethics. At the same time, it is helpful to acknowledge that the therapist appreciates and cares about the child and carer as people, and will continue to remember and think of them even after the relationship has ended.

It is beneficial to endorse how difficult it is to say goodbye and separate from people when there has been a positive and close relationship. Furthermore, the therapist can offset the importance of keeping professional boundaries with the reminder that if the child or family needs help in the future, either they or another therapist will be available.

Most children and carers appear to understand such an explanation. They may experience some relief, because the social situation may be awkward for them as well. Very rarely some clients continue to pursue the relationship outside treatment, and in these instances the therapist may consistently need to reinforce therapeutic boundaries.

The loss of the therapist

As a result of previous separations and losses, the child may be left feeling bereft and powerless. The termination of treatment, in the present, can provide an opportunity for a different, healthier kind of ending. It can be significant in teaching a child that he can experience and sustain a loss and still move on in life.

The loss of the therapist is significant because of the child's dependence on him or her. The meaning of the loss for the child depends to some extent on the strength of the relationship with the therapist, and on the child's relationship with the carer and others in the environment. If a child has a strong support system, it is likely to be much easier to leave treatment.

The way in which this separation experience is processed and resolved will influence how the child processes further separations and losses later in life. West states that the ending of treatment should not further damage the child:

- Particular care should be taken with children who have had bad experiences of previous loss and endings.
- Play therapists sometimes worry that a child who has made an attachment to the therapist may be damaged when play therapy finishes. Attachment is a good thing, and, provided play therapy termination is handled sensitively with careful recognition of the child's feelings and phantasies, the child's ability to attach is transferable.
- Play therapists need to ensure that they do not become over-involved and hang on to the child. (1996: 109)

If the feelings regarding loss are too strong or painful, children may deny, minimize, or disavow their feelings. Some children will do this as a way of defending against painful affect. It is beneficial if the therapist can help the child to understand such behaviour, by making a gentle interpretation about what the child is doing and why. The therapist can also help the child become aware of or express painful affect by talking about the therapist's own feelings regarding ending, for example saying that they feel sad about saying goodbye and no longer working with the child. The therapist can also make interpretations about the child's effort (defence) to protect him or herself. Some children regress to previous levels of affect or previous defences, used exclusively during earlier phases of their treatment.

In some cases, the child may remain unable to connect with or express feelings. The therapist needs to accept that this is what the child needs to do, and not react punitively or defensively. The therapist may feel hurt, unappreciated, and saddened as a result of the child's defensiveness about ending, but needs to process these feelings so they do not interfere with this important phase of treatment.

Some children may disconnect from the therapist and the therapy process prematurely, in an effort to avoid painful affect. The child may become disinterested or difficult to engage, or may not interact in any meaningful way with the therapist during the final session or sessions.

A case example illustrates some of these issues:

Joe, aged seven, had been seen over five months by a counselling student, David, in a school play therapy programme. Joe had been sexually abused by his mother's male friend over a two-year period. Joe's parents divorced soon after his birth, and his father had little contact with him.

Joe had attached strongly to David, and the treatment process had been successful. It was near the end of the school year and David had begun preparing for termination six weeks earlier. David would be finishing his school placement and would not be available to see Joe in the subsequent school year.

Joe had strong loss and abandonment issues related to his father, and these issues were strongly evoked by this perceived loss of, and abandonment by, his therapist. The student felt sad and guilty about leaving Joe, and was able to discuss these feelings during supervision.

Joe was hurt and angry. He began to suffer somatic complaints again, and expressed his anger passive aggressively. It took David longer to engage Joe. Joe began crying during sessions. Much of the subsequent work centred on the loss and abandonment Joe had experienced with his father. He was also able to grieve for his impending loss of David. The termination phase of treatment was ultimately productive and beneficial.

At the final session, Joe and David decided to have a goodbye party. Joe selected food and chose games to play. David had bought Joe a picture frame, enclosing a photograph of both of them. During the final session, Joe was quiet and seemed emotionally distant. He appeared to be apathetic, if not completely indifferent, both about the ending and about saying goodbye.

David was disappointed and tried to engage Joe, but he was unresponsive. At the end of the session they shook hands and Joe left the room without displaying any emotion. David was very perplexed. After thinking about it, he realized that Joe had disavowed his feelings because it would have been too painful to experience them. David was able to accept Joe's behaviour as necessary, and his own confusion and disappointment lessened. He felt he had adequately addressed the termination issues.

Many children are able to stay emotionally connected to the therapist and enjoy the final session. If much of the grieving and emotional preparation for the final session has taken place, it can be a rewarding time for therapist and child. A final case example illustrates this point:

Samantha, aged eight, had been in treatment with Sally for eight months. Samantha had been abused by an uncle, with whom she no longer had contact, and her family had been supportive. Samantha's symptoms had greatly improved. She was proud of the work she had done in therapy, and the last five sessions had been spent talking about the ending of treatment. Samantha had shared many positive things with the therapist, including her mother's wedding in which she was a bridesmaid, her new friends at school, her improved grades, and her excitement about her new tap-dancing routine.

Samantha decided she would like the final session to be the same as previous sessions, but that she would like to perform her new routine for the therapist. Samantha was sad about ending her relationship with the therapist, but also saw the ending of therapy as an accomplishment. She felt fairly confident about holding on to the gains she had made while in treatment.

The final session went well. Samantha appeared to enjoy the session and was excited about giving the therapist a small stuffed animal, which she told the therapist she had spent considerable time picking out. The therapist gave Samantha a notebook to write in, which was inscribed. Samantha had often used a journal in between sessions to record her thoughts and feelings. Samantha appeared sad near the ending of the session, but was comforted by the therapist telling her she would miss her as well. Samantha performed her dance routine, and told her therapist about a fun activity she would be involved in next week.

The therapist congratulated Samantha on her performance and hard work. A few minutes later, therapist and Samantha said goodbye. Samantha did not appear distressed, but was pleased with her experience of counselling and the final session. The lead up to the ending had been negotiated well, and the outcome of treatment had been successful.

The final session

The therapist can afford to tell the child how proud he or she is of them for all the child's effort and work in the therapy process, and plan with the child how they should spend the final session.

If the child desires, have some ritual or ceremony to mark the ending. With young children, it may be a good idea to plan a final session with food, and special activities that have been enjoyed during earlier sessions. Some children prefer to keep the session as it has always been and do not want any changes. Often it is helpful to have a picture taken of therapist and child together, or to give the child a small present and card (a transitional object). Let the child know that they are special to you and will continue to be special and thought about after the process has ended.

During the final session, there can be a short evaluation, including acknowledgement of the work completed together, followed by the planned activities. It is important to allow plenty of time at the end of the session to say goodbye formally.

If work on termination has been adequately processed in the sessions leading up to the final one, it need not be overly emotionally painful for child and therapist to say goodbye. They are both psychologically prepared, and much of the grieving work will have already been done. The final session is usually an emotional one, but it is often rewarding as well.

Summary

In this chapter we looked at the grieving process. It is almost inevitable that the child will have suffered many losses as a result of the abuse. Grieving for these losses is a crucial part of the therapeutic process. The central losses the child may have experienced were highlighted. The stages of the grieving process (Worden, 1991) were also briefly discussed. The therapist may need to broaden, and normalize, the grieving process for the child and carer, and support them through this phase of therapy.

The ending of treatment is very significant, and needs to be negotiated sensitively. The way in which this separation experience is processed and resolved will influence how the child processes further separations and losses later in life. The loss of the therapist may evoke previous losses the child has experienced. The child and carer will need adequate time and preparation for the ending. Therapists need to work through their own feelings of loss and anxiety so that they are able to give a clear message to the child about leaving treatment. Denial of the ending may occur by both therapist and child, and is clearly anti-therapeutic.

Reasons for termination were briefly discussed and how they might impact on the ending of treatment. Evaluation of the process and some guidelines were given. At this time, any progress, or lack of progress, and future goals may be discussed. It is also important to anticipate and predict that some regression may occur: symptoms may re-emerge briefly. These can be understood and explained in the context of the impending separation. The child and carer often experience anxiety about functioning without the therapist's involvement.

The ending of treatment can provide an opportunity for a psychologically healthy ending. It can teach the child that he can experience and sustain a loss, and still be able to move on positively with his life. The therapist can support, acknowledge, and validate the child's feelings and experience. Earlier losses can be worked through during this period as well. It is advisable to allow additional time if the child has experienced significant losses in the past. Two case examples were given, one illustrating a child's disavowal of feelings, and the other demonstrating a child who was able to stay emotionally connected to the therapist in the final session.

Although the ending of treatment is often emotionally painful for therapist, child, and carer, it provides an opportunity to work through some significant issues, and can be a highly productive and rewarding phase of treatment.

Exercise

How do you experience endings?
Is it difficult or painful for you to say goodbye to people?
How do you feel about saying goodbye to the child?
How did you feel when a relationship ended as a child?

Did you have the opportunity to say goodbye?

Were you supported in this experience?

Think of previous losses and endings. How best can this ending be negotiated?

The ending and losses may be experienced as painful for the child, the carer, and yourself.

Acknowledge and process your feelings.

Encourage the child and carer to do the same.

Epilogue

A final poem written by a survivor of childhood sexual abuse; a poem written at the end of treatment:

(To my abuser)

In my thoughts and dreams,
you do not exist.
I have banished you.
Ashes to ashes,
dust to dust.

I am the one
who moves on.
Besieged and defeated,
you can no longer
linger in the shadows.
Farewell.

(For my therapist)

In this room,
an exorcism
has occurred,
harmonious inside,
you have guided me,
tears transformed,
fears dissolved.

I am the
Survivor.

Appendix 1: Answers to the Exercise on Coping Styles and Defence Mechanisms (Chapter 10)

A. Acting out
B. Denial and minimization
C. Devaluation
D. Dissociation (symptoms of depression)
E. Passive aggression/displacement of anger
F. Sublimation
G. Projection
H. Suppression/undoing

Appendix 2: Worksheets (see Chapter 11)

Positive Messages

Try saying these messages out loud!

1. I am absolutely not to blame.
2. What happened was not my fault.
3. Adults should never touch kids in a sexual way.
4. I have a right to my own body and to decide who touches it.
5. There is nothing I did that caused the abuse.
6. I am not alone. Other kids have had the same experience.
7. People care about me.
8. I care about myself.
9. As I talk about my experience of being sexually abused, I will feel better.
10. The only person to blame for my abuse was the abuser.
11. I have a right to my feelings about the abuse.
12. I deserve to feel better, and I am going to take good care of myself!!!!!!!

What other messages could you add?

....

....

....

....

....

Pick a message for the day. Pick the one you would most like to hear.

Copied by permission from *Cartwheels: A Workbook for Children Who Have Been Sexually Abused* (Notre Dame, IN: Jalice) by P. Spinal-Robinson and R. Easton Wickham (1992).

FEELINGS IN YOUR BODY

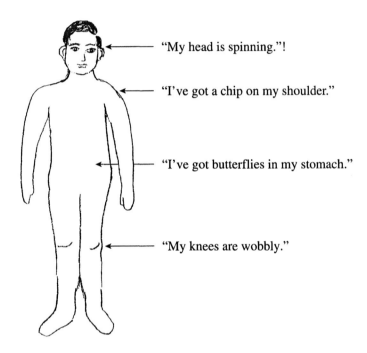

"My head is spinning."!

"I've got a chip on my shoulder."

"I've got butterflies in my stomach."

"My knees are wobbly."

People often feel emotions in their bodies. Can you show where you have feelings in your body? You can use different colours for different feelings and colour them in.

Anger   Embarrassment   Sadness   Fear   Surprise
Nervousness   Confusion   Excitement

WAYS TO COPE

Things to do when I'm feeling afraid or overwhelmed:

1. Take several deep breaths.

2. Find a family member or a special friend to talk to.

3. Say a prayer.

4. Close my eyes. Use my imagination to go to my safe place.

5. Say some positive messages.

6. Listen to some music that I like.

7. Take a walk, play a game, or do some exercise that will help my body to feel more relaxed.

List other ways to cope:

....
....
....
....
....
....

WRITE A LETTER

Write to the person who abused you. Say whatever you feel like saying:

To:...

From:...

Date:...............................

....
....
....
....
....
....
....
....
....
....
....
....
....

....

....

Signed:..

DRAW A PICTURE OF YOURSELF
OR WRITE
SOME WORDS DESCRIBING
YOURSELF:

before the abuse

after the abuse

References

Aldridge, M. and Wood, J. (1998) *Interviewing Children. A Guide for Child Care and Forensic Practitioners*. Chichester: Wiley.

Allen, N. (2000, 3rd edn) *Making Sense of the Children Act*. Chichester: Wiley.

American Psychiatric Association (2000, 5th edn) *Diagnostic and Statistical Manual of Mental Disorders*. Washington, D.C.: American Psychiatric Association.

Ariès, P. (1973) *Centuries of Childhood*. Harmondsworth: Penguin.

Audit Commission (1999) *Children in Mind. Child and Adolescent Mental Health Services*. London: Audit Commission.

Axline, V.M. (1964) *Dibs: In Search of Self. Personality Development in Play Therapy*. Harmondsworth: Penguin.

Axline, V.M. (1969) *Play Therapy*. New York: Ballantine Books.

Bannister, A. (ed.) (1992) *From Hearing to Healing. Working with the Aftermath of Child Sexual Abuse*. Harlow: Longman.

Bannister, A. (1997) *The Healing Drama. Psychodrama and Dramatherapy with Abused Children*. London and New York: Free Association Books.

Barn, R. (ed.) (1999) *Working with Black Children and Adolescents in Need*. London: British Agencies for Adoption & Fostering.

Bass, E. and Davis, L. (1990) *The Courage to Heal. A Guide for Women Survivors of Child Sexual Abuse*. London: Mandarin, Octopus.

Benson, J.F. (1987) *Working More Creatively with Groups*. London: Tavistock.

Berliner, L. (1990) 'Clinical work with sexually abused children', in C. Howells and C. Hollins (eds), *Clinical Approaches to Sexual Offenders and Their Victims*. London: Wiley.

Berliner, L. and Elliott, D. (1996) 'Sexual abuse of children', in J. Briere, L. Berliner, J. Bulkley, C. Jenny and T. Reid (eds), *The APSAC Handbook on Child Maltreatment*. Thousand Oaks: Sage. pp. 51–71.

Bifulco, A. and Moran, P. (1998) *Wednesday's Child. Research into Women's Experience of Neglect and Abuse in Childhood and Adult Depression*. London and New York: Routledge.

Bowlby, J. (1982, 2nd edn) *Attachment and Loss. Vol. 1, Attachment*. London: Hogarth Press and Institute of Psychoanalysis.

Bridge, J., Bridge, S. and Luke, S. (1990) *Blackstone's Guide to the Children Act 1989*. London: Blackstone.

Briere, J. (1989) *Therapy for Adults Molested as Children: Beyond Survival*. New York: Springer.

Briere, J. (1992) *Child Abuse, Trauma, Theory and Treatment of the Lasting Effects*. London: Sage.

Brown, A. (1992, 3rd edn) *Group Work*. Aldershot: Ashgate.

Browne, A. and Finkelhor, D. (1986) 'The impact of child sexual abuse: A review of the research', *Psychological Bulletin*, 99: 66–77.

Butler-Sloss, the Rt. Hon. Dame Elizabeth (1988) *Report of the Inquiry into Child Abuse in Cleveland 1987*. London: HMSO.

Calder, M.C. (ed.) (1999) *Working with Young People who Sexually Abuse: New Pieces of the Jigsaw Puzzle*. Lyme Regis: Russell House.

Carolin, B. and Milner, P. (1999) 'A medley of children's voices', in P. Milner and B. Carolin (eds), *Time to Listen to Children. Personal and Professional Communication.* London and New York: Routledge. pp. 17–28.

Carroll, J. (1997) *Introduction to Therapeutic Play.* Oxford: Blackwell Scientific.

Cawson, P., Wattam, C., Brookern, S. and Kelly, G. (2000) *Child Maltreatment in the United Kingdom.* London: NSPCC.

Children Act (England and Wales) (1989) London: HMSO.

Cicchetti, D. and Rogosch, F.A. (1997) 'The role of self-organization in the promotion of resilience in maltreated children', *Development and Psychopathology*, 9 (4): 797–815.

Cipolla, J., McGown, D.B. and Yanulis, M.A. (1992) *Communicating Through Play. Techniques for Assessing and Preparing Children for Adoption.* London: British Agencies for Adoption & Fostering.

Colclough, L., Parton, N. and Anslow, M. (1999) 'Family support', in N. Parton and C. Wattam (eds), *Child Sexual Abuse. Responding to the Experiences of Children.* Chichester: Wiley. pp. 159–80.

Community Care (2000) 'Act opens up records to public scrutiny', *Community Care* 1313: 4.

Coward, B. and Dattani, P. (1993) 'Race, identity and culture', in K.N. Dwivedi (ed.), *Group Work with Children and Adolescents. A Handbook.* London: Jessica Kingsley. pp. 245–62.

Cramond, J. (1997) 'The nature and role of theory', in I. Horton and V. Varma (eds), *The Needs of Counsellors and Psychotherapists.* London: Sage. pp. 84–98.

Crowe, C. and Kettle, J. (1992) *Survey of Treatment Facilities for Young Sexual Abusers.* London: Department of Health and National Children's Homes.

Cunningham, H. (1995) *Children and Childhood in Western Society Since 1500.* London and New York: Longman.

Dalley, T. (1984) *Art as Therapy: An Introduction to the Use of Art as a Therapeutic Technique.* London: Tavistock.

Dalley, T., Case, C., Shaverein, J., Weir, F., Halliday, D., Hall, P.N. and Waller, D. (1987) *Images of Art Therapy: New Developments in Theory and Practice.* London: Tavistock.

Daniels, D. and Jenkins, P. (2000) *Therapy with Children. Children's Rights, Confidentiality and the Law.* London: Sage.

Data Protection Act (1998) London: The Stationery office.

Davis, E., McKay, B., McStae, L., Pringle, K. and Scott, S. (1991) 'Fostering young people who have been sexually abused', in D. Batty (ed.), *Sexually Abused Children. Making Their Placements Work.* London: British Agencies for Adoption & Fostering. pp. 89–97.

de Mause, L. (1974) *The History of Childhood.* London: Souvenir Press.

Department of Health (1991) *Working Together Under the Children Act.* London: HMSO.

Department of Health (1992) *Memorandum of Good Practice.* London: HMSO.

Department of Health (1995a) *Child Protection: Messages from Research.* London: HMSO.

Department of Health (1995b) *The Challenge of Partnership in Child Protection: Practice Guide.* London: HMSO.

Department of Health (1998a) *Local Authority Circular (LAC)(98)28: The Quality Protects Programme: Transforming Children's Services.* London: The Stationery Office.

Department of Health (1998b) *Our Healthier Nation.* Cm3852. London: HMSO.

Department of Health (1998c) *Modernising Health and Social Services.* London.

Department of Health (2000) *Framework for the Assessment of Children in Need and Their Families.* London: The Stationery Office.

Department of Health, Home Office, Department for Education and Employment (1999) *Working Together to Safeguard and Promote the Welfare of Children: A Guide to Interagency Working to Safeguard and Promote the Welfare of Children.* London: The Stationery Office.

Department of Health and Social Security (1974) *Non-Accidental Injury to Children.* LASSL(74)13. London: HMSO.

Donovan, D.M. and McIntyre, D. (1990) *Healing the Hurt Child. A Developmental-Contextual Approach.* New York: Norton.

Doyle, C. (1997, 2nd ed.) *Working with Abused Children.* Basingstoke and London: Macmillan.

Dwivedi, K.N. (ed.) (1993) *Group Work with Children and Adolescents. A Handbook.* London: Jessica Kingsley.

Edgeworth, J. and Carr, A. (2000) 'Child abuse', in A. Carr (ed.), *What Works with Children and Adolescents? A Critical Review of Psychological Interventions with Children, Adolescents and their Families.* London and New York: Routledge. pp. 17–48.

Eleftheriadou, Z. (1997) 'Cultural differences in the therapeutic process', in I. Horton and V. Varma (eds), *The Needs of Counsellors and Psychotherapists.* London: Sage. pp. 68–83.

Elliott, J. and Place, M. (1998) *Children in Difficulty. A Guide to Understanding and Helping.* London: Routledge.

Elson, M. (1986) *Self Psychology in Clinical Social Work.* London: Norton.

Erikson, E.H. (1959) *Identity and the Life Cycle.* New York and London: Norton.

Erikson, E.H. (1977) *Childhood and Society.* St. Albans: Triad/Granada.

Farmer, E. and Pollock, S. (1998) *Sexually Abused and Abusing Children in Substitute Care.* Chichester: Wiley.

Fergusson, D.M. and Mullen, P.E. (1999) *Childhood Sexual Abuse. An Evidence Based Perspective.* London: Sage.

Figley, C.R. (1995) 'Compassion fatigue as secondary traumatic stress disorder: An overview', in C.R. Figley (ed.), *Compassion Fatigue. Coping with Secondary Traumatic Stress Disorder in Those Who Treat the Traumatized.* New York: Brunner/Mazel. pp. 1–20.

Finkelhor, D. and Browne, A. (1985) 'The traumatic impact of child sexual abuse: A conceptualization', *American Journal of Orthopsychiatry* 55: 530–41.

Fitzgerald, J. (1991) 'Working with children who have been sexually abused', in D. Batty (ed.), *Sexually Abused Children. Making Their Placements Work.* London: British Agencies for Adoption & Fostering. pp. 37–49.

Furniss, T. (1991) *The Multi-professional Handbook of Child Sexual Abuse. Integrated Management, Therapy, and Legal Intervention.* London and New York: Routledge.

Gallo-Lopez, L. (2000) 'A creative play therapy approach to the group treatment of young sexually abused children', in H.G. Kaduson and C.E. Schaefer (eds), *Short-Term Play Therapy for Children.* New York and London: Guilford Press. pp. 269–94.

Geldard, K. and Geldard, D. (1997) *Counselling Children. A Practical Introduction.* London: Sage.

Gersie, A. (1991) *Storymaking in Bereavement. Dragons Fight in the Meadows.* London: Jessica Kingsley.

Gersie, A. and King, N. (1990) *Storymaking in Education and Therapy.* London and Stockholm: Jessica Kingsley and Stockholm Institute of Education Press.

Gil, E. (1991) *The Healing Power of Play. Working with Abused Children.* New York: Guilford Press.

Gil, E. and Johnson, T. Cavanagh (1993) *Sexualized Children: Assessment and Treatment of Sexualized Children and Children Who Molest.* Rockville, MD: Launch Press.

Giles, H. and Mendelson, M. (1999) '"I'm going to do magic ..." said Tracey: Working with children using person-centred art therapy', in P. Milner and B. Carolin (eds), *Time to Listen to Children. Personal and Professional Communication.* London and New York: Routledge.

Gilroy, A. and Lee, C. (1995) *Art and Music Therapy Research.* London: Routledge.

Harper, P. (1993) 'Developmental considerations in therapeutic planning', in K.N. Dwivedi (ed.), *Group Work with Children and Adolescents. A Handbook.* London: Jessica Kingsley. pp. 61–77.

Hawkins, P. and Shohet, R. (2000) *Supervision in the Helping Professions*. Buckingham: Open University Press.

Heal, M. and Wigram, T. (eds) (1993) *Music Therapy in Health and Education*. London: Jessica Kingsley.

Hodges, J. (1999) 'Research in child and adolescent psychotherapy. An overview', in M. Lanyado and A. Horne (eds), *The Handbook of Child & Adolescent Psychotherapy. Psychoanalytic Approaches*. London and New York: Routledge. pp. 105–24.

Hodges, J., Lanyado, M. and Andreou, C. (1994) 'Sexuality and violence: Preliminary research hypotheses from psychotherapeutic assessments in a research programme on young offenders', *Journal of Child Psychotherapy*, 20 (3): 283–308.

Hollows, A. and Armstrong, H. (eds) (1991) *Children and Young People as Abusers. An Agenda for Action*. London: National Children's Bureau.

Holmes, J. (1993) *John Bowlby and Attachment Theory*. London: Routledge.

Home Office/Department of Health (1992) *Memorandum of Good Practice on Video Recorded Interviews with Child Witnesses for Criminal Proceedings*. London: HMSO.

Horne, A. (1999) 'Sexual abuse and sexual abusing in adolescence', in M. Lanyado and A. Horne (eds), *The Handbook of Child & Adolescent Psychotherapy. Psychoanalytic Approaches*. London and New York: Routledge. pp. 347–67.

Howard, A. (1993) 'Victims and perpetrators of sexual abuse', in K.N. Dwivedi (ed.), *Group Work with Children and Adolescents. A Handbook*. London: Jessica Kingsley. pp. 220–32.

Howe, D. (1993) *On Being a Client. Understanding the Process of Counselling and Psychotherapy*. London: Routledge.

Hoyles, M. (1989) *The Politics of Childhood*. London: Journeyman.

Huber, N. (2000) 'Disclosure no longer subject to blanket veto', *Community Care*, 1314: 11.

Human Rights Act (1998) London: The Stationery Office.

Humphries, S., Mack, J. and Perks, R. (1988) *A Century of Childhood*. London: Sidgwick & Jackson.

Hunter, M. (1999) 'The child and adolescent psychotherapist in the community', in M. Lanyado and A. Horne (eds), *The Handbook of Child & Adolescent Psychotherapy: Psychoanalytic Approaches*, London and New York: Routledge. pp. 127–39.

Jackson, J. (1989) 'Joseph Jackson memorial lecture', *New Law Journal*, 139: 505.

James, A. and Prout, A. (eds) (1990) *Constructing and Reconstructing Childhood: Contemporary Issues in the Sociological Study of Childhood*. London: Falmer Press.

James, B. (1989) *Treating Traumatized Children. New Insights and Creative Interventions*. Lexington, Mass., Toronto: Lexington Books.

James, B. (1994) *Handbook for Treatment of Attachment-Trauma Problems in Children*. New York: Lexington Books.

Jenks, C. (1996) *Childhood*. London and New York: Routledge.

Jennings, S. (ed.) (1995) *Dramatherapy with Children and Adolescents*. London: Routledge.

Johns, M. (1997) *NSPCC Study of Children's Recovery Process*. London: NSPCC.

Johnson, T. Cavanagh (1993a) 'Childhood sexuality', in E. Gil and T. Cavanagh Johnson (eds), *Sexualized Children. Assessment and Treatment of Sexualized Children and Children Who Molest*. Rockville, MD: Launch Press. pp. 1–19.

Johnson, T. Cavanagh (1993b) 'Group therapy', in E. Gil and T. Cavanagh Johnson (eds), *Sexualized Children. Assessment and Treatment of Sexualized Children and Children Who Molest*. Rockville, MD: Launch Press. pp. 211–74.

Kaduson, H.G. and Schaefer, C.E. (eds) (2000) *Short-Term Play Therapy for Children*. New York and London: Guilford Press.

Keats, D. (1997) *Culture and the Child. A Guide for Professionals in Child Care and Development*. Brisbane: Wiley.

Kendall-Tacket, K., Williams, L. and Finkelhor, D. (1993) 'Impact of sexual abuse on children', *Psychological Bulletin*, 113: 164–80.

Kennedy, R. (1997) *Child Abuse, Psychotherapy and the Law*. London: Free Association Books.

Kirk, K. (1998) 'The impact on professional workers', in Z. Bear (ed.), *Good Practice in Counselling People who have been Abused*. London, Bristol and Pennsylvania: Jessica Kingsley. pp. 178–92.

Klein, M. (1981) 'The psychoanalytic play technique', in C. Schaefer (ed.), *Therapeutic Use of Child's Play*. New York: Jason Aronson. pp. 125–40.

Kluft, R.P. (1985) 'Making the diagnosis of multiple personality disorder (MPD)', *Directions in Psychiatry* 5: 1–11.

Knapman, J. and Morrison, T. (1998) *Making the Most of Supervision in Health and Social Care*. Brighton: Pavilion Press.

Kohut, H. (1971) *The Analysis of the Self*. New York: International Universities Press.

Kramer, E. (1971) *Art as Therapy with Children*. New York: Schocken Books.

Lamb, S. (1986) 'Treating sexually abused children: Issues of blame and responsibility', *American Journal of Orthopsychiatry*, 56 (2): 303–7.

Lanyado, M., Hodges, J., Bentovim, A. (1995) 'Understanding boys who sexually abuse other children: A clinical illustration', *Psychoanalytic Psychotherapy*, 9 (3): 231–42.

Laungani, P. (1999) 'Client centred or culture centred counselling?', in S. Palmer and P. Laungani (eds), *Counselling in a Multicultural Society*. London: Sage. pp. 133–52.

Lawton, B. and Feltham, C. (eds) (2000) *Taking Supervision Forward. Enquiries and Trends in Counselling and Psychotherapy*. London: Sage.

Lear, R. (1996, 4th edn) *Play Helps. Toys and Activities for Children with Special Needs*. Oxford: Butterworth-Heinemann.

Little, M. (1997) 'The re-rocusing of children's services: The contribution of research', in N. Parton (ed.), *Child Protection and Family Support: Tensions, Contradictions and Possibilities*. London: Routledge.

Livingstone Smith, S. and Howard, J.A. (1994) 'The impact of previous sexual abuse on children's adjustment in adoptive placement', *Social Work*, 39 (5): 491–501.

Macaskill, C. (1991) *Adopting or Fostering a Sexually Abused Child*. London: B.T. Batsford and British Agencies for Adoption & Fostering.

Mandell, J.G. and Damon, L. with Castaldo, P.C., Tauber, E.S., Monise, L. and Larsen, N.F. (1989) *Group Treatment for Sexually Abused Children*. New York: Guilford Press.

Margison, F. (1991) 'Learning to listen: Teaching and supervising basic psychotherapeutic skills', in J. Holmes (ed.), *A Textbook of Psychotherapy in Psychiatric Practice*. Edinburgh and London: Churchill Livingstone.

Maslow, A.H. (1954) *Motivation and Personality*. New York: Harper & Row.

McNichol, S. and McGregor, K.J. (1999) 'Exploring the link between sexualized behaviour and sexual abuse in a clinical setting', *Child Abuse Review*, 8 (5): 339–48.

Mealor, D.J. and Ackert, T.W. (1989) 'The school psychologist as expert witness'. *Communiqué*, 17 March.

Mehra, H. (1996) 'Residential care for ethnic minority children', in K.N. Dwivedi and V.P. Varma (eds), *Meeting the Needs of Ethnic Minority Children*. London: Jessica Kingsley.

Merry, S.N. and Andrews, L.K. (1994) 'Psychiatric status of sexually abused children 12 months after disclosure and abuse', *Journal of the American Academy of Child and Adolescent Psychiatry*, 33: 939–44.

Naitove, C.E. (1982) 'Arts therapy with sexually abused children', in S.M. Sgroi (ed.), *Handbook of Clinical Intervention in Child Sexual Abuse*. Lexington, Mass.: Lexington Books.

NSPCC (National Society for the Prevention of Cruelty to Children) (1993) *The Child Witness Pack: Helping Children to Cope*. London: NSPCC.

O'Connor, K.J. (1991) *The Play Therapy Primer. An Integration of Theories and Techniques*. New York: Wiley.

Oldfield, A. (1999) 'Listening. The first step toward communicating through music', in P. Milner and B. Carolin (eds), *Time to Listen to Children. Personal and Professional Communication*. London and New York: Routledge. pp. 188–99.

Palmer, S. (1999) 'In search of effective counselling across cultures', in S. Palmer and P. Laungani (eds), *Counselling in a Multicultural Society*. London: Sage. pp. 153–73.

Palmer, S. and Laungani, P. (1999) 'Introduction: Counselling in a multicultural society', in S. Palmer and P. Laungani (eds), *Counselling in a Multicultural Society*. London: Sage. pp. 1–5.

Parton, N. and Wattam, C. (eds) (1999) *Child Sexual Abuse. Responding to the Experiences of Children*. Chichester: Wiley.

Payne, H. (1992) *Dance Movement Therapy: Theory and Practice*. London: Tavistock/Routledge.

Peake, A. (1989) 'Child sexual assault prevention programmes in school', in The Children's Society, *Working with Sexually Abused Children: A Resource Pack for Professionals*. London: The Children's Society. pp. C2–C8.

Pearlman, L.A. and Saakvitne, K.W. (1995) 'Treating therapists with vicarious traumatization and secondary traumatic stress disorders', in C.R. Figley (ed.), *Compassion Fatigue. Coping with Secondary Traumatic Stress Disorder in Those Who Treat the Traumatized*. New York: Brunner/Mazel. pp. 150–77.

Pfeffer, C.R. (1984) 'Clinical aspects of childhood suicidal behavior', *Pediatric Annals*, 13: 56–61.

Piaget, J. (1954) *The Construction of Reality in the Child*. New York: Basic Books.

Plotnikoff, J. and Woolfson, R. (1996) *Reporting to Court Under the Children Act*. London: The Stationery Office.

Porter, F.S., Blick, L.C. and Sgroi, S.M. (1982) 'Treatment of the sexually abused child', in S.M. Sgroi (ed.), *Handbook of Clinical Intervention in Child Sexual Abuse*. Lexington, Mass.: Lexington Books. pp. 109–25.

Pringle, M.K. (1980) *The Needs of Children*. London: Hutchinson.

Pritchard, J. (1995) *Good Practice in Supervision*. London: Jessica Kingsley.

Putnam, F.W. (1989) *Diagnosis and Treatment of Multiple Personality Disorder*. New York: Guilford Press.

Putnam, F.W. (1993) 'Dissociative disorders in children: Problems and profiles', *Child Abuse & Neglect* 17: 40.

Putnam, F.W. (1997) *Dissociation in Children and Adolescents. A Developmental Perspective*. New York and London: Guilford Press.

Rasmussen, L. and Cunningham, C. (1995) 'Focused play therapy and non-directive play therapy: Can they be integrated?, *Journal of Child Sexual Abuse*, 4 (1): 1–20.

Reder, P. and Duncan, S. (1999) *Lost Innocents: A Follow-up Study of Part 8 Reviews of Fatal Child Abuse*. London: Routledge.

Reder, P., Duncan, S. and Gray, M. (1993) *Beyond Blame. Child Abuse Tragedies Revisited*. London and New York: Routledge.

Rogers, C.R. (1951) *Client-Centered Therapy*. London: Constable.

Rogers, C.R. (1957) 'The necessary and sufficient conditions of therapeutic personality change', *Journal of Consulting Psychology*, 21 (2): 99.

Roopnarine, J.L., Johnson, J.E. and Hooper, F.H. (eds) (1994) *Children's Play in Diverse Cultures*. New York: State University of New York Press.

Rutherford, D. (1988) *A Lot of Bottle*. London: The Institute of Alcohol Studies.

Ryan, K. (1999) 'Self-help for the helpers, preventing vicarious traumatization' in N.B. Webb (ed.), *Play Therapy with Children in Crisis* (2nd edn). London: Guilford Press. pp. 471–92.

Ryan, M. (1998, 2nd ed.) *The Children Act. Putting it into Practice*. Aldershot: Ashgate.

Ryan, V. and Wilson, K. (1993) 'Child therapy and evidence in court proceedings. Tensions and some solutions', paper given to the *International BAPSCAN Conference*, Padova, Italy, 29.3.93.

Ryan, V. and Wilson, K. (1996) *Case Studies in Non-directive Play Therapy*. London: Baillière Tindall.

Sereny, G. (1999) *Cries Unheard: The Story of Mary Bell*. Basingstoke: Macmillan.

Sgroi, S. (1992) *Handbook of Clinical Intervention in Child Sexual Abuse.* Lexington, M.A.: Lexington Books.

Sgroi, S.M., Blick, L.C. and Porter, F.S. (1982, 1992) 'A conceptual framework for child sexual abuse', in S.M. Sgroi (ed.), *Handbook of Clinical Intervention in Child Sexual Abuse.* Lexington, MA.: Lexington Books. pp. 9–38.

Sharland, E., Jones D., Aldgate, J., Seal, H. and Croucher, M. (1996) *Professional Intervention in Child Sexual Abuse.* London: HMSO.

Sharp, S. and Cowie, H. (1998) *Counselling and Supporting Children in Distress.* London: Sage.

Silverstone, L. (1997) *Art Therapy: The Person-centred Way.* London: Jessica Kingsley.

Skuse, D., Bentovim, A., Hodges, J., Stevenson, J., Andreou, C., Lanyado, M., Williams, B., New, M. and McMillan, D. (1996) 'The influence of early experience of sexual abuse on the formation of sexual preferences during adolescence', *Report to the Department of Health London.* London: Behavioural Sciences Unit, Institute of Child Health.

Smith, G. (1992) 'The unbearable traumatogenic past: Child sexual abuse', in V.P. Varma (ed.), *The Secret Life of Vulnerable Children.* London: Routledge. pp. 130–56.

Spinal-Robinson, P. and Easton Wickham, R. (1992a) *Cartwheels: A Workbook for Children Who Have Been Sexually Abused.* Notre Dame, Indiana: Jalice.

Spinal-Robinson, P. and Easton Wickham, R. (1992b) *Cartwheels. Therapist's Guide.* Notre Dame, Indiana: Jalice.

Stainton Rogers, R. and Stainton Rogers, W. (1992) *Stories of Childhood. Shifting Agendas of Child Concern.* New York and London: Harvester Wheatsheaf.

Stanton-Jones, K. (1992) *An Introduction to Dance Movement Therapy in Psychiatry.* London and New York: Tavistock/Routledge.

Strand, V. (1999) 'The assessment and treatment of family sexual abuse', in N.B. Webb (ed.), *Play Therapy with Children in Crisis.* London: Guilford Press. pp. 104–30.

Summit, R.C. (1983) 'The child sexual abuse syndrome', *Child Abuse & Neglect*, 7: 177–93.

Thomas, L.K. (1999) 'Communicating with a black child: overcoming obstacles of difference', in P. Milner and B. Carolin (eds), *Time to Listen to Children.* London: Routledge. pp. 65–78.

Trowell, J. (1999) 'Treatment', in N. Parton and C. Wattam (eds), *Child Sexual Abuse: Responding to the Experiences of Children.* Chichester: Wiley. pp. 107–22.

Turkel, S.B. and Eth, S. (1990) 'Psychopathological responses to stress: Adjustment disorder and post-traumatic stress disorder in children and adolescents', in L.E. Arnold (ed.), *Childhood Stress.* New York: Wiley.

United Nations (1989) *The UN Convention on the Rights of the Child.* New York: United Nations.

Valios, N. (2000) 'Inspectors highlight lack of quality assurance for children's services', *Community Care*, 1313: 5–6.

van der Kolk, B.A. (1996) 'Trauma and memory', in B.A. van der Kolk, A.C. MacFarlane and L. Weisaeth (eds), *Traumatic Stress: The Effects of Overwhelming Experience on Mind, Body and Society.* New York: Guilford Press. pp. 279–302.

Wadsworth, B.J. (1984, 3rd edn) *Piaget's Theory of Cognitive and Affective Development.* New York: Longman.

Walton, P. (1996) *Partnership with Mothers in the Wake of Child Sexual Abuse.* Monograph. University of East Anglia.

Ward, H. (ed.) (1995) *Looking After Children: Research into Practice.* London: HMSO.

Waterhouse, Sir R. (2000) *Lost in Care. Report of the Tribunal of Inquiry into the Abuse of Children in Care in the Former County Council Areas of Gwynedd and Clwyd since 1974.* London: The Stationery Office.

Webb, N.B. (1999, 2nd edn) 'Assessment of the child in crisis', in N.B. Webb (ed.), *Play Therapy with Children in Crisis.* London: Guilford Press. pp. 3–28.

Wellard, S. (2000) 'Is it time to revise the rulebook on abuse'? *Community Care*, 1350: 10–11.

West, J. (1996, 2nd edn) *Child-Centred Play Therapy*. London: Arnold.

Westcott, H.L. (1993) *Abuse of Children and Adults with Disabilities*. London: NSPCC.

Westcott, H.L. and Cross, M. (1996) *This Far and No Further: Towards Ending the Abuse of Disabled Children*. Birmingham: Venture Press.

Westcott, H. and Jones, J. (1997) 'The Memorandum: considering a conundrum', in H. Westcott and J. Jones (eds), *Perspectives on the Memorandum: Policy, Practice and Research in Investigative Interviewing*. Aldershot: Arena. pp. 167–79.

White, R., Carr, P. and Lowe, N. (1995, 2nd ed.) *The Children Act in Practice*. London: Butterworths.

Wieland, S. (1998) *Techniques and Issues in Abuse-Focused Therapy with Children and Adolescents*. London: Sage.

Wigram, T., West, R. and Saperston, B. (eds) (1995) *The Art and Science of Music Therapy: A Handbook*. Chur, Switzerland: Harwood Academic Publishers.

Wilson, K., Kendrick, P. and Ryan, V. (1992) *Play Therapy. A Non-directive Approach for Children and Adolescents*. London: Baillière Tindall.

Wilson, P. (1999) 'Therapy and consultation in residential care', in M. Lanyado and A. Horne (eds), *The Handbook of Child and Adolescent Psychotherapy. Psychoanalytic Approaches*. London and New York: Routledge. pp. 159–66.

Winn, L. (1994) *Post Traumatic Stress Disorder and Dramatherapy. Treatment and Risk Reduction*. London: Jessica Kingsley.

Winnicott, D.W. (1986) *Home is Where We Start From: Essays by a Psychoanalyst*. Harmondsworth: Penguin.

Winnicott, D.W. (1990) *The Maturational Process and the Facilitating Environment. Studies in the Theory of Emotional Development*. London: Karnac Books and The Institute of Psychoanalysis.

Wolfe, V. and Birt, J. (1995) 'The psychological sequelae of child sexual abuse', in T. Ollendick and R. Prinz (eds), *Advances in Clinical Child Psychology*, Vol. 17. New York: Plenum. pp. 233–63.

Worden, J.W. (1991, 2nd edn) *Grief Counselling and Grief Therapy: A Handbook for the Mental Health Practitioner*. London: Routledge.

Yalom, J.D. (1995, 4th edn) *The Theory and Practice of Group Psychotherapy*. Harlow: Longman.

Yassen, J. (1995) 'Preventing secondary traumatic stress disorder', in C.R. Figley (ed.), *Compassion Fatigue. Coping with Secondary Traumatic Stress Disorder in Those Who Treat the Traumatized*. New York: Brunner/Mazel. pp. 178–208.

Zimmerman, R.B. (1988) 'Childhood depression: new theoretical formulations and implications for foster care services', *Child Welfare*, 67 (1): 37–47.

Index

Printed in the United Kingdom
by Lightning Source UK Ltd.
122264UK00001B/175-192/A